D0732226

□ □ □ □ □ □ □

The Quiet Revolution

WITHDRAWN
UTSA LIBRARIES

Pitt Latin American Studies

George Reid Andrews, General Editor

The Quiet Revolution

DECENTRALIZATION AND THE RISE OF POLITICAL

PARTICIPATION IN LATIN AMERICAN CITIES

□ □ □ □ □ □ □ □

TIM CAMPBELL

UNIVERSITY OF PITTSBURGH PRESS

Published by the University of Pittsburgh Press, Pittsburgh, Pa., 15260

Copyright © 2003, University of Pittsburgh Press

All rights reserved

Manufactured in the United States of America

Printed on acid-free paper

10 9 8 7 6 5 4 3 2 1

ISBN 0-8229-5796-5

Library of Congress Cataloging-in-Publication Data

Campbell, Tim.
  The quiet revolution : decentralization and the rise of political
participation in Latin American cities / Tim Campbell.
    p. cm. — (Pitt Latin American series)
Includes bibliographical references and index.
  ISBN 0-8229-5796-5 (pbk. : alk. paper)
  1. Decentralization in government—Latin America. 2. Political
participation—Latin America. 3. Democratization—Latin America. I.
Title. II. Series.

JL959.5.D42 C35 2003
320.8'5'098—dc21

                        2002015821

Library
University of Texas
at San Antonio

CONTENTS

ACKNOWLEDGMENTS

No one can recover the time and special moments waiting to happen just outside my study as the kids, my wife, my friends would come round and, after peering in and finding me locked onto the keyboard, drift away in quiet understanding. This small note is to acknowledge their patience and our loss—of many rich moments with family, flights of fancy with friends, fun games, banter, and pure enjoyment of life—that ran downstream irretrievable during the years this book was being written. Those moments cannot be recovered, and I wish to pause this moment to imagine what might have been and to express profound gratitude to my wife, Linda, and children, Alana, Kathryn, and Eric, as well as to all those others who felt this loss.

On the other hand, I am confident something has been gained, and my colleagues have given a lot of time and effort helping me, to research this, fetch that, even write passages for me to digest and use. Fernando Rojas, Rafael de la Cruz, Harald Fuhr, Gabriel Aghon, Travis Katz, and Marcela Huertas should be named right away. Joining them are a dozen more, including some at Stanford (no academic order intended here)—Katherine Sternfels, Eric Munoz, Lisa Taber; and Marisa Brutoco; others at MIT, including John Frankenhoff and Sara Freidheim. My gratitude also goes to my very professional colleagues and friends at the World Bank, the ones on the front lines who helped teach me and encourage me over these years: Vitor M. Serra, Teresa Serra, David Vetter, William Dillinger, Mila Freire, Elio Codato, Shelton Davis, Jack Stein, Oscar Alvarado, Thakoor Persaud, Braz Menezes, and Jim Hicks. Still others from around the Bank Mara Morgan, David Gow, Jorge Serraino, Joy Trancoso, Daniel Tailant, Kathryn Bacon, and Piers Merrick.

Thanks also to Nigel Harris, Joseph Tulchin, George Peterson, Judith Tendler, and Terry Nichols Clark for reading parts of the manuscript during various moments of creation. Nita Congress has shown great editorial patience in working through the various drafts.

Acknowledgment also goes to many co-authors of reports and studies prepared during the early years of decentralization (1988–93). It is impossible to be entirely accurate about attributions, but much credit goes to George Peterson for shaping an analytical framework and classifying the decentralization strategies that appear here in chapters three and four. My thanks also to Jose Brakarz for reports he prepared on Chile, to Ken Davey for the same on Mexico, to David Gow and John Frankenhoff for early drafts of chapter five and to Marcela Huertas my co-author for chapter seven. I wish to express special acknowledgement to, and mourn the passing of, Gabriel Aghon for his collegiality, friendship, and help.

PART I □ □ □ □ □ □ □ □ □

The Backdrop of Change
and Overview of Reform

1 □ Overview

WHY REVOLUTION? WHY QUIET?

This book documents two dramatic, but largely unheralded, revolutionary trends in Latin America—decentralization and democratization—and argues that policy responses to them by national and international institutions may be smothering the embers of reform at the local level, reforms that are vital to long-run sustainability of growth in the region.[1] Both trends emerged only in the past decade or so, both were inconceivable just three decades ago, and both reshaped the very nature of governance without a single drop of blood being shed anywhere in the hemisphere. In comparison to revolutionary struggles against the state in the 1950s and 1960s, the upheaval I call the quiet revolution is a restructuring of power that is not as radical as, say, the Tupamaro vision of social change, but is far beyond the changes envisioned by reform-minded public sector officials and policy analysts in the 1970s and 1980s (e.g., Lordello de Mello 1984).[2] Moreover, these revolutionary trends, though not inseparable by any means, were carried out in parallel and calmly, partly because they filled a need for systemic reform shared widely in the region. The quiet revolution proceeded quickly also because government leaders acting in collaboration with their constituents implemented reforms. This is not to say that the two trends were not controversial and filled with local political conflict.

The first of these trends was the transfer of decision-making and spending power from central to local governments. Nations everywhere in the region have extended power-sharing arrangements to cities and regions,

3

backed by automatic revenue transfers that double or even quadruple municipal revenues compared to previous years. From Guatemala to Argentina, local governments began spending 10 to 40 percent of central government revenues. The significance of this trend, one that makes it revolutionary, is that it reversed decades of central government control. For most of the period since the Second World War, public spending at all levels was controlled by central governments.

With decentralization, officials in the lowest tier of government began to play a much more important part in spending decisions. Moreover, this was happening in countries where years of overspending and inflation in the 1980s produced a decade of indebtedness and economic contraction so severe that social and economic progress achieved in the preceding decade was erased. For most of this same period, local officials called repeatedly, but fruitlessly, for a greater voice in spending and political decisions. Then, suddenly, and paradoxically, municipalities were given not only new spending authority but also unconditional new flows of revenues. Automatic transfers in a majority of the countries in the region put money in city coffers that was remarkably free from controls by central government treasuries. Finance ministers were painfully aware of the fiscal instability created by excessive borrowing and spending in the 1980s. Yet, for political reasons central governments devolved powers of spending and finance to local governments all across the region.

The second trend is the region's comparatively quiet and largely universal transition to democracy, a transition evident not just in the selection of national leaders, but in the choice of virtually every mayor and council member in the more than 14,000 units of state, intermediate, and local governments. All but a few islands have completed this transition. Elections at the local level—and, more importantly, electoral reforms in nearly half the countries of the region—constituted a revolutionary shift in power, especially against the backdrop of dictatorial regimes that controlled local affairs as recently as the 1970s.

Swiftly and radically, yet remarkably peacefully, these two trends of decentralization and democratization transformed the entire face of governance in the region. Implemented in various combinations in different countries, these trends have triggered a revival of popular participation at the local level and the rise of importance of local governments in national affairs. These changes, in turn, pose sharp new challenges regarding political control, intergovernmental coordination, formation of public policy, and implementation of public programs. Much depends on how these challenges are met by political leaders, and also by policymakers, voter-taxpayers, and international lending and technical assistance organizations.

Ironically, even while some national and international policy authorities aimed to foster liberalization and reform, countervailing efforts were also mounted, and these effectively limited or blunted the impact of reforms at the local level. Gradually, over the decade of the 1990s, the international policy debate regarding decentralization in Latin America leaned toward what might be called a containment strategy. Though it was not articulated explicitly nor conceived as a master plan of response, the strategic reactions of national and international authorities in the 1990s was, above all, geared to maintain fiscal stability in national affairs. An entire decade of indebtedness in the 1980s had reversed the previous decade of growth, and policymakers were afraid that decentralization might undo the painstaking efforts that had finally achieved restoration of positive growth. Thus, policymakers were focused on stability rather than on responsible local governance. Governments and international agencies only slowly realized the need to stimulate better public choice making and to explore economic growth at the local level. As a consequence, the remarkable impetus for change—the startling shift of trends seen all across the Hemisphere—was dampened and the full benefits of decentralization have not been realized.

International policy did not help much to conceive or promulgate decentralization in the beginning, and once the first major steps were taken to transfer spending powers to local governments, national fiscal stability quickly became the chief policy objective of international advice. International agencies have been focused—mostly successfully—on restraining fiscal excesses at the local level, but this has come at the exclusion of democracy building. Although the international community began to gear up support for local institutional capacity and democratic choice making, agencies were unclear about the pathway to take and unprepared for the scale of effort needed. Nevertheless, many lessons can be learned from the Latin American experience, and this book outlines recommendations for cities and nations in Latin America, as well as for those in newly decentralizing regions, to capitalize on the amazing social energies unleashed by the trends of decentralization in Latin America.

History may well show that the burst of activity and reform that I call the quiet revolution flowered for less than a decade and then fell into remission. Certainly, not all of the reforms were lasting, nor were all of them free from problems. Although decentralization and democratization represented new solutions to difficult issues in the public sector, they also created many new challenges to implement and sustain the best of the reforms. Most important, the quiet revolution made a clean break from the past and produced many promising leads showing a way forward. Ironically, as containment policies began to take effect, cities all around the world were being challenged, as they were in Latin America, to play a more important role in national affairs, international trade, and local economic development, and lessons from the quiet revolution can be helpful to nations elsewhere engaged in decentralization.

Many nations outside the Latin American region are now struggling with the same or similar questions about the origins and processes of decentralization. The Philippines has progressed quite far with local elections and adjustments in shared revenues. India has promulgated constitutional reforms and is experimenting with new relationships of power between state and federal powers. Cities like Ahmedabad, along with scores of others, are testing a newly found authority and autonomy. Nations with centrally planned economies from Albania to Vietnam are also exploring a transition from a highly centralized organization of the state to arrangements that are drastically different from those of the past in terms of the nature of the public sector, the role of private actors, and the intergovernmental division of labor. In general, policymakers at the national level in Asia and Eastern Europe, like those in Latin America, are concerned first with financial arrangements, particularly with controls over spending and borrowing to achieve fiscal stability. Local officials, on the other hand, increasingly look for greater freedom and autonomy, for instance, to break shackles like restrictions on local borrowing that have controlled their existence for many years. Local governments everywhere are now drawn by the ineluctable lure of foreign direct investment and (though suddenly dampened by the Asian currency crisis) borrowing on capital markets. The quiet revolution in Latin America has much to offer by way of perspective and lessons to governments everywhere.

AN OVERVIEW OF LESSONS

The lessons of the quiet revolution from countries in Latin America are sometimes surprising and often applicable to other countries in Africa, Asia, and Eastern Europe. The following paragraphs provide an overview of some of the lessons and insights that will be presented throughout the text.

Political power sharing, not financial or state reform, was the underlying imperative in the move to decentralize decision making and spending in Latin America. The consolidation of political power at the local level was the most important factor in the long-term financial sustainability of decentralized governance. An influx of capital also played an important role in the swing from central to local control in Latin America over the past seven decades. Eager lenders from afar and ambitious national leaders from within the region promoted irresponsible international lending to Latin American countries.

Political leaders in Latin America drew more than a little inspiration from Europe and the Soviet Union, as well as from each other, in charting the shifts in power that have led to a quiet revolution. Decentralization in Spain beginning in 1978 laid the groundwork for change in Latin America. Changes in Western and Eastern Europe, fueled by the collapse of the Soviet empire and provoked by the political forays of Pope John Paul in countries like Poland, Brazil, and Mexico provided further inspiration for reform.

The highly centralized states of Mexico and Chile were two unlikely pioneers in Latin America's decentralization process. They expanded citizen participation and, surprisingly in Chile, even retooled municipalities to focus on social welfare. Most central governments shared revenues with local governments faster than they spelled out local spending responsibilities. In the long run, this may prove to have been a wiser strategy than the rational "finance should follow function" dictum often espoused by international financial assistance agencies like the World Bank. Ready access to shared finances breathed real life into the new spending powers given to local governments.

Local leaders have emerged from political and electoral reforms to produce myriad innovations in governance. These ran parallel—and even exceeded—the breadth of change espoused in the United States as it "reinvented" government. For instance, scores of mayors invented or borrowed ideas in order to implement new and more effective ways to mobilize local finance, to foster institutional change, and to mobilize popular participation in local public decision making.

The most striking of these innovations is the reconstruction of a "contract of governance" between elected officials and voter-taxpayers.[3] In this reconstruction, the contract of governance has been renewed and reinvigorated by voter-taxpayers who have shown willingness to allow local elected leaders to take actions on their behalf in areas of public life in which the same voters show much less trust in national officials. In cities all across the region, voter-taxpayers generally agreed to new tax burdens when elected officials could demonstrate through concrete improvements that tax revenues were at work in visible and verifiable ways. The essence of this governance innovation was fiscal decision making through participatory democracy at the lowest level. Engineering this change could not have been accomplished without the quiet revolution.

For nearly ten years, central governments were coaxed and wheedled by agencies like the International Monetary Fund (IMF) and the World Bank to reform the public sector in order to restore growth. These efforts met with mixed success. The quiet revolution suggests that the arena for the next stage of reforms in the region was shifted to the local level, where new models of governance were being invented. These models were marked by innovation in the governance contract, by widespread participation, and by new forms of accountability in spending.

Mayors and other local leaders have become more proactive in areas of trade, economic development, jobs, and environmental concerns; and local leaders were both eager and able to make more of an impact on national development. Local leaders have followed the priorities of ordinary citizens, with surprising results. Cities are interested in economic development, jobs, and poverty. Environmental quality also proved to be more important than often thought, but not for the reasons that international nongovernmental organizations (NGOs) talk about. Rather, environmental issues were understood by ordinary citizens in terms of survival, of water supply, infant mortality, traffic hazards, and air pollution, and not in terms of global green issues such as greenhouse gasses and forestry loss.

Most international lending and technical assistance organizations followed rather than led the process of decentralization in Latin America. In the past, these organizations were limited to actions in the domains of economics, finance, and social development. They had not played a strong role in the area of public choice making, which is at the heart of the quiet revolution. This is because the charters of most multilateral lending agencies rightly prohibit (partisan) political concerns from affecting economic and technical judgments. But lessons from the quiet revolution suggest that much scope of action is open to development institutions to strengthen democratic public choice making, such as electoral processes, public interest policy analysis, and education of the public, among others.

Many, if not most, of these findings are surprising challenges to the conventional wisdom about decentralization in the region, particularly about its origins, the political nature of reform, and the role—or lack of a role—of development agencies in the early years. Very few of the initial steps taken by governments to decentralize were recommended by development assistance agencies. Indeed, the prevailing wisdom in several key areas ran exactly contrary to the decisions taken by many of the region's governments. For instance, governments moved quickly, not with slow deliberation as they were advised. They enshrined decentralization in national constitutions, not in more easily modifiable national laws. They transferred revenues to local authorities long before the true costs of delivering services were known, and they were soft on spending rules throughout political liberalization, exactly contrary to recommendations of one of the World Bank's main reports on the subject (1999). In some areas, such as participatory democracy, local governments in the region even invented through trial and error new ways of doing political business. They reformed democratic institutions quickly and effectively, creating new pages in the manuals of prevailing wisdom in agencies like the World Bank.

QUIET REVOLUTION IN HISTORICAL PERSPECTIVE

Ironically, after fifty years of centralized governance since the Second World War, the quiet revolution has established an arrangement of power not so different from that in place during the inter-War period. Then, wealth in countries like Argentina and Brazil was generated in specific regions by rubber, cattle, coffee, mining, and bananas. Central states had not yet consolidated power into bureaucracies and the legislative branch of government. Profligate spending, aided and abetted by foreign banks in a manner disturbingly similar to the debt crisis of the 1980s, was a key factor in breaking the power of regions. The distribution of power in the region's governments has swung back and forth over this century. In the 1930s, private banks in Europe and the United States lent large amounts to subsovereign governments. Many loan obligations were pushed imprudently onto cities like Belém and Buenos Aires. With the depression and intervening recessions, most local governments could not meet their obligations, and the central government had to assume the debt. In the meantime, central governments were launching state-led strategies of growth, beginning a process of centralization and consolidation of financial and political power that fed the authoritarian state (Malloy and Seligson 1987; Collier 1979). Nickson (1995, p. 16) speaks of "de-municipalization" in the 1950s and 1960s, as important functions of cities were transferred to central governments. Today, eager foreign lenders, and equally eager city and regional borrowers, could trigger a crisis in finance and start the pendulum swinging back.

However, one key difference in decentralization traditions today, compared to previous eras, is that decentralization has cascaded downward to the grassroots level. Local governments today increasingly feel the need to involve citizens in making public choices about local infrastructure, environmental quality, primary health care, and schooling. Remnants of the old, centralized system, such as high turnover of local public officials, make it harder for good governments to take root. A new generation of skills and techniques is needed in local government, building on the innovative spirit of the quiet revolution, to strengthen communication between local constituents and their elected leaders. Can the many changes put in motion in Latin America teach new policy lessons about managing the next stages of reform? Can these changes be sustained? Can this experience help guide other countries going through similar processes? These and other questions are addressed in this volume.

The Quiet Revolution places the historical transformation of Latin America in a policy perspective, explores the many dimensions of reform in the region, and reflects on the lessons of the quiet revolution in relation to similar events in other regions—notably Eastern Europe, Asia, and parts of Africa. The book documents the drama of decentralization, illustrating the give and take between central governments and local constituents as they gradually came to realize, and then to exercise, the newly found power that came to cities with the stroke-of-the-pen reforms known as decentralization.

The text focuses on leading cities, those that made the most of decentralization. Less attention is paid to the broad mass of local governments and the failures and reversions to poor performance or weak management that have occurred in many cities and towns tend to be understated. The idea is not to explain the success of decentralization in side-by-side comparisons of cases of neighborhood action, participation, or finance. Rather, the purpose is to show that the many varieties of experiments and innovative solutions engineered by local leaders in the region demonstrate a systemic response to a new set of incentives put in place with decentralization. In effect, the body of practice established a new standard of government at the local level. Moreover, prevailing approaches and theory—for instance, fiscal federalism, new institutional economics, and participatory development—are not always adequate to explain this response nor sufficient to guide future policy for decentralized democracies. In this connection, this volume fits into the family of literature on political economy and new institutional economics (see for example, Gage and Mandell 1990; North 1991; Fox 1994; Grindle and Thomas 1991; Ostrom et al. 1994; and Tendler 1997). Also, references are made to local finance (Bahl and Linn 1992; Mouritzen 1992; Clark 1994).

This method of examining leading cities has the drawback of understating the pitfalls, obstacles, and dangers in the story of Latin America's decentralization and of producing a rather rosy picture. The author is aware, as should be the reader, that decentralization has created many problems for governments, national and local alike. The optimistic tone of this volume should not be misinterpreted as a statement of policy success. Rather, the tone is a consequence of concentrating on how leading governments overcame the well-known problems and pitfalls of decentralized governance, for instance, poor leadership, distorted incentives, and unclear rules of the game.

Finally, the text provides a comparative and useful perspective on political transformations in other regions. Many dimensions of the changes in Latin America, such as those involving fiscal relations, political reform, local leadership, participation, and innovation process, apply to political systems in Africa, Asia, and Eastern Europe, making a comparative perspective possible and helpful.

The analysis in the book draws on first-hand knowledge in several key areas of local government, particularly the voicing of demand by voter-tax-payers; modes of holding local officials accountable; and employing, and then reforming, electoral processes and local leadership. The book broadens and extends a 1991 study by the World Bank's (then) Technical Department for Latin America and the Caribbean, and builds on a half-dozen subsequent papers, many of them woven into or cited in the text. Other sources include government documents, national legislation, analytical reports, and a vast amount of "gray" literature, published and unpublished papers such as policy and position papers produced by practitioners and observers of the quiet revolution.

Personal interviews provided another very important source of information in drafting this book. Hundreds of elected officials, local authorities, citizen and community group members and leaders, business people, NGO representatives, university researchers, and national officials were interviewed between 1989 and 1997. The focus of these discussions—particularly at the onset—was on response at the local level to decisions, policies, and mandates from central governments. Later, the focus shifted to innovations and reforms at the local level. Note, however, that this book is not a report based on systematic data gathering through surveys, interviews, or opinion polls, nor is it based on published quantitative data on subjects like municipal finance. Where relevant and available, however, such sources are of course incorporated into the text.

The book is organized in four parts, the first of which sets the historical context and policy framework within which decentralization strategies in Latin America were developed and from which it is possible to gauge both the meaning and import of decentralization as a social and cultural phenomenon. The second part covers the varieties of decentralization strategies exhibited in the Latin America region, including the means of sharing economic and decision-making power among levels of government. These political arrangements are compared to other parts of the world and traced in detail in the specific cases of Chile and Mexico. These two countries, both relatively right wing and strongly centralized, found ways to accommodate decentralizing impulses in the political structure. They may have pointed the way to political regimes in other parts of the region then contemplating next steps.

The third part of the book dissects key dimensions of decentralization strategies. Modes of political participation—electoral and voice—are still emerging in the region. Priorities of cities change as leaders focus on issues of poverty, violence, social development, and environmental quality. These issues inform the day-to-day struggles of local populations, and participatory democracy has helped bring them squarely into the political arena at the local level. At the local level a new fiscal bargain is being forged, breaking an impasse about local taxation following years of mistrust.

The final part presents the similarities in the operating styles of leading local governments, and describes a new model of governance characterized by stronger leadership, more competent technical skills, and a willingness to innovate. The broader array of policy in the developmental agenda is presented and alternatives to conventional wisdom proposed about managing local governments in decentralized democracies.

The broad comparative treatment of the material and the emphasis on spotting leading trends and common features in the region's decentralization experience fills a gap in the scholarly and institutional literature. Until now, most publications on this subject—whether produced by the World Bank (which has generated much of the literature), or associations, NGOs, and universities—have either covered specific issues in a set of countries or a specific sector such as finance or education in a particular country. Excellent studies have been produced by Aghon (1996) on fiscal decentralization, de la Cruz (1994) on Venezuela, Hausmann (1998) on macro policy and decentralization, and Rojas (1995) on various topics. But little has been said about the overarching trends in a region. This text seeks to do just that by reviewing and appraising the impacts of reform that have washed over Latin America since the 1980s.

2 □ The Backdrop to Revolution and the Seeds of Reform

Early in the 1980s, a startling transformation in governance began to occur in scores of countries in Latin America. In subsequent decades similar changes took place in many other countries around the world. National and regional leaders, in executive and legislative branches alike, seemed simultaneously to reveal—and then to act upon—an impulse to abrogate some or many central state prerogatives that had dominated virtually all developing nations since the Second World War. Nations began to shift important new roles to their local governments by conferring on them new powers and new sources of finance that had been firmly nested in national systems dominated by central states for fifty years. Of course, actual cases make this sweeping view of entrenched nesting and symphonic change much more rutted with idiosyncrasy and local circumstance. But, in fact, a thread of common influences ran through Latin America's governments and, in less than a decade, produced startlingly similar results across the region. Swiftly and silently, the nature of governance was altered, and so too was the way of doing business, the modalities of conducting politics, and the perspectives of viewing governments at every level in Latin America. What unseen signals penetrated the many spheres of power across the continent and led to a revolutionary shift of national authority?

Decentralization could have happened when it did for a number of reasons. Certain factors—by and large different from those found in the literature—might explain this transformation in government. One of the most commonly accepted explanations is voiced by Foxley (1984), who refers to deep indebtedness and "the collapse of the neoliberal model and the authoritarian state." Other analysts have pursued a variety of explanations ranging from global trade to local democracy. For instance, Malloy and Seligson (1987) address globalization of trade and capital markets as forces that move governments to act more quickly on reform and to give up important substitution policies. Frieden (1991) covers interest-group pressures to demonstrate the mechanical transmission of demand for change. Still others identify new distinctions and subtleties that might be seen as transitional mechanisms transforming into fully democratic regimes. Terms such as "low intensity democracy" and "delegative democracy" (O'Donnell 1993) or "political learning" (Remmer 1992) reflect these strains of thought. Recently, scholars have also begun to address the outcomes of decentralization, to explore its impact on governance, and to address degrees of decentralization (e.g., Willis et al. 1999). But none of these sources throws much light on why decentralization appeared so widely, so closely together in time, and so swiftly.

The most immediate, and undoubtedly the most visible, backdrop to the sweeping changes of Latin America's quiet revolution was the series of gripping events in the former Soviet Union and beyond. The new federalism, even Reagan era governance in the United States, along with perestroika and glasnost were taking shape at about the same time as Solidarity was gathering strength in Poland, and these caused ripple effects on the Velvet Revolution in Czechoslovakia. Perestroika and glasnost also influenced the demise of Ceauşescu in Romania, the fall of the Berlin Wall in Germany, and even the events in Tiananmen Square in China. We can only imagine the weight these events had in the political calculus of leaders in Latin America. Reformist policymakers and political leaders in the region could have easily been encouraged by these upheavals. However, a glance at the sequence of events suggests that the roots of the quiet revolution took hold before, not after, the collapse of the Soviet empire. Decision making in Latin America began to be swayed a full decade earlier.

THE CONTEXT FOR DECENTRALIZATION IN LATIN AMERICA

Subtle transformations of power had taken place in state houses and national congresses in Latin America a decade before Gorbachev's perestroika. Chile had already begun municipal reforms in the late 1970s, Mexico had constructed an elaborate funding mechanism to support local governments at about the same time, and Colombia began deliberations to strengthen local governments in the early 1980s. So the seeds of reform leading to decentralization in Latin America had been sown early and in many places. But how and why? These questions can be answered in two ways. First, it is important to understand changing contextual factors, large-scale shifts in demographics and urban development that were taking place for decades and that affected the entire region. But other factors were also at work, factors that can be seen as more immediate causal events. This second set of factors includes the impact of debt, the influence of Spain's return to democracy, and the stirring messages of Pope John Paul II. These also played a role in answering the questions of how and why.

Local Governments within National Political Systems

In order to appreciate the scope and pace of change in the region, it is important to understand the historical role that cities have played in a centralized system of government in Latin America. Cities have been seen as highly dependent subnational units in an ossified system of hierarchical control dating back to the Spanish conquest (Veliz 1981). Mayors were elected in some large and many capital cities, but they were frequently from the opposition party and therefore subjected to a politically hostile national government. For the most part during the interwar period, selection of city executives by higher authorities was a matter of appointment to posts of confidence, and the role of city executives was largely to manage the city's affairs under the supervision of governors or ministries. In this scheme, mayors were subject to the political control of the party in power and to the administrative control of the ministries of interior, government, and finance (Nickson 1995). It was possible for appointed mayors to take initiatives, but the purse strings were always tightly held by central governments and loosened only when it was convenient at the center to do so. According to one recognized authority (Lordello de Mello 1984), local government was characterized by a "pathological syndrome," meaning it was not allowed to strengthen its institutional capacity. For would-be reformers under these arrangements in the 1970s and 1980s, the scope for innovation was tightly constrained. To be effective, local authorities had to be willing to bargain for resources from central government and prepared to give something in return, for example, concessions, return of political favors, or loyalty.

The ability of local governments to respond to change depended very much on the size of the city and the larger political system in which cities were imbedded. For cities with over a half-million in population, or in federated systems where states (or, in Argentina, provinces) played a significant role, local authorities had legitimate political powers. Four of the largest nations in the region—Argentina, Brazil, Mexico, and Venezuela—were (and still are) comprised of states with their own constitutions and prerogatives, including the creation and regulation of municipalities. Brazil is a notable exception in the region for the equal footing given to cities by the then (and present) Brazilian constitution. The rest of the countries in the region are unitary states, meaning that cities are administrative branches of the central government. These systems do not have the intergovernmental complexities of federal systems, and they must also cope with local interests and local loyalties in dealing with social and political change. But even though big-city authorities were given some scope to introduce initiatives to solve problems, most operated within the confines of a political and administrative system designed to control the timing and scope of local actions.

Yet the onus of response to big-city problems always fell first on local authorities. Many studies have documented the political, social, and environmental pressures that were put on cities and governments starting after the 1960s (see, for example, Turner 1968, Leeds 1967, Lomnitz 1974, and Perlman 1976). For most of the postwar period, governments at all levels were playing catch-up with regard to water supply, schools, health care, and the fulfillment of other basic needs (Ringskog 1995). Political expression occasionally reached a boiling point and burst into riots or civil unrest in many Latin American cities. And though they have always been the first to feel pressure, the role of local authorities had traditionally been one of transmitting these pressures up the authoritarian line to national leaders and then of implementing policy decisions and programs conceived by central authorities.

The Maturing Urban System

Many decades of rapid urban growth produced an expanding and maturing urban system in Latin America, and this factor has been overlooked as an explanation for decentralization. For decades, cities in Latin America have set the world pace for rapid urban growth. During the second half of this century, particularly in the 1960s, some cities in the region were growing at 5 and 6 percent annually, producing some of the world's great megacities as rural migrants squatted in the interstices of mature, built-up cities and filled in vast tracts of land on city peripheries. Wherever and however they settled, they laid a foundation for future growth that is still under way today.

After the 1960s, rural-to-urban migration slowed somewhat, and natural increase became once again the driving factor in city growth. In fact, for nearly two decades, the largest share of the numerical increase in city populations has been produced by the offspring of urban residents. Data from the United Nations (1991) indicate that, beginning in the 1970s, more than one million new urban households were added each year in Latin America, and that this "natural" growth increased in the 1980s and 1990s. This dual trend of fewer rural-to-urban migrants and continued natural increase is projected to continue into the next century. By the year 2010, urban populations will increase by nearly 60 percent over the 1990 level (UN 1997).

The features of Latin America's growing and maturing urban system can be seen as initial conditions for—and perhaps could even be regarded as the triggering factors of—the quiet revolution. With each passing decade since the great wave of migrations in the 1960s, Latin America has not only become an urbanized region, it has also become a region of city residents born into urban cultures. In a broad sense, urban populations have grown more mature about the city and about their role in it as citizens. In this view, Latin America's urban residents can be seen as more steeped in the ways of the city, more connected to the fate of the city than their parents had been as migrants, more knowledgeable about city and neighborhood life, and more apt to take part in organized community groups. This last hypothesis is explored and supported by writers such as Carroll (1992), Reilly (1994), and McCarney (1996), all of whom contend that NGOs, a measure of local activity, have grown in strength and effectiveness since the 1970s. Whatever effect the maturation factor might have had on the timing, speed, or depth of the quiet revolution, a region of city-born residents is a notable factor in the initial conditions of change before decentralization in Latin America.

Yet another important change taking place—the growing number of big cities—was largely ignored in the literature. Beginning sometime in the early 1980s, the largest cities were no longer growing more rapidly than secondary cities and towns. Most of the major metropolitan areas were growing at less than 2 percent per year, while the secondary cities—those with a million or less in population—were growing at twice that rate. The spreading of the urban population into the middle ranks of cities meant that by 1980, the number of cities in this range had grown by nearly 100, from 117 in 1960 to 205 in 1980 (UNCHS 1987). One hundred new executives and urban constituencies were brought into the public sphere in the decades before decentralization, joining the ranks of significant population centers with growing wealth and a stake in self-determination. These cities also had an increasing need for professional management. Both the largest cities with established orders and the smaller, more recent members of the big cities club became stakeholders in, and the arenas for, the quiet revolution.

Social Complexities of the City

Another factor connected to the growth of cities is that city authorities began to face an increasingly complex set of social issues. One was the troubling trend toward the urbanization of poverty that began in the latter part of the 1980s and came into full view in the past decade.[1] Poverty has been growing faster than population, particularly during the economic stagnation of the 1980s. Over the last two decades, the number of urban residents below the poverty line grew by 50 percent, rising from 80 million in 1975 to more than 125 million in 1995. Data from the Economic Commission for Latin America and the Caribbean show that extreme poverty was on the rise more rapidly in urban than in rural areas from 1980 to 1986, increasing by 12.4 million people in cities versus 2.9 million in rural areas. Additionally, the nature of poverty began to change around this time, adding to the complexity of social issues. The number of poor households headed by women increased and new problems of drugs and violence began to draw notice. If these features of poverty were present during the 1970s, they were simply not mentioned by the standard literature of the time. Valladares's review of literature on urban development in Latin America over the past several decades found fewer than 90 citations of the subject of violence out of more than 3,000, and virtually all of these appeared in the late 1980s (Valladares and Coelho 1996).

IMPETUS FOR CHANGE

Unlike these context factors that evolved gradually over decades, others became evident more recently and more suddenly. The debt crisis in the 1980s appeared within the span of a few years. Reforms in Spain, new republicanism in the United States and Britain, the tide of change in Eastern Europe fostered by the Pope, and glasnost may all have had an impact on triggering the quiet revolution. Though speculative and by no means proven, each of these factors has been cited by informants during the course of research and professional work on decentralization. Further investigation is required to explore and test the relative weight these factors might have had on the spawning or pace of the quiet revolution.

The Dead Weight of Debt

Certainly one proximate cause of change was the shattering effect of a decade of debt. A hemispheric debt crisis, brought on by excessive borrowing during the 1970s, paralyzed economic growth in the 1980s and wiped out gains from the previous ten years in Latin America. During this "lost decade" of debt, Latin America's nations quadrupled their combined long-term foreign debt, which rose from $45 billion to $176 billion between 1975 and 1982. During roughly this same period, current account deficits doubled from 2.2 percent of gross domestic product (GDP) to 5.5 percent (Edwards 1993).

State enterprises, set up as a complement to import substitution policies in the 1970s, nearly tripled their indebtedness. Overborrowing and fiscal mismanagement in many of the region's countries produced hyperinflation, peaking at 40,000 percent a year in Brazil in the late 1980s. Edwards (1993, 8) argues that the region's public sectors had become bloated and overloaded: "instead of protecting the public from external shocks, [they] had greatly weakened the ability of these economies to react."

A reference point outside of the region by which we can gauge this failure is the occurrence of sudden growth spurts in Asia in the late 1980s. There, the alternative export-promotion models of economic development were put into practice earlier in the decade. Key countries in Asia made macroeconomic adjustments and opened their economies to trade. These policies bore fruit. As reported by the World Bank (1993), East Asia's economies quickly recovered from their own debt crisis and grew faster than any others in the world. Chile was the first country in South America to make such reforms, and the demonstration effect was quite strong. President Augusto Pinochet had already begun to reform taxes and liberalize trade in 1975. The results of those experiences—a return to vigorous growth in Chile after 1985 and an annual growth in exports in the range of 10 percent in Asian countries—began to spread throughout the hemisphere. These lessons added a new reason to solve the debt crisis. More importantly, they accelerated the impetus to reform and to offload the burdens of the central state apparatus (Edwards 1993, 31).

Spain as Inspiration

After the death of General Franco in 1975, Spain began to build a new state and to create regional autonomy within the republic. Because of its many historical ties to Latin America—cultural, religious, institutional, legal, and linguistic—Spain is viewed as a role model in Latin America (Nickson 1995, 7). Spain's move toward local autonomy, reforms in local governance, and more aggressive foreign policy to capture the promise of trade and commercial markets in Latin America, all worked to make the Spanish experience a source of inspiration and, later, of technical and financial assistance for decentralization in Latin America.

Spain's move toward decentralization reached an important milestone in 1980 when Catalonia, the Basque Country, and Andalusia, among other regions, were granted autonomy after constitutional reform. This transformation can be seen as both pioneering and inspiring, although not necessarily a blueprint for decentralization in Latin America. The shift to autonomy in Spanish regions effectively created a quasi-federal regime in which the central government shared power with local and intermediate levels of government. And although it was and remains a constitutional republic and monarchy, Spain accorded more power to its regions after 1976 than had ever been enjoyed by the states in Latin America's four federal republics (Argentina, Brazil, Mexico, and Venezuela).

Spanish authorities drew on various European experiences—German, British, and French—in designing fiscal policy and the political apparatus of the state. European practices were copied or modified to set up systems for setting and collecting local taxes, arranging intergovernmental fiscal relations, and setting prices for public goods and tariffs. Implementation of these ideas in Spanish cities such as Barcelona, Madrid, San Sebastian, and Seville established an environment of creative experimentation. For instance, according to Rojas, benefit levies were introduced in some cities as a way of capturing value increases in private property created by public investments.[2] These and other experiences were known in the region through literary and consultative channels (e.g., Borja 1988).

In addition to recognized practitioners such as Borja, many institutions served as vehicles to carry Spanish influence to Latin America. For instance, the Institute of Ibero-American Cooperation was charged with seeking and deepening ties between Spain and Latin America as one element of Spain's foreign policy. Other vehicles were (and still are) the Spanish associations of local governments, which have extended technical assistance to national and international associations of local authorities in Latin America—mayors, councils, governors, and other public officials. The international treasurers' association, international institutes of public administration, and the International Union of Local Authorities all helped (and continue to help) in transmitting ideas and exchanging information between Spain and Latin America.

In this context, Brazil borrowed some elements of Spain's urban legislation in its constitutional reforms after 1985. Colombia later passed similar legislation drawing on the Brazilian and Spanish experiences. Similarly, the expansion of public-private partnerships and public participation in urban affairs—evident, for instance, in the planning and financing of neighborhood renewal in Basque and Catalan cities—inspired numerous mayors and municipal councils throughout Latin America. As a final Spanish fillip, some financial assistance to Latin American nations came from Spanish banks such as Banco Santander, Banco del Bilbao, and Banco Vizcaya.

Elements of the Spanish experience came to light for Latin American leaders at about the same time the impacts of macroeconomic reform and liberalization were being felt in the region. Evidence from Asia, from the fruits of experiments of early pioneers like Chile, and the transformation in Spain were all mutually reinforcing, offering policy-makers in many countries compelling evidence to extend reforms to the subnational level.

New Republicanism

Few references were made in personal communications about the new Republicanism as a direct influence on decentralization of the state, but it is hard to imagine that the political shifts engineered by Ronald Reagan did not have some influence over thinking by leaders of the Latin American region. In 1980, Reagan campaigned on a platform of limiting the role of federal government, and in one analyst's words, it "became a central objective of his first term." (Liner 1989, 5). Even in the 1970s, the Advisory Committee on Intergovernmental Relations had issued frequent warnings about the congested intergovernmental system and finally, in 1985, recommended a shift of responsibility and revenues back to states and localities in the United States.

Divine Inspiration: Papal Message of Individual Freedom and Responsibility

During the 1970s and 1980s, Pope John Paul II was a factor in fostering reform. The Pope traveled extensively and worked to strengthen the Roman Catholic Church in authoritarian states while spreading a message compatible with, if not outright supportive of, decentralized democracy. This open, albeit restrained, papal championing of human freedoms and individual responsibility can be seen as an implicit challenge to the authoritarian and, to a lesser extent, centralized states. The Pope's visits to forty-five developing countries between 1979 and 1987 may have inadvertently turned into political support for decentralization. Repeated visits by Pope John Paul II to Poland in 1979, 1983, and 1987 were decisive factors in the rise of solidarity and political opposition to the Jaruzelski regime. Kwitny (1997) cites Gorbachev as having said, "Everything that has happened these past few years in Eastern Europe would have been impossible without the Pope." His visits in the 1980s to scores of other countries—including Mexico, Brazil, and the Philippines—carried a message of individual freedom and responsibility. His words reached millions of people and may have helped erode the moral and political grip of authoritarian power in Latin America.

A New Standard of Assistance after Perestroika

The breakup of the former Soviet Union produced more than a dozen newly independent states interested in reform and eager to decentralize. The attitude of the former Soviet states changed the political and institutional climate between donors and aid recipients. Development institutions saw in the states of the former Soviet Union a set of conditions quite unlike those commonly found in borrowing nations: large endowments of built capital, an educated labor force, and relatively strong, if inexperienced, institutions directed by governments eager to reform. This situation created a new competition for development assistance funds. Capital market flows, and particularly concessional assistance, were already being diverted from the Latin American region (Cumby and Levich 1987) in favor of countries in the former Soviet Union. The prospects for a major redirection of official assistance, as well of private capital, were so strong that nervous leaders of the developing world published a declaration in 1991 reminding public interest institutions like the World Bank of the dangers of capital drain away from Africa and Latin America. These fears grew more real with the 1993 accession to the World Bank of seventeen former Soviet republics and Eastern European countries.

The gravitation of the new states to a capitalist mold, and the flow of international finance to these states, meant that reform—of the macroeconomic system, public sector, and trade policies—as well as decentralization took on a new importance. In effect, state reform, democratization, and decentralization became more important components in, if not a new standard to qualify for, official assistance. Those Latin American countries that did attract capital—Chile, Mexico, and Argentina—did so by accelerating the liberalization of their markets and loosening the reigns of centralized state power and control.

Bilateral Democracy Builders

After the mid-1980s, technical and financial assistance from Spain was complemented by sustained and focused assistance from bilateral donors in North America and Europe. France, Canada, Sweden, Holland, and the United States were interested in promoting democracy, good government, and fiscal stability. Germany's foreign assistance agency, GTZ, had been operating since the 1960s in local community development and institution building in Bolivia, Ecuador, Venezuela, Colombia, Peru, Paraguay, the Dominican Republic, and nearly all of Central America. The Friedrich Ebert Foundation, Ford Foundation, Adenauer Foundation, and F. Naumann Foundation all launched programs addressing issues related to decentralization. These foundations and bilateral donors found it easy to increase emphasis on democratic decision-making as the influences of state reform and decentralization began to spread across the region.

Horizontal Influences

Countries also began to influence one another. Exchanges between and among various national and subnational governments were important in framing issues, formulating approaches, and designing legislation and institutions. Authorities and policymakers in (unitary) states such as Peru and Bolivia, to cite two examples, were intrigued with the promulgation of Colombia's first laws on competencies and resources in 1986.[3] Various decentralization laws in Colombia accorded powers to cities and regions that approximated those normally given to states in federated republics, much as Spain had done to strengthen the autonomy of its regions. Nearly all nations learned from—and, certainly, policymakers and legislators commented about—the Brazilian constitution of 1988 and the Bolivian national participation law promulgated in 1991. (Both of these are examined in more detail in chapter 7.)

Venezuela's first commission on decentralization was headed by the internationally respected jurist and historian Carlos Brewer-Carias. With ministerial rank and highly respected for his integrity, Brewer-Carias was able to attract top academic and administrative experts from Europe, the United States, Mexico, and Chile for consultations in 1988 and 1989. In the early 1990s, as the attention of the region's policymakers turned to more narrow sectoral concerns of local government, like supplying drinking water and delivering health care and education, many of the countries in the region began to draw more heavily on experiences of neighbors. For instance, the Chilean experiences with decentralized health, education, and social welfare (see chapter 3) became the source of new ideas about how to mobilize community resources for housing and local improvements in Argentina, Brazil, Ecuador, Costa Rica, and El Salvador. Many countries learned from squatter upgrading experiences in Brazil, Guatemala, and Venezuela and from experiences with social funds in Bolivia and Mexico. Networks of professionals and local authorities came to play an important role in dissemination around the region. Dissemination of experiences among a few pioneers—Mexico, Chile, Colombia (as discussed in chapter 3)—was a key factor in shaping policy choices and encouraging leaders to take action toward decentralization.

SMALLER FACTORS OF CHANGE

Many other factors may have helped to make the decision about decentralization easier or faster. Factors mentioned by practitioners and suggested in the media include the fear in military regimes of a political backlash, the poor or unpopular management in Argentina, and brutality in Chile during the Pinochet regime. A second factor has been the growing awareness among regions and peoples about their relative places in the distribution of wealth and share of power in the national scheme of things.

Military

The military did not impede decentralization and state reforms in most instances, at least not publicly. Indeed, in Chile the military regime promoted decentralization. But where the military was not in power, sweeping state reforms and decentralization provided the occasion to test the long-observed military prerogative of "protecting the constitution" when the state was threatened. Military forces ran Brazil, Argentina, and Chile for more than a decade before decentralization. And military forces moved on student uprisings in Mexico in 1968 and in Bolivia repeatedly in the 1970s and 1980s. Perhaps the first signs of caution shown by the military appeared when the Raul Alfonsin administration took steps to prosecute military officials in criminal courts following the Malvinas War in 1982. President Augusto Pinochet in neighboring Chile had, until that year, declared an intention to stay in power for a sixteen-year period. His abrupt about-face, along with the rising tide of popular support for the Patricio Alywin government, can be interpreted as recognition by Pinochet and other military leaders of a shifting tide of support away from military control.

In Brazil, the election of Tancredo Neves can be interpreted in part as a repudiation of the military powers that backed his opponent. The upswelling of popular enthusiasm after Neves's victory in the 1986 presidential elections was another note in the chorus of liberalism echoing around the region. A similar posture of deference was expressed differently in Peru. There, military leaders themselves struck out on a decidedly leftist path. The Peruvian council of government sought to reform political and economic spheres of the public sector. Gillespie (1989) also argues that the military withdrawal from power in Peru was due to the loss of support for them from economic elites. In short, military governments for various reasons did not stand up to block the sharing of power that came with decentralization.

Regional Interests and Rising Awareness

Some observers give weight to the effects of improved social communications (Skidmore 1993) and particularly to the rising awareness and growing power of regions led by groups outside the centers of power in national capitals. Improved awareness through news media and other communications was said to aid and abet regional elites whose economic fortunes were based in the "hinterlands" (Torres 1986; de la Cruz 1994). Virtually every country in the region has an equivalent to the financial power center of Monterrey, Mexico, a robust economic base of a Valle de Cauca in central Colombia, or the natural resource base of the eastern llanos cattle country in Venezuela. In these examples, regional interests began to rise in prominence just at the time when many other factors mentioned earlier were beginning to precipitate the decision to decentralize. In Mexico, the process of decentralization was described by former President de la Madrid as "strengthening federalism"— that is, bringing together various regional interests into a (federal) whole. The converse view was expressed eloquently by two newly elected state governors in Mexico and Venezuela in 1988. They described the new power arrangements in their states in virtually the same words: "Before [elections], when the president called, we would go. Now [after elections], we decide if it is convenient for us." This simple tale, repeated at the local and regional levels with many variations throughout the continent, reveals a willingness to articulate regional interests and concerns over and above national priorities.

RELEVANCE OF THE QUIET REVOLUTION IN OTHER WORLD REGIONS

The trends toward decentralization and democratization in Latin America developed in the context of a highly urbanized population living in hundreds of large cities and thousands of small ones. And even though the sizes of cities, powers of states, conditions of social classes, and arrangements of political power vary greatly from one country to the next, the nations in Latin America seemed to respond to similar forces. The Latin American region is often seen as being a decade or more ahead of other regions in the world because of the scope and speed of change accomplished there, or because the urban transition is just beginning elsewhere, as in Africa, or has not yet been completed, as in Asia. For these reasons as well, Latin America's contextual factors help us gauge the distance it has come and take measure of the prospects for change and issues involved in decentralization in other regions.

Eastern Europe and the Newly Independent States

Though each of the states in the former Soviet bloc has its own cultural, historical, or provincial features, all the Eastern European nations are attempting to redefine the state and to reestablish legitimacy in governance after the political bankruptcy of communism. A reaction to excessive concentration of power in the Communist Party may explain the drive to decentralize into excessively small, atomistic units of local governments. For instance, cities in Hungary were minced into small municipal units with populations of a few thousand people. Municipal units of such small size are perhaps useful for consultation, but impossible in terms of economic viability and financial sustainability. They are unlikely to prove workable. The Budapest metropolitan council consists of thirty-two elected mayors from surrounding municipalities, presided over by an elected official. The smaller municipal domains enjoy powers—control over national assets like the building stock and metro rails—that were reserved for the central government in even the most liberalized Latin American countries. Cities in Hungary have been given control over such assets, created originally by national officials in the previous regime (and ultimately by Moscow's control). But no permanent income source is yet authorized to cover the large recurrent costs required to maintain these buildings and railways or to sustain local investment (Bird et al. 1995). These are but a few examples of the many policy issues in Eastern Europe that are strikingly parallel to those still under debate or already resolved in the quiet revolution.

Asia

Many Asian governments moved toward decentralized arrangements almost at the same time as Latin America. However, except for the Philippines, countries in East Asia and many in South Asia made adjustments that reflected a sharply different view of the state—one less inclined to give up central control—in order to retain national political coherence between central and local governments. Beginning with the overthrow of Ferdinand Marcos, democratic reforms in the Philippines were accompanied by a series of legal and administrative changes that gave greater weight to local governments, much as in Latin America. But more recent political upheavals in Indonesia, punctuated by the currency crisis beginning in 1997, produced a marked reduction in expectations about the capacity of the state, but growing expectations about local autonomy among regions and in local government. Specific reform legislation in the Philippines, Indonesia, and Thailand and to a lesser extent the Doi Moi reforms in Vietnam, has called for new functions at the local level and novel financial arrangements between local and national levels of government. Constitutional amendments in India (numbers 73 and 74) and laws in Indonesia (numbers 22 and 25) reflected familiar shifts of power toward states and local governments as in Latin America, but much more administrative and bureaucratic drag in the implementation. Though institutionalized models of autonomy in local finance and decision making have been slower to emerge in Asia than in Latin America, a few outstanding examples of local governments have emerged in all of these countries. Often forged by outstanding local leaders—for instance, in Hyderabad, Bangalore, Peshawar, and Kathmandu—the trailblazers in South and East Asia appear to have been a little further out in front of the broad mass of local governments and not to have been supported by consistent central policies. The acid test of power sharing—whether local governments are allowed to fail and be held accountable by local, rather than national, authorities—has not yet been attempted anywhere in Asia.

Africa

The impulse to decentralize is now emerging throughout many African countries, but in more muted form, partly because of staggering impoverishment in the continent. Overwhelming problems of national, even global, scope like the AIDS virus and civil and tribal warfare also contribute to slow progress. Intermediate and local governments are exceedingly weak in institutional terms, and decentralization has sometimes taken the form of deconcentration, that is, placing central bureaucratic controls at local levels. Mechanisms for voicing local concerns have been put into place and more substantial progress has been made in several countries, for instance, in South Africa, Mozambique, and Uganda. South Africa has invented an entirely new system of government for Johannesburg, but on the whole, power sharing in the mode of Latin American governments has been approached much more cautiously in Africa.

Countries in these and other regions can benefit from the experience of the quiet revolution. Though many of the sparks of change were flickering in regions all around the globe in the 1980s, particularly in Eastern Europe, none shone as brightly or endured as long as in Latin America. Anecdotal information suggests that national leaders drew inspiration from the Czech Velvet Revolution and from other, more purely economic management reforms in Asia. Even more lessons can be extended from the Latin American experience to inform policy decisions in other parts of the world as the quiet revolution matures and the momentous changes experienced in that region are absorbed by countries elsewhere.

PART II □ □ □ □ □ □ □ □ □

National Strategies
and Local Response

3 □ Unlikely Pioneers

Mexico and Chile are two unlikely pioneers in the quiet revolution. Both countries explored ways to reshape local government and to share power between local and central entities as early as the 1970s. Both Mexico and Chile created an opening in their two respective centralized, monolithic structures of government, and both set in motion a transformation of governance. In a matter of years afterward, similar changes could be seen throughout the region. Like much associated with Latin American decentralization, these pioneering efforts were fraught with irony. For one thing, Mexico and Chile were two unlikely candidates because decentralization in those countries was accomplished under relatively restrictive political circumstances. The absence of political freedoms in Chile and of pluralism in Mexico during the time decentralization was being launched might lead us to the conclusion that these nations would be followers rather than leaders in the move to decentralize. But because the governments were either genuinely interested in improving public sector efficiency (as in Chile in the 1970s) or because imperatives of sharing power with emerging regions were no longer resistible (as in Mexico in the late 1970s), both countries found ways to begin sharing decision making or spending power while maintaining control from the center.

A handful of other countries is included in this pioneering group for reference and comparison purposes. Colombia is included because it also acted early, and its unitary system is much like Chile's and offers convenient comparison. Also, civil unrest and violence in Colombia built pressures for change and instigated national laws and political reform that, beginning about 1968, took a very different direction from those in Chile. Brazil and Venezuela are included because, like Mexico, they are federated republics, and Brazil was moving out of a military dictatorship into a new democratic "opening" that marked a new level of local participation in public affairs. Venezuela was the only country to create a lead agency to guide the decentralization process.

The review of these countries affords insight into the similarities and special problems faced by their governments.[1] For all of these pioneers, the stimulus for decentralization arose from particular circumstances in each country and was fostered with varying degrees of urgency. But although these countries responded to circumstances distinct to their own political and historical milieu, each adopted similar methods or techniques to solve their problems. For instance, each of the states was in search of an alternative to the exhausted model of centralized government. For each of them also, Spain's experience with regionalization was an important source of inspiration and learning. The five pioneers also explored greater participation by the private sector, and one, Chile, invented a market model of private-sector involvement and competition in public services and infrastructure.

The resemblance of their approaches contains a second irony. Despite their similarities, the states seemed to learn little from each other's experience, at least in the first decade of change. In other words, the fruits of experimental trial and error spread slowly and in a piecemeal fashion through the region. Not until a decade after these changes began did efforts by countries and outside agencies begin to achieve some economies in scale of learning. Even though they were struggling with the same problems and taking similar approaches, these five countries did not benefit from a systematic attempt to disseminate their lessons and learn from their neighbors. A structured learning process might have accelerated the timetable of implementation.

CHILE

Compared to other countries in the region, Chile is more urbanized and its cities are growing more slowly. About 85 percent of the nation's population live in cities, and most of the country's 13 million people are concentrated in cities of the temperate central zone. Population growth and birth rates, in decline since the 1960s, have remained under 2 and 3 percent, respectively, since the 1970s. Chile today is organized administratively into 13 regions, 51 provinces, and 335 comunas, or municipalities.[2] Modern principles of municipalities were established in Chile's constitution of 1925. Before the

Pinochet years (1973–90), the traditional hierarchy of the Chilean government structure consisted of a president presiding over the national government, *intendentes* (governors) heading the provincial governments, and mayors at the local level. (In 1965, there were 25 intendentes and 227 mayors.) Under that hierarchy, like most administrative systems in unitary states, municipalities were the most local and the first line of contact between the populace and central ministries.[3]

Two-thirds of the municipalities in the 1960s had populations of fewer than 20,000, and the average municipal budget was around US$8 per capita (1965 dollars). Municipalities were primarily responsible for trash collection, traffic control, street lighting, street and neighborhood markets, and parks. Provincial administrations headed by intendentes named by the president provided coordination among municipalities in the same geographic region.[4]

One of the major objectives of the first efforts in decentralization was to clean up local government. Political partisanship and politicization had severely weakened local governments during the 1960s. A system of political patronage had gradually infected municipalities and paralyzed their ability to perform their basic functions. Before 1973, municipalities had followed a strong council model with council members (known as *regidores*) elected by direct vote with powers to approve local budgets and supervise implementation. The mayor was selected from among council members and could be replaced at any time by council resolution. Many observers of different political tendencies believe that this system led to a number of ills, including excessive turnover of mayors, excessive party posturing, and strongly partisan influences in municipal affairs. Aghón (1996), Castaneda (1990) and Friedmann (1976) all note that, by the early 1970s, local party politics were marked by partisan wrangling. These factors were harmful both to actual efficiency and to the public image of local governments. Politically inspired job creation had undermined local government budgets. In fact, according to Friedmann, neighborhood groups were seen by the Frei administration (1964–70) as a base for popular participation in national affairs. Intensive efforts were made to organize and confederate grassroots interest groups along partisan lines. Allende (1970–73) built upon similar local political groupings to advance social programs, such as the neighborhood food distribution system. These grassroots movements and central government supports were also mobilized to play out national political battles in the municipal arena. This state of affairs ended abruptly with the military coup in 1973.

Implementing a New Model of Government

Pinochet's strategy for government was aimed at creating a greater central control and greater discipline at the local level. One of several major components to his model of government was aimed at rooting out partisan favoritism at the local level and replacing it with efficient, private sector–like local units of government operating on market principles (i.e., minimizing costs, staying within a budget). The Pinochet model of government also deconcentrated some functions, meaning that central agencies set up local offices throughout the country. The model also changed the intergovernmental financial system, and, to enhance effectiveness of centralized control, created a more direct chain of command. All of these steps helped to maintain control over macroeconomic management. These changes were launched with decrees in July 1974 (laws 573 and 575).

The Pinochet military regime acted quickly to remove the partisan character of local affairs and to convert the local government system into a more service-oriented, even private-sector model, in which efficiency and service delivery were emphasized. The campaign by the military government against partisan influence began by establishing a rigid template for the size and functions of local government, backed up by a budgetary discipline that was enforced with impunity. The templates prescribed the number of professional staff, size of councils, and range of specific functions a given municipality should have according to its population size. Soon after taking power, the military government dismissed existing mayors and regidores and established a system of governance in which mayors were named directly by the president. Municipalities were thus brought under central administrative and political control. Local officials were told to fit the prescribed number of personnel corresponding to the size category of the city. For most, this meant downsizing. Objective standards of qualification for many jobs were also introduced. Mayors could be sacked for failing to stay within budget limits.

Changes in municipal manpower illustrate the dramatic transformation in local government between 1975 and 1988. During this period, the total number of municipal employees actually decreased, while Chile's population increased by about 13 percent. But the proportion of professional level personnel moved from about one in twenty to seven in twenty, while numbers of unskilled staff moved in the opposite direction (Castaneda, 1990). Middle level staff remained about the same. These proportions represented an utter transformation in local government and signified success in Pinochet's campaign to increase competency in local administration.

These austerity measures spilled over into the arena of civil participation, weakening or destroying collective expression of demands by neighborhood groups. Instead, the market model of local government was to operate on the principle that citizens interact with government primarily as individual consumers of municipal services. The military regime created corporate bodies (for instance, local advisory councils) that were supposed to represent the interests of different local groups in an orderly manner. But the "representatives" of these groups were appointed from above, often without popular support, and always without a mandate to express group demands that conflicted with governmental priorities.

Chilean municipalities were expressly removed from the political role they had played before 1973. Under the military regime, local governments did not have opinions on national political questions, were not supposed to represent organized political sentiment, and were expected to be apolitical in their delivery of services and hiring of workers. Municipal leadership, after all, was appointed from the ranks of those generally supportive of the military government, and steps often were taken to dismiss opponents of the national regime. But the very fact that the expressed ideal of local government in Chile involved insulating it from political pressures sets the Chilean experiment in decentralization apart from others in the region. Local government, at least in theory, was supposed to be a technically skilled, politically neutral, and efficient provider of services.

Local Government as Service Delivery Agent

The decentralization model applied in Chile is a very good example of the *principal agency model* of administration. In this model, local governments act at the discretion and under the control of a "principal," in this case, the central government. This model contrasts sharply with a local public choice model in which local governments enjoy some degree of autonomy within which local needs are expressed by voter taxpayers and met by local authorities within the resources of tax and other revenues available to them. With the exception of the very wealthiest localities in the Santiago area, Chile's municipal governments did not have a meaningful choice as to the type of services they would provide and almost no discretion over the revenues they could raise. They also had very little legal flexibility in taking on new service functions or in declining functions the central government might choose to assign them. Local governments were, above all else, to be cost-effective providers of local public services.

Municipalities were to refrain from interfering with local economic markets and from planning economic development. As if to drive home the point, some larger municipalities in the Santiago metropolitan area were split into several smaller municipalities. This was done to divide political opposition and to make the jurisdictions more efficient for service delivery. But carving up large municipalities greatly weakened their potential for local economic development because some were left without a tax base of commercial and manufacturing districts.

At the same time, Chilean municipalities were bound by law to handle social welfare concerns. This obligation sewed the seeds of another irony. Within a few years, Chilean municipalities began to build a stronger, professional capacity for social service provision to low-income groups. In its drive for efficiency, the Pinochet regime inadvertently laid the groundwork for effective poverty targeting and program delivery at the municipal level. Like other posts in large municipalities, social workers with professional qualifications became an obligatory part of local government. They were meant to keep track of the poor and see to it that state subsidies for shelter, food, and schooling were rationed fairly. By the 1990s, Chile had installed an innovative practice of integrating municipal and national efforts to provide targeted assistance—in welfare and subsidies—directly to the poor (Castaneda 1990).

The Chilean model of local service delivery might be called a market model. Local governments, like other levels of government, were expected to cease engaging directly in providing service functions whenever these could be performed by the private market. This policy built upon and expanded the *principio de subsidiariedad* (principle of subsidiarity or subordination), according to which government in Chile should become involved in service delivery only when the private sector or voluntary groups of citizens cannot do so adequately.[5] In its own operations, local government was supposed to act as much as possible like an efficient private-sector firm. This meant placing an emphasis on cost minimization rather than following the theretofore customary practice of providing services at any cost up to the limits imposed by budgets plus negotiated grants and off-budget resources.

The application of the principle of subsidiarity shaped local government activity. Municipalities withdrew altogether from some service functions and entered into open competition with the private sector in others, for instance, education. They were asked to serve as halfway houses on the road to full privatization for still other functions. Consequently, local governments drastically cut back their permanent labor forces in favor of contracting with the private sector.

Local transit and slaughterhouses fell into the first category of services abandoned by local government. Primary and secondary education were the chief examples of services that were provided by local government in competition with the private sector. When the central government decentralized schooling to the local level beginning in 1979, it also provided that central government per-pupil payments would be available on exactly the same terms to public and private schools alike, in the expectation that the two sectors would compete for customers and upgrade school quality in the course of their competition. The Pinochet government indicated that education also fell into the third category—services that eventually could be taken over entirely by the private sector. It reorganized water services to the same end, breaking up the national water authority into regional bodies and reorganizing them as public corporations. These were intended to be preparatory to selling the water companies to private investors, but the onset of civilian government in 1990 delayed this privatization.

Hierarchy of National Administrative Control

The strengthening of local government service responsibilities took place at the same time that national administration intensified control over many aspects of the Chilean public sector, including local government. With the installation of *intendentes* in the thirteen newly created regions (composed of clusters of municipalities), and with the new limitations on local government, the national ministries could more effectively transmit national policy and national decisions to the local level. The number of provincial governors rose to 51, and the number of mayors grew to 335.

President Pinochet made the true meaning of these arrangements unambiguously clear to one of his appointed regional intendentes, noting that they were created "to be the representatives of the President in the regions, not representatives of the regions before the President" (Campbell et al. 1991). The hierarchical structure is a classic representation of the principal agency model described earlier. Chilean authority proceeded downward from the dictator to his appointed intendentes, onward to his appointed municipal mayors, and thence to the subjects. Mayors were responsible to the regional authorities and, through them, to the president in a direct chain of command. One aspect of the Pinochet emphasis on coordination and control— the involvement of municipalities in regional investment decisions—led to improved capacity in local governments to plan and evaluate investments. But emphasis was on control, not on managing a system of free-thinking local governments.

The strategy of delegating important new functions to local government while tightening central administrative control was unique to Chile within the Latin American region. (A somewhat parallel development occurred in

Indonesia, where fiscal and service decentralization were achieved under a highly centralized system backed up by military authority {Hull, 1999}). In the other countries of the region, decentralization typically has carried with it an increase in local political power, either voluntarily granted by the central government or forced from it by political realities.

Macroeconomic concerns were driving factors behind Chile's strategy of decentralization. Pinochet was the first leader in the region (in 1975) to undertake liberalization of trade and fiscal reforms. Without tight controls, municipalities were seen as potential obstacles to fiscal discipline. Consequently, municipalities were kept on a very narrow fiscal course. They were given virtually no control over local revenues. (They are still prohibited from borrowing.) Personnel ceilings were dictated by the central government. Salary levels, except those for health and education workers, were prescribed by national law. During most of the military regime, local government budgets were subject to line item authorization by both regional authorities and the Ministry of the Interior. As a result, very few fiscal surprises were possible in the Chilean system of local government. The budgetary discipline imposed on the local public sector in Chile was without precedent in Latin America.

The evolution of decentralization in Chile took a dramatic turn in 1990 with the accession to power of the Aylwin conciliation government. A new phase of decentralization was launched with appointment of then-opposition mayors in key cities and with the gradual dismantling of the hierarchical system put in place by Pinochet.[6] Municipalities were given more autonomy in personnel and finance issues and were allowed to engage in a wider spectrum of political and economic activities.

More than a little irony can be found in the harsh downsizing and tight-fisted control imposed over municipalities in Chile. Pinochet's measures forced the creation of lean and mean local governments bound by duty and militaristic obligation to deliver specific services efficiently, and not to engage in political and economic business. These measures severely circumscribed political freedoms and participatory aspects of local government, effectively eliminating the one argument—improved resource allocation at the local level—most governments in Latin America recognized as an unquestioned rationale for decentralization. Despite this limitation, Chile produced the first "re-invention" of local governments, reversing the ratio of unskilled to professional personnel and converting them to high performers not seen anywhere else in the hemisphere. Along with it were planted seeds for later reforms, for instance, in contracting out many services, participating in the planning of regional investment projects, exercising expenditure control, and forging a role in implementing the government's poverty assistance program. All of these reforms led eventually to new, more proactive roles by local governments in the years following conciliation.

MEXICO

Mexico became a highly centralized state at the very inception of its revolution in 1910. Strong leaders and a single political party financed by oil wealth (vastly expanded after discoveries in the 1970s) embarked on nation building controlled from the center. Mexico has been the third largest oil exporter in the world for decades. Its oil wealth has generated the largest part of the country's income for most of the postwar era. These political and resource factors translated into a monolithic structure of centralized control, and although the Mexican political system was challenged at various times in its history, it was only in the late 1960s that fissures in the system began to appear. The student demonstration for increased political freedoms in 1968 was but one visible episode. Overreaction by the Mexican military to otherwise peaceful street marches discredited the centralized leadership. But the major give-and-take in Mexican decentralization took place between the states and the central government. In these battles, municipalities were secondary, but direct beneficiaries of the shifts in power wrested from the central government by the states. As a federated republic, the states are the most important interlocutors with central government in Mexico, as they are in Venezuela, Brazil, and Argentina.

As in Chile, decentralization started in Mexico nearly a decade ahead of the rest of the continent. And although both countries were reacting to fiscal concerns and both displayed a strong instinct to maintain control at the center, the motives for and mechanics of Mexico's decentralization were quite distinct from those in Chile. While Pinochet appropriated control over municipalities as part of the administrative apparatus of the state, the Mexican government, during several consecutive presidential administrations (each a six-year term), gradually evolved to a new balance of power with states. Mexican states have their own independent assemblies and law-making powers. Of critical importance also was the outcome of the 1988 elections, which were lost by the Partido Revolucionario Institucional (PRI) in key urban centers. Decentralization and power-sharing arrangements left the states with more say in how public investments were made in their jurisdictions. Attention to and changes in municipal government followed directly and indirectly from this shift in power.

Regional Tensions in the Centralized State

Mexico City is one of the largest cities in the developing world, and Mexico has often been cited as the archetype of the "macrocephalic" state, where national political and economic life is dominated by an oversized center. For decades, Mexico City has produced about 40 percent of the country's gross domestic product, has housed half the nation's industrial plant, and has accounted for more than half of the financial transactions in the country. However, beginning sometime in the 1970s, changes in demographic and productive structure began to appear that reflected a subtle shift in power.

The rate of population growth in Mexico City began to shrink, and cities surrounding it began to absorb a larger share of new growth. Cities like Puebla, Toluca, and Queretaro began to experience what one Mexican planner called "spontaneous deconcentration."[7] Because there were no specific policy interventions, growth was spilling over into cities surrounding Mexico City. Most likely, social and economic forces were driving up the costs of living and doing business in Mexico City and driving away businesses and residents from the center. In fact, population movements to these satellite cities came at about the same time as structural reforms—such as the elimination of subsidies for drinking water, gasoline, and foodstuffs—were being implemented in the country. These kinds of subsidies had a strong impact on decisions of firms and households to locate in a particular place (Kelly and Williamson 1984). To cite an example, the price of water sold to residents in Mexico City in 1970 was about one-quarter the cost of producing it (Campbell 1981). Whatever the cause, the population of three of the cities around Mexico City grew at over 4 percent per annum in the 1980s —Puebla (4.4 percent), Queretaro (5.9 percent), and Toluca (4.7 percent).

The rates of growth in other large metropolitan areas also began to sink below those in the rest of the country, and new centers of power and wealth were consolidating their places in Mexico's economy. Mexico's system of cities can be categorized in three groups. First is the big four, the largest cities, Mexico City and the three next largest metropolitan areas, Monterrey, Guadalajara, and Leon. Each of these last three is the center of industrial and commercial production that is distinct from that of Mexico City. Next are about sixty medium-sized cities and state capitals of between roughly 100 thousand and one million residents. The third group consists of more than 100 smaller towns that serve as agricultural supply and service centers spread throughout the country. Major changes in demographic dynamics in the 1970s—a decrease in birth rates in the big cities and a shift in the intensity and direction of migration—began to reflect an alteration in the growth pattern in the country.

Many cities and regions in the country began to consolidate comparative advantage in economic production, and often these regional cities were also centers of a distinct cultural identity or even ethnic population. For instance, cities of the central arid states, like Monterrey and Chihuahua, were based on irrigated agricultural and livestock for export. Monterrey and Guadalajara began in the 1960s to take on a new level of importance as financial, industrial, and manufacturing centers with markets in United States, Europe, and Japan. Cities in the southern mountain states of the southwest, like Tuxtla Gutierrez, became and remained largely supply and trading centers in agriculture production and centers of Mayan culture. Secondary cities were also growing up around their own economic resources or markets, such as Veracruz and Tampico, the centers of oil production, and coastal resort cities like Acapulco and Cancun. In each of these places, migration in the 1970s and 1980s accounted for well over half the annual population increase, helping to push growth rates to levels twice as high as the big four.

One of the most dramatic displays of regional growth took place along the border with the United States. Mexico's northern border region consists of about a dozen cities with more than twelve million total urban population. Tijuana and Juarez became centers of "in-bond"[8] industrial production, where investments for the manufacture of electronics and consumer goods created 100,000 jobs in the 1980s. Industrial investment in Nuevo Laredo, for example, grew in excess of 5 percent in the 1970s and 10 percent in the 1980s. In a sense, the northern part of Mexico began, in a metaphorical way, to turn away from the political center in Mexico City and toward the north, to face future markets for its exports.

Thus, while Mexico City was still the major economic force in the country, it was gradually losing its centripetal pull as new economic powers began to diversify the economy and consolidate their strength and political influence. Little by little over several decades, regional forces began to exert pressure on the monolithic structure of political and financial control. A breaking point was reached with the 1988 elections. The hand-picked candidate of the PRI, Carlos Salinas, lost much of the urban vote, including Mexico City. Although he won a national plurality and was elected into office, his poor showing in Mexico's major urban centers was unexpected, and the PRI began to redouble its efforts to win popular support, partly by power sharing and decentralization.

Institutional Reforms

Reforms can be traced back to the fiscal crisis triggered by the 1976 devaluation of the peso.[9] This crisis played an important role in Mexico's initial decision to begin sharing power with the states by allowing them to have more influence in expenditure decisions. Mexico's decentralization policies were implemented as three separate reforms. The first was the *Ley de Coordinacion Fiscal* of 1978. This law strengthened and expanded revenue sharing between central and local governments. The law also reaffirmed a suspension of state and local levies. These overlapped with the newly introduced value-added tax, the IVA, which became the principal source of income shared among the states. The law not only guaranteed state and municipal governments a share of federal revenue, but subjected these transfers to a formula free of discretionary allocation—at least so far as the distribution among states was concerned. Distribution of 20 percent of each state's share went to municipal governments under terms that each individual state was allowed to define for itself.

The second instrument of reform was the amendment of Article 115 of the constitution in 1981. This conferred upon municipal administrations prime responsibility for the provision of urban infrastructure and services. It also conferred authority to municipalities over land use and development and revenues from taxation of property. Although emphasizing continued subordination to state law and policy, the amended article established a clear role for municipal administrations in the management of local affairs. Together with the Ley de Coordinacion Fiscal, it gave local governments access to public tax revenues. The amendment to Article 115 can be seen as a direct outgrowth of an upswelling of popular sentiment for more local control over local affairs. This sentiment was expressed forcefully by citizens and organized groups during *consultas populares,* or public fora, organized by Miguel de la Madrid as a part of the presidential campaign of 1982 (Torres 1986).

The third reform improved the institutional arrangements to carry out the new functions and to manage shared revenues at the state and local levels. Of particular importance were new mechanisms—contractual agreements between planning bodies in states and their counterparts in central government—set up to determine investment needs and to manage grants from the central government to finance regional development (these are described in more detail, below). Federal branch offices for most ministries were opened in each state in 1985 to facilitate this cooperation.

Each of these three reforms can be seen in relation to the growing strength of regions, each with a distinct identity, and most of them anchored by one or more rapidly growing cities. Regional authorities, private sector actors, and civil society were growing stronger and making claims for more influence over the way the nation's resources were being spent. At the same time, Mexico's pioneering matching grant program was one of the most elaborate and effective programs anywhere in Latin America for financing public investment at the local level with strong state and local participation. The grant programs grew to the $2 billion level by the 1990s. They had such significant impact on local affairs and political ramifications for mayors, governors, and presidents in Mexico that they deserve more detailed examination.

Matching Grants: Financing Decentralized Participatory Planning

Beginning in the 1970s, the government started a modest program to provide central government financing on a matching basis to state and local governments. The foundations of the matching grant system grew organically out of regional development and special-emphasis programs of programming and budgeting ministry (known as SPP for Secretaria de Programacion y Presupuesto) in the 1970s. Regional development strategies were undergoing a shift, moving away from growth poles and regional river basins patterned after the TVA in the United States, to more targeted investments in rural and regional development in programs such as PIDER.[10] In 1978, a system of bilateral contracts—known as *convenios unicos de cooperacion* (CUCs)—was put in place to coordinate federal investments in states implementing the PIDER and other federal programs.

A few years later, these arrangements were extended to all states and broadened to cover general program assistance. To qualify for the funds, local governments were obliged to implement a planning process that engaged a large number of interest groups, agencies, and organizations in the decision over public spending. Each state was to develop detailed plans that were signed as unified development contracts, known as *convenios unicos de desarrollo* (CUDs). CUDs were yearly agreements that stipulated the size, terms, and conditions of investment projects financed jointly by federal, state, and local governments. Investment programs proposed in the CUDs were negotiated between the SPP in the federal government and each state.[11]

Comites Estatales de Planeacion para el Desarrollo (COPLADEs) were normally chaired by the governor and consisted of a permanent technical staff and representation of an elaborate array of sectoral and regional authorities as well as representatives of the private sector. In a variety of consultative fora, the COPLADEs decided on investment projects and ranked them in order of priority. Some states extended the COPLADE further by creating municipal counterparts (COPLADEMS or COPLAMUNs).[12] At both the state and municipal levels, meetings and planning exercises followed a year-round schedule, and in some states and cities they involved thousands of people and organizations. By the late 1980s, about a fifth of the public sector investment budget was channeled through this program.

The importance of these grants was not their size, but that they were controlled in coordination with local officials. The regional development budget and matching grants were the smaller of the two major instruments for fiscal decentralization in Mexico (the other, larger program was the revenue-sharing system mentioned earlier). In per capita terms, matching grants grew from US$3 to US$11 during the 1980s. State and local contributions would further increase per capita levels by perhaps 40 percent. By comparison, transferred revenues to states ranged between 23 percent and 31 percent of the total federal budget over the same period. These funds reached about US$67 per capita in 1990. Unlike transferred revenues that were to be used freely by states and municipalities, matching grants were restricted to capital investment. State and local authorities could place these investments wherever they pleased. Transferred revenues, in contrast, were used mostly for recurrent budgetary expenditures, offering local authorities little by way of concrete, visible projects.

At the municipal level, the uses and importance of CUD matching grants showed great variability. Within the municipality of Chihuahua, for example, more than 90 percent of CUD matching grant financing in 1989 was devoted to improvements in the water supply. In Juarez (also in the state of Chihuahua) in the same year, water supply claimed less than 10 percent of CUD resources, because federal and state authorities required Juarez to pay for most of the expansion of the water distribution system from local funds. Juarez's much lower level of CUD support was used principally for criminal justice facilities, electrification of marginal areas, and cultural and recreational facilities. After the 1988 elections, CUD matching-grant financing was transformed into a new program, known as *Solidaridad*, or Solidarity. This change can be seen as part of the effort by the federal government and PRI to win back support of low-income urban populations.

Mexico as Pioneer

Even though a number of reforms in revenue sharing and functional responsibilities formed a core part of Mexico's decentralization overtures, its use of matching grants was a pioneering development in the region. The matching grants were not entirely new inventions. Many countries have used these tools before. But they were new at the time in the region and were adapted to the circumstances of decentralization—to involve state and local governments more directly in decision making. In effect, the central government dosed out a sizeable fraction of its investment budget in a controlled sharing of power, in this case over responsibility for local investments. The federal government defined sectoral priorities, controlled allocation among states, set the rules under which projects were approved and funded, and authorized and processed financial disbursements according to progress in project implementation. From the states' perspective, matching grants became an important part of financing for core infrastructure, giving governors and mayors new ways to exercise their political power.

A SECOND WAVE OF PIONEERS

A handful of countries joined in a second wave of decentralization, beginning in the mid-1980s. Brazil, Colombia, and Venezuela were quick to launch initiatives in state reform with strong components of decentralization, although neither moved as soon or as far as did Chile and Mexico. A little later, toward the end of the 1980s, Bolivia and several Central American countries also started a process of transferring power of decision making and spending to local governments. Guatemala and Honduras are the best examples. But Brazil, Colombia, and Venezuela also made their mark on early efforts, and because Colombia is a unitary state and Brazil and Venezuela, federal, they offer a useful comparison to the pioneering efforts of Chile and Mexico.

Colombia

Responding to a destabilizing insurrection in the early 1960s, the Lleras administration (1967–70) initiated a constitutional reform in 1968 that can be seen as marking the beginning of the decentralization process. But, unlike Chile, Colombia moved in fits and starts. For instance, although the more than ninety central government agencies, most notably in the education sector, were shifted to field offices in the early 1970s, local governments were not given authority over basic services until 1987. Furthermore, far from promoting decentralization, administrative deconcentration to regional offices actually swelled the size of the centrally controlled bureaucracy. Although deconcentration brought the bureaucrats who managed services closer to local users, it kept authority over personnel, financing, and policymaking exclusively in the hands of national ministries.

The Betancur and Barco administrations (1983–86 and 1987–90, respectively) launched fresh new efforts to decentralize political decision making, financial control, and management authority over most public services to Colombia's more than 1,000 municipalities. Almost thirty laws, legislative acts, and decrees were enacted to implement decentralization policies. Law 14 of 1983 strengthened the capacities of departmental and municipal governments to generate their own revenues. Law 12 of 1986 authorized the transfer of increasing shares of national sales tax revenues directly to municipal governments. In 1986, Legislative Act 1 and Law 78 mandated popular election of mayors. Another major step came in 1987 with Decree 77, which established the partial or total transfer of financial and administrative responsibilities for water, sewerage, sanitation, agricultural extension, education, health, and public works services to municipalities.

President Gaviria (1991–94) embraced the challenge of decentralization as the yardstick against which the state was to be measured. By 1991, with a new constitutional assembly, the centralized state in Colombia was formally (if not practically) ended. The constitutional assembly (comparable to the Brazilian assembly five years earlier) engaged in extensive debate about the new rules of decentralized government and provided guidelines for the devolution of political, fiscal, and administrative responsibilities at each level of government. The assembly also authorized popular election of governors.

In the course of the 1980s, Colombia provided a nearly complete blueprint of decentralization, a blueprint far more to the liking of local governments than, say, the Chilean model would have been. But like the Chilean model, Colombian decentralization was part of a broader process of economic liberalization. Viewing the traditional patrimonial model of state-centered development as inefficient and ineffective, Colombia sought to structure a modern state that reduced the role of government as the primary instrument of development (Rojas 1996a). But unlike Chile, Colombia envisioned decentralization as a mechanism to promote allocative and productive efficiency in the use of public resources, stimulate local resource generation, and promote capital investment by local governments. And Colombia's reforms, like Mexico's, were stimulated by growing powers of regional forces. For instance, elites in regional capitals—Cali, Medellín, Manizales, among the most wealthy and politically influential cities in the country—were effective in pressing national government to cede financial and administrative autonomy. Another internal force was the recurring violence in outlying areas where public services were poorly provided—if provided at all. These factors may have been as important to spur decentralization as any enlightened belief in a theory of public fiscal choice.

When the 1986 decentralization policies were launched, it was assumed that each level of government would be capable of paying for its own responsibilities, either entirely out of its own revenue sources or with credit financing and, if necessary, higher unconditional transfers or block grants from the central government. Shortly after the value-added tax was implemented in 1986, transfers were raised substantially. The primary goals of these reforms were to achieve fiscal independence among layers of government while avoiding building up fiscal pressures on the central treasury by local governments. According to Rojas (1996b), as long as the most substantial sources of income, such as income tax, remained under the control of the central government, it was thought that no local or regional level of government with significant responsibilities could ever be fully independent financially.

The initial ideal of fiscal autonomy was gradually replaced by the goal of coordinating fiscal matters—both income and spending—between central and local governments. Several new instruments were introduced to achieve this goal. The *Ley de Competencias y Recursos* provided for reassignment of expenditure responsibilities and a better fit for revenue sharing. For instance, local governments were made executing agents for many social services, and national government took a supervisory role. *Departamentos* were also made responsible for complementing municipal action, cofinancing, advising, training, or temporarily acting on behalf of those local governments unable to assume these duties themselves.

Colombia also chose to use performance criteria as conditions for transfer payments, and these were made explicit in the law (and therefore more difficult to adjust and fine tune than if they were set administratively). A formula with twelve separate factors was used to calculate how much central government revenue would be transferred to a given municipality. The performance criteria included such items as administrative costs and service levels for health, education, water, and sewerage. Colombia then created new cofinancing mechanisms known as social funds, which were inspired by the Mexican experience with matching grants.[13]

The Complications of Federated Pioneers: Venezuela and Brazil

Four of the largest countries in the region—Argentina, Brazil, Mexico, and Venezuela—are federated republics, meaning that these countries are composed of states with independent powers of legislation and administration. Except in Brazil, municipalities are creatures of the states, not of the central government, as is the case in a unitary system. (All the rest of the countries in the region are unitary states.) And in Brazil, municipalities are given a coequal status with the central government and the states, though in many respects, this is more of a de jure distinction than one that has much practical significance. The constitutional composition of federated republics makes them politically and administratively more complicated than their unitary neighbors. In unitary countries, all subnational units of government—for example, the Departamentos in Colombia, and the regions and provinces in Chile—were (and remain) administrative branches of the central government and therefore responsible for administering policy down to subnational entities. Decentralization in federated countries, on the other hand, had to be negotiated or shaped to fit a variety of states, each a semi-independent entity. Venezuela and Brazil each made efforts not long after Mexico to reform their governments, but each was hobbled by special complications—a presidential crisis in Brazil and unprepared states in the case of Venezuela.

Decentralization in Brazil was accompanied, and its earliest stages even overshadowed, by the virtual makeover of the republic. The major steps in the decentralization effort in Brazil—including elections of mayors and governors, the fiscal reform law of 1986, the dismantling of the federal bureaucracy in 1988, and the promulgation of the 1988 constitution—were intertwined with efforts to reestablish democracy after more than a decade of military rule. Bold as they were, the major steps in decentralization became secondary, insofar as national policy was concerned, to the renewed foundation of the state. The constitutional convention in 1988 to rewrite Brazil's constitution was a major step in the process of restoring democracy. But the convention produced many of the same kinds of rigidities that were seen in Colombia at about the same time. Later, the death of Tancredo Neves, the first popularly elected president following nearly two decades of military rule, dealt a stunning blow to the nation. His loss came precisely at the time of greatest need for his vision and strong leadership to move forward with reforms of democratization.

In the early 1980s, Venezuela was also preparing for decentralization. The country has enjoyed a petroleum-based source of wealth strikingly similar to Mexico's. Venezuela's pattern of growth among its regions has also been similar to Mexico's in the sense that agriculture, tourism, and commercial and financial development was taking place in regional centers and was championed by states and urban centers. At stake in Venezuela was the share of revenues from the country's oil exports.

Many reasons lay behind the upsurge of interest in and actions toward decentralization in Venezuela. The private sector was increasingly engaged in the debate over the proper role of the state in such matters as state enterprises, tariffs, trade policy, subsidies, and protectionism (COPRE 1988). In addition, the development of private-sector and economic interests outside of Caracas created a new interest group discontented with the centralized decision making of a closed group of party-oriented officials in the center.[14] Small businesses also disliked the favored role that state monopolies were given in such areas as ports, cement, telecommunications, and other sectors. Worker groups since the 1980s had grown more vocal in their demands to share power with state enterprises. Local community movements, cooperatives, consumers, and environmentalists also sought access to decision making at the state and municipal levels (COPRE 1988, de la Cruz 1998).

Although the constitution (of 1961) provides for a three-tiered system of government with democratically elected national, state, and local authorities, in practice, the power structure of the country operated for decades more like a unitary state. For example, for more than thirty years, the president appointed governors, and states had no independent source of income other than transfers from the central government. Local leaders, though elected, were (until 1989) preselected by a closed party list system (meaning options for voters were narrowed to a few party favorites). For these and other reasons, the apparatus of state administration had grown progressively out of touch with, and therefore had a low capacity to respond to, the real needs of the citizenry. Neither governors, who owed their allegiance to the president, nor the state legislatures, which were controlled by political parties, were directly responsible to the public at large. This loose connection opened possibilities for corruption and inefficient administration. Decentralization in Venezuela can be seen as an effort to resuscitate political legitimacy and strengthen federalism.

To seek these ends, Venezuela pioneered the use of a specialized presidential commission, known as COPRE (Presidential Commission for State Reform),[15] to spearhead reform of the state. COPRE was established by presidential decree in 1984 and given ministerial rank. Its mandate was to hold hearings, conduct policy analysis, do research, organize conferences, and publish materials aimed at informing decision makers and the public about the issues and options in Venezuela's state reform. COPRE's first minister, Alan Brewer-Carias, set about to produce extensive documentation to explain the nation's reform process and to explore issues in decentralization. He canvassed the literature and consulted extensively with colleagues in Europe. Although extremely knowledgeable about the issues in many countries, he exchanged ideas with his colleagues in Latin America only sporadically.[16] COPRE developed model legislation covering municipal governments and offered assistance to states to do the same. The commission drafted the central legislative framework for reform and prepared a strategy to implement the reform process. Other countries organized high-level agencies to spearhead or manage decentralization—Bolivia created a cabinet post for this purpose—but no country provided the same scale of resources or breadth of mandate that Venezuela vested in COPRE.

Straight thinking in Caracas was often derailed, however, by political power plays and bureaucratic inertia. After a long process of debate and public discussion, for instance, the centerpiece of national legislation for reform—the Decentralization Act of 1989,[17] which had been in preparation for a period of several years—was introduced into the legislature and enacted rather suddenly at the end of 1989. COPRE and the legislative leaders may have felt pressure to have this central legislative framework in place before moving on to elections of governors and mayors. Political pressures for electoral reform were building quickly. In November of 1989, several opposition congressional representatives introduced a bill to authorize elections of governors and mayors, and it was quickly enacted into law.[18]

Together, the two acts created significant new centers of political power in decision making, spending, and revenue at subnational levels of government. The Decentralization Act authorized states to request transfer of any functions then under central government control, for instance, ports, tolls roads, and school system and health-care facilities, only on the condition that the state legislators ratified the request (Brewer-Carias et al. 1990). The act also mandated a scheme of revenue sharing and investment coordination.[19] Creating new power bases in the states, as open elections and revenue sharing suddenly did, gave new incentive to governors to take over services. The central government was not prepared, politically, administratively, or technically for the sudden groundswell of interest in the states for assuming these functions. Governors from many states moved quickly to claim control over services and infrastructure that was of importance to them for economic, political, and, sometimes, historical reasons.

The central government had not worked out the processes of transfer, and local governments had not worked out financial and administrative consequences of suddenly absorbing new responsibilities. For instance, the governor of the State of Lara, Mariano Navarro, moved quickly in 1990 to take control of the primary education system.[20] He was eager for the opportunity to introduce a stronger regional flavor to the educational curriculum. But he learned within the first year that with this control came the responsibility to grapple with powerful teachers' unions and their demands for salaries as high or higher than those previously provided by the central government. Before two years had passed, the governor relinquished control over primary education in the state to the central government.

Both Mexico and Venezuela were moved by voter turnout and public opinion to take strong steps to decentralize, but in many ways the two countries moved in opposite directions. It is somewhat ironic that Venezuela repealed its law of state investment coordination at about the same time that Mexico was sharing decision making in subnational investments with the central government. In addition, like Mexico, Venezuela had devised a revenue-sharing scheme dating to the late 1970s, only to later scrap it in favor of a value-added tax.

DECENTRALIZATION IN REVIEW

Chile and Mexico were clearly the first to move out of the blocks in the course of decentralization in Latin America. Colombia and Venezuela followed suit, as did Brazil. The experiences of these countries help to round out the picture of how decentralization began and to demonstrate the differences in policy and administrative challenges posed by unitary and federated republics.

Looking back, it is surprising that Mexico and Chile were early reformers. This anomaly is in some measure explained by their own brands of reform (including liberalization of national economic management). Each state took actions to decentralize in response to a broad array of specific political circumstances—growing wealth in some regions, impatience with a failing central state, and military rule. Perhaps not surprisingly, no dominant model emerged to serve as a template—of how much power to devolve, how quickly, in what sequence, and under what controls—to enlighten reform elsewhere in the region. On the other hand, although each of the early reformers responded to circumstances unique to its own political and historical milieu, the courses each followed seemed to be guided by a common set of shared values, for instance, strengthening federalism, providing greater local autonomy, and improving resource allocation (except in Chile). These similarities seem to suggest a common source—the language, the market, liberalization and reform of the state itself—yet no single agent of change, no lending program, nor coordinated technical assistance program from international donors helped to facilitate and guide these early responses.

Furthermore, the countries seemed to learn little from each others' experiences. Their experimental trial and error spread in an ad hoc fashion and was disseminated in bits and pieces. Colombia adapted parts of the Mexican matching grant system, and Venezuela consulted mainly with European rather than with Latin American colleagues. Often, ideas were transmitted by personal communication and sometimes by official visiting delegations. It's an open question as to whether more ordered processes of dissemination and learning about decentralization might have been possible or more effective. Perhaps international development assistance agencies could have played an important role in heading off mistakes or cutting the time lost by developing common approaches to achieve more rapid or more efficient solutions. This lesson might be applied productively to countries in Africa, Asia, and Eastern Europe to illustrate good ideas and mistakes, as well as to disseminate the most promising ideas of Latin America.

The very nature of decentralization impeded the degree to which states were able to exercise the influence needed to keep progress moving smoothly. In other words, the pioneers were left without the very elements—strong vision and leadership in management at the center—they needed most to guide the process. Without a strong and visionary leader, sustaining the reforms proved difficult. For this and other reasons, each of the early pioneers was in some way knocked off course: the loss of a visionary leader in Brazil, Venezuela's failed attempts to transfer functions to the states, and Colombia's efforts to improve revenue raising and spending at the local level. Venezuela became ensnared in too open a system, one that allowed more choices and outcomes in states than administrators could handle. All the countries were committed to reforms, yet the pace and depth of change varied greatly, and in all cases, the process took much longer than anticipated. Most countries believed that they could implement functional reassignments and revenue transfers in a period of four or five years when, in fact, adjustments are still being made in many countries. Surprisingly, few states created specialized agencies to handle the complexities of decentralization.

Brazil and Colombia organized constitutional assemblies to chart out the new state. The little evidence available shows both the merits and demerits of this route. Constitutional conventions can anchor reformation of the state, but also open the process to capricious ideology. In Brazil, this tactic introduced fiscal traps, such as mandated spending on regions and specific levels of revenue transfer. Once enshrined in the constitution, these mandates preempt the choices of local officials and make any modifications or adjustments very difficult.

Chile's approach to decentralization is virtually inconceivable in a federated republic not under total military rule. In effecting its reforms, the central government did not have to be concerned with intermediating levels of political and financial powers, as did Brazil, Mexico, and Venezuela. States and provinces with their own constitutional roles can make change more difficult. Almost always they create a wider variety of institutions and policies than in unitary states. On the other hand, in unitary states, a single set of institutional arrangements applies throughout the country. When these arrangements are changed, the entire local sector and all intergovernmental relations automatically change with them. The transformation of local government was swift and definitive in Chile. By the same token, with the onset of democratization, unitary states can take on features of federated republics, if, for instance, localities begin to use a local political base to exert preferences different from national government, as happened in Colombia.

With the possible exception of Chile, these pioneers never saw themselves as innovators. They saw themselves as reformers of the state, working step by step, to cope with the exigencies of governing under changing circumstances. Only in retrospect do we begin to see a pattern of concession to local levels of government, of the awkward sequencing of revenue transfers, and, later, democratization. After the early 1980s, many more players entered the process of reform and began to show a pattern of handling first the fiscal and then political aspects of reform of the state.

4 □ National Decentralization Strategies

Following the lead of the pioneer states, many Latin American countries moved swiftly in the latter half of the 1980s to introduce changes in the structure of government. By the end of the decade, more than half of the governments in the region had begun or were planning major reforms in spending responsibilities, financing, and power-sharing arrangements. Although many national and civic leaders recognized the need for change and moved quickly to replace the state-led model of development, restructuring the state proved to be more than difficult. Restructuring was much more a process than a single event or even a set of predetermined steps. This was because the reform process was turbocharged in most countries by pressures from within the national political systems to share power.

Indeed, the power-sharing arrangements constituted the core of the revolution of decentralized governance in Latin America. But though political reforms have proven to be the most profound changes in the region, they were mixed inextricably with changes in financial arrangements and functional responsibilities. Because many stand-alone and comparative studies have already documented subnational reform in specific countries, this chapter examines the patterns of change in a large cohort of countries as of about 1990, rather than reexamine the details of reform in specific countries.[1] These patterns are composed of several elements in the political and financial organization of the state. One important element is the extent to which the political system is open to change from below, for instance, the extent to which overtures by local governments in spending or revenue raising were tolerated by the national system. Another element, linked to this openness, was the degree of autonomy granted subnational governments, that is, the extent to which municipalities had the power and authority to act independently in setting taxes, choosing officials, and organizing the size and composition of the local government.

Another factor in the pattern of change was the speed and scope of change itself. Large systemic reforms of the kind involved in decentralization produced quick, surprising movements that had a sudden effect throughout the system. The record shows that reactions and false starts and countervailing forces arose quickly in the inevitable give and take, as social and political interest groups adjusted to the new rules of the game and the shifting distribution of powers and wealth. The fits and starts of national reform seen in many countries resulted in part from ad hoc and often uncoordinated changes in these fundamental parts of the political organization of the state. Because all countries that engage in decentralization must face these choices, the patterns of choice observed in Latin America will provide some guidance to countries in Africa, Asia, and Eastern Europe that are currently embarking on decentralization reforms of their own.

FINANCE AND EXPENDITURES: STRATEGIC DEGREES OF OPENNESS AND AUTONOMY

Two of the most important dimensions of subnational reform—revenue arrangements and expenditure responsibilities—may be seen as constituting, implicitly or explicitly, the heart of national strategies in decentralization.[2] This chapter begins with a discussion of these dimensions and then moves to a consideration of political reforms that, uneven, incomplete, but widespread, are possibly the most important strategic component of decentralization strategies because they change the environment of incentives facing local authorities.

Latin American cities and municipalities have long been weak in revenue collection and historically, thanks to revenue transfers, they have spent more than they collect in taxes. With the shifts in spending and service responsibilities that came with decentralization, local governments were flooded with added income and new expenditure responsibilities, at least in the early stages of decentralization. For the better part of the past decade, the entire region was engaged in restructuring a financial equilibrium to cover what are known as horizontal and vertical gaps. Horizontal gaps refer to discrepancies in levels of basic services—water, drainage, sewerage, education, and health—across all the municipalities in a country. Vertical gaps refer to

Table 4-1. Expenses by Level of Government for Selected Countries

	Argentina		Brazil		Colombia		Chile	
	1980	1991	1980	1991	1980	1990	1980	1991
National level	66.3	55.6	64.8	51.8	67.7	69.5	96.1	87.6
Intermediate level	28.3	35.7	26.2	30.7	22.8	18.2	1.1	1.0
Local level	5.4	8.7	9.0	17.5	9.5	12.3	2.8	11.4
Total	100	100	100	100	100	100	100	100

Source: Aghon 1996

shortfalls in income needed to cover the costs of basic functions within municipalities. In most countries, funds are transferred from central sources to regions and cities to cover both horizontal and vertical gaps.

With decentralization, funds are transferred in a combination of automatic sharing of revenues with some restrictions on their use or as grants designated for very specific purposes. Most often, grants were destined for basic needs, such as water supply or primary health or education. The combination of transfers and grants after the 1980s swelled municipal coffers by a factor of three or four in a very short period of time. Guatemalan municipalities saw revenues jump by 400% literally overnight. Table 4-1 illustrates the degree to which these funds increased spending by local governments in key countries of the region.

It is surprising, and therefore somewhat revolutionary, that a large financial shift should have been such a prominent and early feature of decentralization in so many countries. Macroeconomic and fiscal balance of the kind described by Bird (1978) has always been a cardinal concern shared widely in the development community, and this concern dominated financial and macroeconomic perspectives of influential institutions of multilateral assistance like the World Bank and the InterAmerican Development Bank. Macroeconomic stability became the overriding policy objective during the "decade of debt." Authors such as Aghón (1996), Burki and Perry (1997), and Weisner, (1994) explain or exemplify this concern, framing policy issues in terms of matching income with expenditures and controlling local spending. Yet revenue transfers ran ahead of spending responsibilities in the late 1990s in virtually every country then undergoing decentralization.

Table 4-2 summarizes the two principal fiscal dimensions of decentralization strategies in the region. The table first distinguishes between the revenue side of decentralization and the expenditure, or service delivery, side. This distinction is drawn to show the asymmetry in decentralization strategies, at least in the early stages of policy implementation. Governments everywhere

Table 4-2. Summary of Decentralization Strategies: Revenues and Expenditures, Early 1990s

Country	Revenue strategy		Expenditure strategy		
	Increased or reorganized fiscal transfers or revenue sharing	Increased local ability to levy taxes and fees	Significant transfer of functions from central government or parastatals	Increase in local flexibility to select/manage service delivery	Significant central earmarking for local capital investment
Argentina	Reorganized	Varies by province	Yes	Yes	Yes (for housing)
Bolivia	Reorganized and increased	Existent	Yes	Unclear	Unclear
Brazil	Increased	Existent	Not explicit but some de facto	Yes	Yes
Colombia	Increased	Yes	Yes	Yes	Yes
Chile	Increased	No	Yes	Yes	Yes
Ecuador	Reorganized	No	No	No	Yes
Guatemala	Increased	No	No	No	Yes
Honduras	No	Yes	No	Some	No
Mexico	Increased	No	No	No	No
Venezuela	Increased	Yes	Negotiable	Yes (states)	Yes

Source: Campbell et al. 1991

were carried away with the notion of sharing power, particularly spending power, and they began transferring finances far in advance of any concomitant change in functional responsibilities.

The strategies of revenue decentralization can be pictured in two polar approaches. In one approach, the central government allows local governments to raise taxes and fees on their own as they see fit. It can do so by granting subnational governments control over new tax bases or fees, as Venezuela has done in a limited way with ports and certain toll roads. In Honduras, this allows local governments greater latitude in establishing rate structures and permits them to revalue traditional tax bases (e.g., the property tax base) more aggressively. In the alternative approach, the central government retains revenue-raising responsibilities—as, for instance, in Brazil—but shares a larger proportion of its receipts with lower levels of government, either through tax-sharing arrangements or new intergovernmental transfers. Usually, these changes in revenue-sharing arrangements are fundamental enough to be incorporated into the basic municipal law or, in the cases of Brazil and Colombia, to take the form of constitutional modifications.

Consecrating this tactical variable in the constitution, as was the case in Brazil and Colombia, builds rigidity into the fiscal system. This, in turn, locks central governments into arrangements that may become increasingly inappropriate to the widely varying circumstances of subnational authorities. For instance, both Ceara and Parana in Brazil have been aggressive in reform and hindered by constitutional limitations on revenue raising. (In the end, Brazil edged ever closer to unmanageable debt burden created by state and local governments, and was forced in 1998 to pass landmark legal restrictions known as a fiscal pact to control indebtedness and spending by local governments.) Constitutional rewrites also impose unrealistic spending mandates on municipalities, sometimes penalizing any efforts they might otherwise have made to reach service standards at a lower cost. Of course, the two revenue strategies—granting powers and sharing revenues—are not mutually exclusive. Central government may, as in Venezuela, simultaneously cede local governments more revenue-raising authority and increase revenue transfers from centrally collected funds.

A parallel choice of strategy applies to the expenditure or service delivery side. The role of local government can be strengthened permissively by allowing local governments to expand service responsibilities at their discretion, as in the states of Venezuela, or through negotiated agreements with parastatals (state-run corporations) and other centralized providers. It can also grow stronger through obligatory arrangements as in Chile, where the central government formally transfers service functions to lower levels of government. An intermediate strategy followed in the United States during the Reagan administration involved the central government's unilateral withdrawal from certain functional responsibilities or a sharp reduction in central funding for these activities, forcing states and localities to decide whether they will step in to assume the central government's role.

Table 4-2 provides a summary of the picture in selected governments. The first column, revenue strategy, indicates whether significant transfers of service responsibilities were made from the central level to the subnational level. The second column indicates whether local governments were given more discretion in deciding which services they will provide or how they will provide them. Examples of this discretion include the scope given to local governments to decide which service functions will be provided locally and how these will be managed institutionally, and whether local governments are to be allowed the freedom to contract with private sector firms or parastatals for service delivery.

In practice, one of the most common decentralization strategies, devised to forestall the fears of runaway spending, was for central government to require that a large part of its revenue transfers be dedicated to local capital investment in infrastructure facilities. Consequently, an index is included in the table to show whether there was significant earmarking of centrally provided funds for local capital investment.

Classification schemes always carry the potential for oversimplification. Several of the measures in table 4-2 are more properly continuous variables than yes/no indices. For some variables, there are other logical alternatives than the ones recognized in the table (e.g., country decentralization plans could move in other directions than either clearer aid formulas or greater use of negotiated agreements). However, for most countries and most measures, the appropriate classifications seem to carry little controversy.

All of the region's decentralization programs, compared to the 1980s, involved new and substantially larger central government transfers to local (sometimes state) government. This pattern is surprising in light of the fiscal constraints operating on most nations in the region. Highly indebted nations in general were cutting back on the growth of central government budgets (World Bank 1988). A central-level commitment to decentralization would have been compatible with this cutback if a decentralization strategy had been designed primarily to shift financing responsibilities to the local level. However, for the countries reported in table 4-2, this was not true. Revenue transfers generally ran well ahead of expenditure or functional transfers, implying that over the medium term, at least, decentralization would add to central government costs.

The transfer of central government functions under conditions where local governments must then finance service delivery generally proved difficult to implement. As a consequence, many countries transferred resources to the local level, but recipient governments were not required to take on specific functional responsibilities of comparable cost, and central government bureaucracies were not required to formally abandon their involvement in service provision. Although some progress was made in privatization and state reform, duplication of roles contributed to driving up the costs of the public sector. Peterson estimated that the central government in Brazil would have had to reduce real expenditures by one-sixth to offset its loss of retained revenues in the late 1980s (Campbell, Peterson, and Brakarz 1991).

It is paradoxical that decentralization strategies were adopted at a time of severe budgetary pressure on central governments and against a backdrop of budgetary retrenchment, yet designed to impose large net costs on central budgets. To compound the paradox, the decentralization plans put into effect were plainly designed to stimulate local government spending as well, especially for infrastructure projects. In most cases, all or part of the new revenue transfers were to be spent on local capital investment. Formal requirements were written into the transfer terms to try to ensure that this investment was additive—that is, that central government transfers did not substitute for local funding. These provisions met with mixed reactions. Many local authorities cut back on local revenue collection and substituted central transfers for own-source revenues. Others, many of them larger cities, began to increase own-source revenues. But the intent of decentralization was to increase local capital spending, and this outcome was achieved to a significant degree.

In the early stages of decentralization, many analysts (e.g., Prud'homme, 1994; Bonfim and Shah, 1991) predicted that local revenue raising would be enervated because automatic revenue transfers would substitute for local income. The record in fact shows that many localities raised their income despite these increased transfers. But the first waves of decentralization reform took much less action to grant new revenue-raising authority to local governments than to increase centrally financed resource transfers. Indeed, table 4-2 is likely to overstate the practical significance of the changes in local revenue-raising authority. In several cases where local governments were granted more tax- or fee-setting discretion, the influx of central resources made use of this new taxing authority unnecessary. Yet local governments began responding to unforeseen incentives triggered by the decentralization process. This, in turn, led to surprising efforts among leading governments to increase local resource mobilization despite heavy flows of transfers.

The magnitude of revenue sharing with subnational entities was the most prominent feature of the region's decentralization initiatives. Revenue-sharing rules were transformed to increase local governments' share of nationally collected revenues and to decrease the share retained by central government. Revenue transfers ran far ahead of expenditure transfers, and ahead of specific agreements as to expenditure responsibilities that would be transferred in the future. Some observers cite this asymmetry in income and spending as a way to "buy off" local governments, to silence critics of the centralization of power, while at the same time creating new political obligations from grateful recipients at the local level (Bailey 1994; Rodriguez 1993; Cornelius, Craig, and Fox 1994). Others see the transfers as the result of hasty or careless policy design (Aghón 1996; Peterson 1997 and Weisner 1994). Closer examination shows that strings, conditions, and controls were seeded in virtually every country to safeguard the otherwise apparent free hand on spending given with shared finance (Peterson 1997). The continuing concern with macroeconomic stability up through the 1990s, however, shows that strings, conditions, and controls have not always worked effectively.

For countries that still have the choice, revenue transfer schemes should be designed to be fiscally neutral, that is, not to allow either revenue or expenditure transfers to run far ahead of the other. Yet the net fiscal gains enjoyed by lower-level governments in Latin America have served a political purpose. They account in part for the broad support that decentralization received at the subnational level. Moreover, they may be responsible for fueling the renaissance in leadership and participation that has come with the quiet revolution. On the other hand, a strategy of imbalance of this kind necessarily triggers political debate over future rounds of fiscal adjustments and heightens uncertainty about the fiscal sustainability of decentralization policies. Finance should follow function in decentralization design. That is, decisions should be made first at the levels of government that can most efficiently perform different kinds of services. Revenue transfers then should be constructed so that the appropriate levels of government end up with the resources they need to carry out their responsibilities. Experience in the Latin American region reversed this order by first transferring revenues and then negotiating expenditure uses.

INSTITUTIONAL AND POLITICAL REFORM: VERSIONS OF POWER SHARING

While financial and expenditure responsibilities were at the forefront of the policy change during the initial stages of reform in Latin America, political reform was given expression in many countries as well. Power sharing has been the ineluctable concomitant to decentralization in Latin American and Caribbean countries, as elsewhere in the world, and this imperative was perhaps the cause of more missteps and trepidation than any other facet of decentralization in the early stages of the quiet revolution. Political and institutional pitfalls, like conferring too much spending power on weak local governments, were discovered everywhere in the region.

And yet, curiously, the political realm—of voice and choice making—became the fulcrum on which the balance of power was being tipped in favor of local governments in Latin America. Though power sharing underlay virtually all of the initial steps in decentralization, true political reform—in some cases, buttressed by electoral reform—came to be implemented only in the end of the 1990s. This is because the stroke-of-the-pen reforms in the financial arena had immediate, almost overnight, impact on local governments. Changes in spending took somewhat longer to implement. But results

Table 4-3. Summary of Decentralization Strategies: Institutions and Democracy

Country	Intermediate levels of governance created or activated			Intergovernmental institutional arrangements				Electoral reform					Democratic participation			
	Councils	New functions	Elected officers	Formulas	Negotiated agreements	Strengthening	Associations	Ballot choice	Election timing	Terms of office	Renewable term	Reform years	Mayor elected separately	Mayor elected by council	Formalized participation	Terms
Argentina		x		x		x							Terms & procedures vary by province			
Bolivia	x	x		x	x	x				x	x	1994			x	3
Brazil		x		x	x¹	x			x			Vary by state				3
Colombia	x	x	x	x		x	x	x	x	x		1983 1985 1991	x		x	3
Chile	x	x	x	x		x	x	x	x	x	x	1983 1991	x		x	4
Ecuador	x	x	x			x	x					1988	x			2
Guatemala	x	x		x		x	x			x	x	1988	x			4
Honduras	x	x	x	x	x	x	x			x	x	1982²	x			4
México	x	x		x		x				x				x		3
Venezuela	x	x		x	x	x	x	x	x	x	x	1989	x		x	3

¹States are responsible for municipal strengthening, and efforts vary from state to state.
²Until 1990, local elections were tied to votes cast for parties in presidential elections.

of changes in democratic and electoral rules of the game became visible only after several rounds of local government elections. Some of the most startling consequences of the quiet revolution were seen only after the impact of electoral reform. The most important aspects of these institutional and political reforms are depicted in table 4-3.

The table shows the changing institutional presence of the state at intermediate levels of government—elected authorities and councils, as well as non-elected participation by the general public in departments, provinces, states, and regions. The table shows the extent to which states have either filled in intermediate levels of administrative tiers to buttress the presence of the center or inserted wholly new governmental functions to expand the levels of government accountable to local voters. The table also indicates changes in the basis of fiscal cooperation—whether intergovernmental relations moved toward greater reliance on fixed and clear formulas in allocating aid and service functions or moved toward greater use of negotiation and agreements (convenios) between levels of government.

These alternative strategies are extensions of, but quite different in character from, the fiscal side of decentralization mentioned earlier. New tiers of elected officials expanded the operative levels of government. They also created a stronger presence for and increased control by central authorities at the local level, sometimes in competition with locally elected officials. Colombia is a good example of a country where a fixed and transparent intergovernmental aid system cleared the way for independent choice making by local governments, but added elements of control at the level above municipalities.

Another index indicates whether the central government introduced new direct links between community-level participation and the central government structure in an attempt to set development priorities outside the local voting process. The planning structure typically brings together central government, local, and community officials, as well as representatives of other collective entities (e.g., business groups, unions, and political party leaders). For instance, an agency of the executive branch in Peru channeled more spending directly to the local level than any other single ministry. In a similar way, the convenios negotiated by the PRI in Mexico guaranteed closer contact between central government and grassroots groups.

The final set of indices in the table concerns the nature of political accountability and democratic participation in local government. Political and electoral reform has been the most intriguing dimension of decentralization because it widened the spectrum of political participation in intergovernmental affairs. The table displays some of the innovations in electoral regimes that increased accountability of local government to local electorates. Reforms included such changes as new formats of ballots in order to more easily distinguish individual candidates from their parties. Before reforms, some ballots (in Venezuela, for instance) merely listed a party slate of candidates without individual names. Other changes affected the timing of elections and terms of office. The table notes (re-)introduction of local elections and the lengths of elected terms as well as whether mayors are elected by local councils in a collegial system or directly by the voters.

The key features of institutional and political reform are the "filling in" of organizational elements and improvements in choice-making capacity at the subnational level. These took many forms. Councils were formed at the intermediate level, and officials were named to carry out more detailed decision making at the local level. Many countries made efforts to buttress weak local governments with a variety of training and institutional strengthening programs. Elections and electoral reforms were introduced to enhance the capacity of local governments to decide what services they wanted. Some of these strategic directions held pleasant surprises in that they led inadvertently to more highly qualified candidates and to a wave of reforms at the municipal level. In general, policymakers were concerned with adding new organizational units to carry out—sometimes to control—governance at the local level. They were less effective inventing new political incentives to induce reform. Strategic choice in decentralization policy turned on questions of how much autonomy to grant local governments. To what extent should intermediary and lower levels of government (states, departments, and municipalities) have freedom to choose officials, rotate them, decide on the mix and scope of services, and recover costs in taxes and fees?

Intermediate Levels of Government

More than half the countries in the region have moved to bolster intermediate governance, both to strengthen the presence of government from the point of view of the center, as well as to give citizens the opportunity to take part in, watch over, and hold responsible those parties officially accountable for public sector decisions and actions. In a handful of countries, this was accomplished with the creation of nonelected councils at the intermediate level of government, that is, in regions or provinces above the municipal level. Councils were a mechanism to solicit views and advice, and they generally had no executive authority. Election of intermediate-level officials is a decisive criterion against which to judge the extent of devolution of powers. Whereas most councils have assigned new responsibilities and increased financing of local governments, only about half in the region provided for fully elected officers at the intermediate level. Of this group, Chile balked at first in the timely implementation of some of the provisions for elected councils, first discussed in 1990 (World Bank 1992). Instead, Chile, like Bolivia, retained a hybrid model consisting of a presidential appointment of a governor answerable to councils elected indirectly (that is, councilors were named or elected from among lower-level officeholders). Similar arrangements were proposed (but never implemented) in Guatemala.

Whether elected or appointed, intermediate officials acquired new status and were presented with new political possibilities. They could play a role in deciding how public money was to be spent. They were often empowered to name members of boards and executive directors of regional authorities.

Compared to past experience, they could exert stronger influence on the national agenda because the nature of their role, their very legitimacy, especially for elected officials, was strengthened.

Most countries began adjusting finance before functional responsibilities were changed, and most adopted simple formulas for revenue sharing. The most common arrangement was to divide the total amount to be shared into two parts. One part was distributed in equal proportions to each jurisdiction. The other part was distributed in direct proportion to the population. In many cases, weighting was given (inversely) to the relative wealth of the jurisdiction. Some formulas grew much more complicated, taking into account levels of service, administrative cost, and other factors. Colombia's formula had twelve components of this kind.

More transparent and stable formulas for distributing revenues created the potential for greater local autonomy in expenditure choice. In effect, this "financing-first" strategy might be labeled a hands-off approach to guiding the local response to decentralization. In Mexico and Venezuela, the basic approach to decentralization was to negotiate agreements between federal and subnational authorities. These agreements covered investment priorities and assignment of functional responsibilities, as well as the amounts and forms of intergovernmental aid. In Venezuela, the process was designed to be transitional; the gradual, negotiated agreements were begun to create clear and stable guidelines for future allocation of funding and functional responsibilities. In Mexico, the negotiation process was incorporated into national planning arrangements and was intended to be permanent. As discussed in the previous chapter, Mexican officials at the federal, state, and (less extensively) municipal levels negotiated mutually acceptable investment and financing priorities. This strategy established the basis for the federal government as the senior partner in these arrangements, and it continued to exert control over subnational expenditure priorities.

A common factor in the strategy of intergovernmental relations was to strengthen the capacity of local governments. Virtually every country emphasized the need to increase the level of professionalism and efficiency in local management, and every country listed in table 4-3 increased the scope or capacity of a national institute for municipal government. Colombia's law 357 of 1993 stipulated that a fixed fraction of shared revenues going to municipalities must be invested in capacity strengthening (including support to associations of local governments). The Brazilian Institute of Municipal Affairs entered a boom market following the 1988 constitution and related decentralization policies. Associations of local governments, as strengthening agencies, lobbying groups, and agencies for information exchange, appeared almost everywhere. Some associations were organized along the lines of political parties, such as Asociación de Municipios de México (AMMAC) in Mexico, and others along professional lines, such as the Chilean association of city managers formed in 1997. Still others were organized around economic issues, such as the association of mayors of cities in Mercado Comun del Sur (MERCOSUR), a trade bloc formed in the early 1990s. These innovations were responses to new incentives felt by many local authorities.

New Leadership with Political and Electoral Reform

Perhaps the sharpest turnabout in national political administration is that more than half the countries in the region introduced major modifications in their nation's electoral regimes. New laws were adopted in many countries that changed the way local officials were nominated and selected (Shugart 1996). Most countries have extended the short terms of office for mayors, and some have made the terms of local authorities renewable in successive administrations. Previous to the reforms, an elected official would have to wait through an entire political term before seeking re-election. Election of mayors separately from councils (except in Chile and Mexico) is another aspect of this reform.

With these changes in the way nominations and balloting are conducted, many electoral reforms have—either deliberately or inadvertently—brought about secondary effects. For example, a new generation of leaders was being elected into office in Colombia. Mayors and departmental governors in Colombia ran campaigns and won under new political coalitions whose very existence is attributable to electoral reform. One analysis shows that changes in nominations, balloting, and vote counting make it more difficult for traditional elites, organized in party machines, to sustain control over local nominations in Colombia (Shugart 1996). In the three rounds of Colombian elections beginning in 1988, political outsiders sought nomination, many for the first time in their lives. They were advanced as candidates under new civic alliances and gained office in 300 of the more than 1,000 municipalities in the country, including Bogota and many other large cities. Surveys in Central America and Colombia showed that newly elected mayors were four times more likely to have professional backgrounds than their predecessors. A survey of more than 100 mayors in Central America found a strikingly similar result (Selligson 1994).

Many countries enacted legislation designed specifically to strengthen the management and administrative capacity of municipalities. Colombian legislation required a minimum expenditure of transferred revenues on training and technical assistance. Many countries in Central America expanded the mandate of municipal strengthening institutions, organizations created decades ago, many by USAID, aimed at offering training and technical assistance to local government. But electoral reforms had surprising effects on institutional strength in some places. The new wave of leadership elected into office in Colombia cascaded reforms downward. The significance of this change is that the new generation of elected officials were strengthening municipal administration because it was in the interest of mayors to do so, "to deliver the goods" according to the mayor of Manizales. Reforms resulted from a new, democratic set of incentives, not because they were induced by conditions of central government or by conditions of grants or transfers. For the first time in decades, mayors became direct stakeholders in stronger institutional capacity.

One former mayor of Manizales, Colombia (population 275,000), illustrated these new traits of leadership and participation. The mayor entered office on a reform platform and made the unprecedented promise to *increase* taxes if and when he was able to solve the city's extremely congested traffic flow in the downtown area. In effect, the mayor was proposing to restructure the political compact with his electorate. By borrowing funds from domestic banks, the mayor retained consultant services to diagnose city transit problems and propose remedies—new arterials and improved traffic management—that were also financed in this way. Barely eighteen months into his term, the mayor had substantially removed congestion bottlenecks. True to his promise, he went public with a campaign to impose a gasoline surcharge. This levy, coupled with administrative improvements in tax collection, more than quadrupled city revenues. The revenue gains were dedicated to a long-term transit plan and health care reforms for the city, priorities the mayor knew to be uppermost in the voters' minds.

Many of the countries enacted legislation of one kind or another to emphasize political participation, such as holding open town hall meetings (in Central America and Venezuela) or regulating standards and types of community organizations (in Chile and Venezuela). But mayors in hundreds of cities across the continent began to act on a political mandate grounded in popular election. They began to tap into public sentiment to seek confirmation about community needs. Perhaps the single most striking feature separating postdecentralization mayors from their counterparts before the 1980s is participation of voice. A. O. Hirschman (1970) invoked the term *voice* to describe the communication of preferences, need, and complaint by local electorates to their government. In postdecentralization governments in Latin America, the voice of the people became an important source of information to verify preferences about service and infrastructure needs and willingness of the voters to pay. Many mayors sought independent confirmation of preferences in opinion polls. In the past, mayors would often claim that they, as native sons and daughters, had a sense of what the people wanted, even though they rarely bothered to verify their views with independent information. Participation as a political objective was also mentioned in many of the statutes and laws. In some countries, it was made obligatory through open town hall meetings and publication of expenditure records. The widespread practice of participation, however, appeared to have emerged as a result of incentives created with elections, electoral reform, more open nomination, and spending powers for local executives.

Electoral and financial reforms increased the focus on local executives and heightened the importance of local office. This in turn attracted new, often more qualified office-seekers willing to contest the established order. Stunning reversals in local political practice have already been noted in Colombia with the emergence of mayoral candidates who competed successfully with the traditional elites. A similar development took place in Mexico. By the early 1990s, Mexico's opposition party, Partido de Accion Nacional (PAN), held mayoral offices in more than half of the country's largest cities outside of Mexico City. In only a decade, propelled in part by decentralization, the major opposition parties in Mexico mounted a significant challenge to the ruling party at all levels of government. The record of local leaders was also given more scrutiny. Public opinion polls in Central America and Colombia showed that voters trusted local officials elected under decentralization reforms by a wide margin over national figures. The role in local office appears to have taken on new significance. At least one study (Seligson 1994) suggested that local officeholders considered experience in city hall as a more important step in a political career than serving in state assemblies and even national congressional office.

A countercurrent has built up in several countries—Peru, Mexico, Chile under Pinochet, and Guatemala—that does not identify "closeness to the people" with multiparty local democracy or separation from central government authority. In these countries, decentralization was accompanied by newly created central government agencies dedicated to channeling investments directly into community investments, thereby short-circuiting the intent of decentralized government. The Social Fund of Peru is perhaps the archetype of this model. The fund was set up as a superministry linking the central authority with local governments. More than two-thirds of the 1990 public investment portfolio was channeled through this fund. Such arrangements were effective ways to project a strong central government presence in the form of investments at the local level. Mexico exhibited a similar, but more subtle form of central authority at the local level. There, the matching grant arrangements that have been evolving since the 1970s were used occasionally to steer central government investment funds directly into politically sensitive districts. These forms of decentralization attempted to strengthen, rejuvenate, and legitimize the role of the central government and the political party that controlled it by establishing direct links to the community and organized populace. This short-circuiting of the political process subverts objectives of local autonomy.

Devolution to local governments and political reform also built up a new presence of government at the subnational level and unleashed a fresh wave of energy and innovation in many cities. Perhaps the most intriguing lesson—certainly an evocative question to be verified and explored in more detail—is the effect that reforms had on political leadership. A new generation of leaders sought and won office. They then propagated a secondary wave of reforms in participation and service delivery at the local level. Among the most promising of these secondary effects was the mobilization of community participation and resources. These changes flowed from the realization that for the first time in decades, the decisions of local authorities had real meaning for community welfare. With decentralization, local leaders suddenly had within their reach a much broader scope of action, with financial resources well beyond those of any point in their contemporary history. With transferred revenues and authorization to deliver services, mayors found they could effect change in the lives of their constituents. In this sense, an important objective of decentralization—local self-governance—was realized in many cities and brought within reach of many more. Future empirical research can establish the veracity of this proposition and the extent to which these changes have been sustained.

The increase in autonomy of local governments may have motivated local leadership, but it did too little to support newly elected leaders by strengthening municipal administrative capacity. These weaknesses are more painfully obvious than before, especially in small municipalities that constitute the vast majority of local governments in the region. Though some local governments have benefited from reform mayors, most municipalities are still hobbled by such impediments as restrictions in qualified personnel, a lack of civil service or merit systems to guide staff development, inadequate data, and weak analytical capacity. With a few notable exceptions—Bolivia and Colombia, to name two—decentralization reforms aimed at strengthening local institutional capacity have been largely ineffective or ignored by national governments, and this may well prove to be the Achilles' heel of decentralization.

STAGES OF REFORM

One additional pattern can be detected in the wave of decentralization that occurred in Latin America during the latter half of the 1980s. Implementing new policies and statutes was quite different in practice than the linear sequence that might be suggested by the mere mechanical logic of shifting spending functions, restructuring intergovernmental finance, and implementing democratic reforms. Though the style of governance differed from country to country, most nations went back and forth in policy and administration of reforms during of the first decade of decentralization. As reforms were proposed, both local and national actors struggled with the details of implementation, advancing on some fronts, falling back on others. No systematic measurement of this rhythm has been attempted. Even more variations may still be in the offing. It is useful to note these periodic swings if only to understand that decentralization is a complicated and time-consuming process. Public excitement can quickly turn to confusion and then frustration. Political momentum for reform can then be lost. The rhythmical patterns seen in the Latin American region may be useful to analysts and policymakers in other countries where reform in intergovernmental and political affairs is pending. At least five stages or phases of reform can be identified from the Latin American experience: euphoria, disassembly, crisis of confidence, innovation, and renovation and reconstruction.

During the euphoria phase, local governments everywhere in Latin America eagerly embraced the new "autonomy" they were given in spending and decision making in the first major reforms of the early-to-mid 1980s. (The rough benchmarks for these reforms range from 1983 in Colombia to 1989 in Honduras.) Many constitutional and national statutes were enacted during this period. Financial transfers were the proximate cause of the euphoria. Transfers doubled, even quadrupled, the annual income of municipalities. For instance, several Guatemalan mayors spoke with incredulity and barely disguised glee when the ministry of finance approved the statute authorizing the transfer of 8 percent of total government revenues—about US$40 million in 1988—to be shared among the nation's 326 municipalities. Similar arrangements were implemented in Venezuela, Brazil, and Colombia with similar reactions. Venezuelan municipalities collectively began to receive 16 percent of national revenues in 1990, rising to 21 percent in 1998.

On the expenditure side, legislators identified a broad range of responsibilities for local governments, such as water, wastes, schools, and health, notwithstanding the fact that, in principle, many local governments had always been at least partly responsible for such services. The new flow of finance and the renewed dedication to these services were accepted by state and local governments with enthusiasm, partly because local governments have often felt they were subjected to or dependent upon central government whims. Also, neither the local governments nor the central authorities were very precise about the true costs of the functions being devolved to local authorities. After the first wave of decentralization, mayors were suddenly much more in control over their municipal destinies.

Disassembly occurred within a few years' time, and the image of a decentralized system of government—one that was stronger with a layer of institutions at the base—began to come apart. Very soon, the explicit and implicit costs of discharging the new functions and strengthened roles came into the brighter light of the annual operating and investment budgets of local governments. Euphoria evaporated, and the many pretenders of local service provision began to melt away from the new functions they were eagerly clamoring for only a few years earlier. The real meaning of decentralization, the new costs and demands, drove the intended partners in decentralization, the state and local governments, into disarray. Some local governments no longer wanted to be a part of the new system. Demands for higher wage scales by teachers' unions in Venezuela and medical professionals in Colombia are typical examples of the stumbling blocks that impeded the smooth transition from centralized to decentralized service provision. Only about a third of the departments and municipalities in Colombia—mostly the largest ones—were successful in incorporating the wage bill and benefits burdens of health workers and educators. They did this mostly by bargaining new arrangements with unions and calling for innovative ideas; cost sharing between departments and municipalities; concessions by some unions; and effective use of outside resources, foundations, the private sector, the church, and others. In Venezuela's public education system, offers and counteroffers were repeated many times between various states and the central government until, within 18 months of the original proposals, the arbitration process had come to a standstill. Similar problems affected the health-care system. The high costs of central government salaries and benefits were suddenly transferred to local governments. At the same time, many of the transferred funds were intended for investment, not recurrent costs. Many state and local governments voluntarily abdicated their options, and concentrated instead on functions and activities tied to their own revenue base, such as mines, toll roads, bridges, and ports.

The process was slow and uncertain, and myriad other unpredictable factors figured into the course of events. The crisis of governance at the top in

Brazil and Venezuela, for instance, deeply affected the interplay of division of labor and reform in states and localities in those countries. Armed rebellions in Peru, Guatemala, and—to a lesser extent—Mexico, have accentuated the stakes in the devolution process in those countries.

During these years of adjustment and negotiation, central and local governments grew increasingly distrustful of each other in a crisis of confidence as each tried, but failed, to hold up their end of the bargain. Meanwhile, some central governments continued to spend money on local services. Peterson (1997) and Perry and Huertas (1997) have estimated the rising costs to the public sector as Colombia decentralized. Perry and Huertas showed that as revenues were transferred, spending by central government was increased, particularly on the national police in order to combat crime and the drug trade. This episode clearly depicts the differences in prerogatives, and sometimes differences in priorities, between levels of government in Colombia. Federated systems were especially problematic. They were not able to control the powers and prerogatives of states with legislative and indebtedness powers. Some states—like Cordoba and Sao Paulo—became ungovernable in terms of maintaining macroeconomic stability because they were able to arrange new forms of debt (by borrowing from their own state banks and securing suppliers' credits). Many local forces—such as associations of mayors, legislators, and local governments—pushed for further reform as revenue transfer formulae were brought into question, and national leaders (as in Brazil, Venezuela, and Mexico) were challenged on grounds of corruption or malfeasance.

A growing realization thus sank in after the disassembly stage: Not only was decentralization not a panacea, but the process and outcomes had severe limits. Ironically, one of the conclusions from this period was that the central state needed to be stronger, not weaker as might have been imagined. But new strength was required in many different areas than before decentralization. For one thing, central governments needed to be clearer on how to help local governments, how to set up and implement a regulatory system to manage intergovernmental affairs, and how to help local governments increase capacity and even negotiate assumption of their new powers. Most governments were largely unprepared for these roles. They began to explore this regulatory terrain at the end of the 1980s with the privatization of water and power utilities. Meanwhile, constitutional conventions in Brazil and Colombia consecrated some of the worst ideological instincts by writing revenue transfers and mandated spending into constitutional provisions, making them much harder to change and adjust over time.

Just as the reforms appeared to have created impossible new tasks for central and local governments alike, a flowering of innovative practices began to bloom in many cities across the continent. The new generation of local leaders began to exercise power, motivated in a larger measure than before by the idea of delivering services. For instance, participatory budgeting in a half-dozen Brazilian cities began to draw the citizenry more closely than ever into the process of deciding how to spend public money. Reform in Valledupar (Colombia) led to the election of police inspectors, and some six cities started up homegrown versions of neighborhood improvement funds. Quito created a budgeting and management information system on par with developed country standards. Dozens of cities invented and began to export these innovations through conferences and publications. In other words, some of the political reforms began to take hold with innovation at the local level just as the process of decentralization began to lose its luster. At the same time, new alliances were being forged at the regional level. In a horizontal way, between and among local governments, together with private-sector partners, and civil organizations, the spending powers and new authority opened new possibilities to local and regional groups to begin exploring their shared stake in development (Campbell and Fuhr, 2003). The innovations and consolidation among local governments were successful in forming a more solid tissue of local institutional capacity where the prescriptions and mandates of national policy had failed.

National, regional, and local governments next had to face renovation and reconstruction. They began to piece together their own solutions to issues such as health care, education, and institutional development. The innovations of the past might have begun to sow seeds of hope. Certainly events at the global level, for example, the accession to formal recognition by local governments in UN meetings beginning with Istanbul in 1996 and the opening of global trading and deal making with liberalized trade regimes, have given local authorities new status and new responsibilities. These conditions were not yet at hand to help resolve the crisis of confidence in intergovernmental affairs and to negotiate settlements in the early stages of decentralization. Mayors have begun to claim a place at the table of the national policy debate over developmental strategies. They are forming clubs such as MERCOCIUDADES, an association of mayors in MERCOSUR countries, and engaging in implicit and explicit competition for investments and trade. New coalitions and regional alliances such as the International Union of Local Authorities, the Union of Mayors of Capital Cities of Ibero-America, and the Federation of Municipalities in Central America (FEMICA) are beginning to grow stronger. Indicators of this last stage will include the gradual acceptance of a plural role in debate— an agreement to jointly manage federalist tensions rather than to control and react.

INTERGOVERNMENTAL IMPASSE AND A NEW AGENDA FOR POLITICAL AND INSTITUTIONAL REFORM

Looking back over fifteen years of decentralization, we see a somewhat herky-jerky pattern in strategies of decentralization. National strategies of decentralization were composed of an awkward and uncoordinated mix of financial and political reforms that produced confusion and setbacks as they were implemented. After all, national governments, which in the past had kept local governments weak, were suddenly attempting with decentralization to reverse forty years of practice. Political and electoral reforms, coupled with changes in finance and spending in the 1980s and 1990s, set in motion a dynamic of innovation in governance that was largely unexpected. At least it was not advertised widely in national strategy nor foreseen in public debate.

Decentralization has swung the strategic balance of power decisively away from the center, but the direction and force of the pendular moment is now in question. After a decade of devolution and restructuring the terms of power, governments have arrived at an impasse. A cloak of controls—over intergovernmental finance, investment approvals, and planning—is placed around cities by central government structures that effectively create impediments for cities to achieve reforms even when governments want them to change. Cities do not have the latitude to prove their ability to perform well. National officials are not inclined to loosen strictures until they see evidence of greater responsibility by cities. Stronger incentives are needed to break the impasse now holding cities and the nation back from faster growth. Making the incentive system more effective requires making the system more transparent and the rewards stronger. To go further now means that central governments are facing, and many are reacting to, the consequences of power sharing. The ultimate test in these new arrangements is that local governments may fail in their duties, that is, prove incompetent and make poor choices. They even may go bankrupt. National governments have not devised ways, political or financial, to allow them to fail without recourse to central bailouts. Some local governments, on the other hand, have shown that they can structure new, productive arrangements with voter-taxpayers, but will the new arrangements be reliable over the long run?

To break this impasse requires that the system of governance—national and local governments and their electorates—must reach a new level of mutual trust. This must be buttressed by assurances that local governments can manage local affairs responsibly. Creating these assurances—by improving choice making, managerial skills, professional capacity, and strengthened political and economic incentives among officeholders, in addition to other items—are the highest priority items on the agenda of decentralization in the region. The present conditions—short terms of political office and restrictions on spending—may limit fiscal mischief, but they also propel the revolving door of municipal personnel and sharply devalue training and technical assistance. Increased skills are drawn into higher pay outside local government. This does not mean that political influence in appointments can be eliminated, but rather that appointees, whether friends of the mayor or not, must meet minimum qualifications of service. Without stronger professional skills, local governments will have little hope of winning the trust of citizens and acquiring greater capacity needed to convince national governments that the impasse can be broken.

PART III □ □ □ □ □ □ □ □

Dimensions of Reform

5 □ Political Participation and Local Government

Fiscal Choice and Expressing Voice

VOICE, CHOICE, AND ACCOUNTABILITY

The expansion of popular participation was part of the political and institutional strategies of mayors responding to decentralization. Energies of grassroots groups and organized communities were unleashed all across the region as new arrangements for governance were being implemented. With the return to elections for local government officials, parties and candidates began to alter the pattern of dialogue in the political and choice-making processes. Specifically, with more power and money at their disposal, local officials began to see the importance of listening to voices from "below," that is, tapping into the sentiments of voters, citizen groups, and neighborhood organizations as a part of making plans and budget tradeoffs. These grassroots expressions of preferences and need, as well as the use of participatory and electoral processes to make choices, grew to be essential elements in the stock and trade of decentralized governance. Moreover, it became evident that as citizens began to play a more important role in local affairs, in some places they signaled a willingness to be taxed for local services and infrastructure.

All of these modes of participation—direct and electoral expression as well as fiscal consent—were on the cutting edge of change for leading local governments. Not all cities achieved these new modes of participation, and the experience of leading cities does not clearly define surefire factors of successful decentralization. Drawing conclusions about how to best decentralize requires more controlled analyses of successes and failures. The purpose of this analysis, however, is not to devise successful decentralization by means of comparative analysis; rather it is to understand key changes in local governance that came with decentralization.

This chapter maps out the most important forms of participation and examines the purposes to which they were put. This survey of the broad panorama of participatory interchange starts at the bottom, that is, by looking first at how grassroots organizations, barrio and neighborhood groups for instance, have been brought into the processes of decision making and spending. At the other, national, end of the spectrum is sweeping legislation, such as the Bolivian Participation Law and the Mexican Solidarity Program that spent billions of dollars a year on programs that depended upon widespread citizen or beneficiary participation. This incorporation of participation in governance was one of the outstanding features of decentralization in Latin America. The change of attitude regarding participation was a relatively sudden transformation that reversed long-standing trends in the management of local affairs. The legacy of local governments inherited from decades of central control was one of being aloof, opaque, and closed to citizen input. Participation quickly became the chief propellant for the quiet revolution.

The energies released through popular participation could not be mobilized merely by flowing decision-making and spending power to local levels. Explicitly or implicitly, in Latin America—as elsewhere in the world—the designers of national strategies recognized the practical political impact, if not the moral high ground, of making room in decentralization policy for local inputs. For decades, street demonstrations, union movements, and organized neighborhood groups had achieved political gains, but only by exerting strong efforts that usually targeted very specific and often highly visible issues. These took the form of squatter invasions to gain property, housewives banging pots in the streets of Santiago over austerity measures and price increases, and university and worker demonstrations over wage levels or political freedoms. The loud chorus of citizens demonstrating or demanding change had ample precedent and was not invented in the quiet revolution (Castells 1983; Perlman 1976). But before decentralization took effect, political leaders and policymakers at the local level created and implemented policy with incomplete or ill-founded images of what citizens wanted; after decentralization, participation became part of the steering mechanism in many local governments.

What was new in the quiet revolution is that, metaphorically speaking, a higher fidelity voice was tuned into the central channels of government and was being heard there with greater frequency and clarity. More than that, the voice from below was stimulated by local and national figures, and orchestrated by an increasing number of NGOs and others in the civil sector who understood that, through the amplification of voice, political and social objectives could be won.

Voice and participation came in many forms and from many groups, and before going further here, it is useful to define the scope of civil society being discussed in these chapters. Neighborhood block organizations, student groups, labor unions, and other interest groups (women, church, sports, political parties, and others) were the typical actors in civil society before decentralization. As decentralization policy was being shaped and provisions implemented, new, more variegated organizations sprang to life, some linked to functional interests (sports, women's groups), others to specific places (neighborhood improvement associations). Decentralization breathed new life into existing organizations and led to the formation of many new ones. Many different kinds of public and private groups are referred to with the conventional term nongovernmental organizations (NGOs). The term NGO is inadequate to capture the wide variety of neighborhood and community-based groups, however. Carroll (1992) invoked the more encompassing term *civil sector* to cover the gamut of actors that have played a role in decentralization and participation. Carroll's civil sector is a class of actors with organized input in policymaking, implementation, and service delivery and comprises the nongovernmental and not-for-profit, but private groups operating in both neighborhoods and at national levels. In Carroll's scheme, grassroots, community-based, issues-oriented membership organizations are distinguished from the rest, because they are linked to local places, neighborhoods and residential areas, and consist of self-motivated actors working on specific issues of importance to them. They organize around local issues they themselves feel strongly about, not because they are moved to do so as clients or proxies of outside groups with no long-term stake in the community.[1]

VOICES AND ACTION FROM BELOW

There were six broad kinds of participation mobilized at the local level during the quiet revolution. Arranged in terms of complexity and formality, they are tapping into grassroots opinion, mobilizing grassroots groups, beneficiary contributions, citizen-initiated contact, the electoral and voting system, and the legal and judicial system.

The most common form of participation, and in some senses the most easily arranged, was that of tapping into popular sentiment, grassroots opinion. This method was typically practiced by local authorities simply by visiting local groups or inviting them to city hall, conducting opinion surveys,

Table 5-1. Mechanisms of Participation and Their Functions

Participatory mechanism	Area of Effectiveness			
	Policy and planning	Demand preferences and budgeting	Implementation and oversight	Accountability
Tapping into grassroots opinion	Surveys (Valledupar, Versailles, Colombia) Consultations (Conchali, Chile; Asuncion, Paraguay) Advisory councils (Puerto Madero, Mexico) *Cabildos Abiertos* (Venezuela, Central America)			
Mobilizing grassroots groups	Participatory budgeting (Brazil)		Implementation committees (Mexico)	*Comites de Vigilancia* (Bolivia) Community organization laws
Beneficiary contributions		Mayor's funds (Chile)	Condominial systems (Recife, Brazil)	
Citizens initiated contact				Rating systems (Colombia)
Electoral and voting process	Programmatic campaign (Colombia)			Referenda (Mexico)
Legal and judicial system				Impeachment (Colombia, Brazil)

consultations, and by staging hearings at which organized groups could voice their views and opinions.

Mobilizing local grassroots groups is next in terms of effort and resources. This effort required dedicated resources, often in the form of a community or social affairs secretary with staff in the municipal government. Although no quantitative statistics are available, municipal secretaries of community affairs began to proliferate after decentralization.

Beneficiary contributions from an organized community along with material contributions is the next step in the deepening participation. A typical example is the formation of community labor gangs to open trenches and lay water pipes. Donation of land and materials is another typical, but less common, form of contribution, for example, for the creation of a community center. Again, it is difficult to compile statistics to demonstrate the financial or economic impact of such contributions, but anecdotal evidence shows these contributions were substantial in economic terms. They also became widely observed around the region in the late 1980s and early 1990s. This is significant because it shows a stronger partnership between citizens and local authorities.

In the same vein, citizen-initiated actions, like published ratings of local governments, showed that citizens were also taking decentralized government seriously and were looking for new ways to keep government accountable. Although few report-card systems have been formed, many new efforts were mounted to publish the results of local government performance. (See Epstein 1984 for an overview of performance-based governance.)

The electoral and voting system also became more accessible to the population. Participation has been extended to the electoral domain both in selection of local leaders at the ballot box as well as in the use of voting mechanisms to make public choices. Some countries have reformed the electoral process and made the experience easier.

Participation in the legal and judicial system has also been institutionalized legally in a number of ways. Some countries offered legal recognition of local groups and "regulate" their behavior in administrative and legal terms. Others have made it easier to pursue certain legal actions, such as impeachment.

The coverage in this chapter does not pretend to be comprehensive by category of issue or by country. Rather, the examples are chosen because they are outstanding cases and because they illustrate emerging trends in the region. Also, the reader will notice that some modes of participation, generally those employed at the local level, would fit for several kinds of public business, for instance, tapping into public opinion can be useful for planning as well as holding officials accountable. It should also be noted that the discussion leaves some serious gaps. For instance, political parties are not discussed (except for brief mention), nor are the press and news media. All of these institutions are important, but outside the scope of this analysis. With these limitations, we turn to specific illustrations.

Tapping into Grassroots Opinion

Incorporating grassroots community groups into local improvement programs was the most commonly observed form of participation in local government, and within this category a wide variety of methods has been observed—direct consultation in situ, town meetings, polling, and surveying of preference, and others. In the main, these tools helped to generate a voice in the purest sense for stock taking, reading the pulse of voters, and gauging preferences. Grassroots groups were also engaged in cost sharing for small works or mobilized to take responsibility for ensuring that neighborhood-level projects were completed on budget and to the group's satisfaction.

Some newly elected mayors orchestrated elaborate arrangements with local community groups to discover and verify preferences. A good example is the city of Valledupar in Colombia. The newly elected mayor in this city of 247,000 in the northern floodplain of the Magdalena River, financed extensive surveys of the population to determine priority areas of concern from among the population. Citizens were asked about their desires for public services and their opinions about the public sector. Meetings with community representatives were held to deepen the understanding of information gathered in sample surveys.

A somewhat more structured routine was established by new leaders in Versailles, a community of 27,000 in central Colombia. Citizens there were polled annually to determine preferences for capital investments. The results of the surveys were published and discussed in focus groups. A yearly operational plan emerged from this process. Some short- and long-term rolling investments were verified based on direct, objective, and widespread input from citizens. The survey in Versailles was conducted annually for several administrations. Citizens became familiar with the process and its purpose and became accustomed to responding to a focused set of questions. Mayors in hundreds of cities regularly or sporadically tapped into community sentiment in this way. Mayor Joaquin Lavin in Las Condes (adjacent to Santiago), Chile, included a concise, sophisticated questionnaire about service and priority needs and attached the survey to the annual tax notices mailed to every property owner.

Still other local governments, for instance La Chacra in metropolitan Caracas, Venezuela, Mayor Irene Saenz instituted performance measurement programs to gauge the quality and efficiency of government. This was all but unthinkable before decentralization. In these examples, local governments gather information on the performance of their administrations and determine, through a citizen survey, public satisfaction or dissatisfaction. Incorporating citizen feedback on services has been shown to foster credibility and legitimacy in the U.S. political system (Hatry et al., eds. 1977, 1981).

A more direct, if less powerful, way to gather information about public opinion and needs is to stage face-to-face meetings with citizen groups. This of course was done commonly even before decentralization. It became more widespread and more important after mayors were elected. With a popular mandate, they began seeking not only more information, but also more direct contact with citizen groups. Mayor Marie Antoinette de Sa is a good example.

In the early years following the return to civilian government in Chile, many municipalities like Conchalí, a working-class area of 140,000 low-income residents in the north-central part of metropolitan Santiago, were headed by appointed mayors eager to reach into community sentiment after years of neglect during authoritarian military rule. Against this backdrop, the first appointed mayor in Aylwin's conciliation government undertook her leadership task with special zeal.

A native daughter of Conchalí, Maria Antoineta de Sa undertook her task with a special skill in community relations and a keen sense for first-hand understanding of community needs. In the early stages of her administration, the mayor held a long series of community hearings, consisting of visits by the mayor and her staff to each of the barrios in Conchali. Her visits were scheduled well in advance, and organized neighborhood groups were alerted to be ready to speak their minds on local issues. The meetings were heavily attended by local residents. According to Mayor de Sa, "I was shocked at the outpouring of opinion and surprised to discover the depth of need for resources and assistance for households with more than one working parent, often female-headed households trying to earn a living and concerned about child care, security, and jobs."[2]

Based on these hearings, the mayor and her staff completely revised the recurrent and capital investment budgets for the municipality. Up until the time of the hearings, the budget, like municipal budgets elsewhere, had been dominated by salaries for teachers, police, and municipal staff and by investments in water, streets, and lighting. After the meetings, far greater resources were put into community services, particularly to assist working women with families. Programs were expanded or created to provide assistance to the aged, teenagers, child care, multipurpose community centers, and primary health and nutrition. The mayor actively recruited national and international assistance from nongovernmental organizations for this purpose. Within eighteen months, seventy-five NGOs were working directly or indirectly in consort with the mayor, her staff, and community organizations in Conchalí.

Scores of mayors adopted citizen panels and community advisory boards to provide counsel regarding the impact of government programs. Asuncion Mayor Carlos Filizola broke entirely new ground in the late 1990s by holding formal public hearings on citywide issues. Hearings included experts and community groups who testified on city planning proposals and other public issues. Up until that time, such hearings were unheard of in Paraguay. Elsewhere, community inputs were also provided by advisory councils, some of them elected. Elected advisory councils were implemented in Chile and

Mexico City. Advisory councils were meant to represent a broad cross section of the community and to provide input into public issues. For instance, in Puerto Madero, Mexico, as in many Mexican communities, municipal committees represented both sectoral and geographical interests. The council meets more or less continuously throughout the year to discuss priorities and reach consensus in planning and spending. In yet another twist, the mayor of Machala (Ecuador) founded a foro civico (civic forum) to help build legitimacy in official decisions and to fortify his efforts to prevail over striking public employees.

Town meetings, or *cabildos abiertos*, became increasingly common in the region as mechanisms for institutionalizing public voice. These were literally meetings of council and mayor held before the public. The decentralization process in Venezuela, Honduras, Chile, and El Salvador all produced laws that require municipal governments to hold regular public forums of this kind. In Venezuela, the Ley Orgánica de Régimen Municipal 1989 required local governments to hold town meetings every three months, provided that a minimum of ten citizens request such a meeting in writing. Not only is the council obliged to answer the questions raised beforehand, but citizens are free to present their own opinions, demands, and propositions during the meeting (Brewer-Carias et al. 1990). In one case, the mayor, Fernando Chumaceiro of Maracaibo, advertised his intention to hold a cabildo abierto, specifying the date and time well in advance. He also made it known that the proceedings would be televised. The meeting turned into a ten-hour marathon in which an endless parade of citizens and groups spoke before the council and the public.

In El Salvador, a program supported by the U.S. Agency for International Development (USAID) required that the selection of city projects to be financed be done in consort with citizens through *cabildos abiertos*. A USAID study of citizens' and mayors' views on cabildos illustrates their positive and negative characteristics. Citizens found them to be genuinely open and representative of the community, but were critical of their limitations. Citizens could voice their opinions and project demands but had no concrete role in project selection or general planning for development. Mayors, on the other hand, "did not see the meetings as beneficial, . . . actively resisted citizen involvement in the priority-setting process, [and] as a whole did not convene the number of meetings (five per year) that they were required to hold under the municipal law." (Peterson 1997)

With decentralization, existing and new grassroots groups were quick to identify themselves, declare their intentions, and to be received and courted by incoming mayors eager for new ways to understand community needs.

Mayors, recognizing that grassroots groups were essential building blocks of participation, not only recruited them, but created them to assist in virtually all the key functions of local government: policy making and planning, expressing demand and preferences, implementation of programs, and feedback mechanisms for project supervision and quality control.

Mobilizing Grassroots Groups

Participatory budgeting is a process by which neighborhood residents are incorporated into the decisions about capital investment in their city.[3] Many cities in Brazil began to experiment with participatory budgeting after the demise of the military government in the early 1980s. None carried the process further than Porto Alegre. Opposition candidates for mayor and councilors posts in Porto Alegre, led by Mayor Tarso Genero, felt that their competitive advantage over the ruling party lay in drawing government closer to the people and in providing services people say they need, rather than splashy civil works the community might not really want.

After winning the elections in 1988, Genero and his colleagues set about to build on the work of previous labor party mayor Olivio Dutra and to implement a system of participatory budgeting for each of its barrios in the city (Singer 1998). A series of meetings was held in each neighborhood. Residents were notified in advance of the meetings. Existing neighborhood organizations were invited to take part, and some new groups were created so that the entire city was represented by neighborhood groups. A public education campaign, including cartoon style booklets, was mounted to inform citizens of the many steps in the participatory budgeting process.

At the initial meetings, the mayor and his staff presented the city's budget, including both recurrent and capital expenses. These figures were portrayed in simplified form on large poster boards and other visual aids. The meetings focused on how to invest in the budgeted amount for capital expenses that would affect each neighborhood. City representatives were on hand to explain the costs of services and infrastructure. Residents were also told that the preferences expressed by surrounding neighborhoods should be taken into account. This information also was divulged to each neighborhood unit. This feedback often had the effect of moving individual neighborhood priorities to convergence with others, once participants realized that bargaining with other neighborhood groups could improve their position or that joining forces with neighboring districts could effectively lower the price of some services (for instance, multidistrict schools or clinic services could be delivered more cheaply).

Technical staff subsequently developed an investment program, the high-lights of which were then presented at yet another follow-up meeting, this time with a council of representatives elected from each region. The council's job was then to monitor the city's efforts to comply with the budget deci-sions. According to (then) Mayor Tarso Genero, participatory budgeting reached a stage in the local politics of Porto Alegre where "no serious con-tender for mayor could ignore it."[4]

Participatory budgeting had transformed the idea of best practice about budgeting and even moved it beyond conventional budgeting practices in the region. The technique spread to many cities in Brazil by means of political party connections and through courses at the Brazilian Institute for Munici-pal Administration. The practice has even been exported to cities in Argen-tina, Chile, and Colombia. A delegation of local government officials from Germany visited Porto Alegre to study participatory budgeting for use in German cities.

Only a small step separates participation in the budgeting of local works and participation in their execution. Most local governments have taken this step, which consists of setting up project execution committees (called *co-mites ejecutivos* or *comites de implementacion*) at the neighborhood level to act as the eyes and ears of the community in the supervision of small civil works. Implementation committees were not entirely new after decentraliza-tion, but they were given new authority and new prominence. They were to see to it that contractors complied with regulations and completed civil works as agreed, on time, and within budget. In some cases, the contractor needed the signature of the committee before city payment could be released. It was not uncommon to hear complaints by neighborhood groups of poor engineering, substandard equipment, or shoddy finishing by contractors who sometimes cut corners to complete jobs and increase profits. The short-comings of their work were noticed right away by residents, and mayors and communities were full of stories of refusals to sign for contractors who had not complied with agreed standards.

The joining of forces and tapping local resources is reminiscent of self-help housing of several decades ago (see Turner and Mangin 1967). Com-pared to housing, two features of local community improvements place them in a separate category. First, they are collective works, not individual house-hold improvements, and they are combined with resources with municipal sponsorship. Although some self-help housing involved community organi-zation, shelter itself was an individual undertaking. Second, the partnerships formed to create community works had exhibited a new closeness between governed and electorate. Self-help housing and barrio improvements were often (though not always) done in opposition to local and national governments. From survey, to consultation, to comites ejecutivos, with the quiet revolution, city hall began reaching out in a more fruitful, more collaborative dialogue with citizens.

Organized community groups have also been authorized by national law to increase accountability of local government. The most striking example of this was legislated as national law adopted in the Bolivian Congress in April of 1994. The Popular Participation Law called for the creation of vigilance committees *(comites de vigilancia)* or watchdog groups at the municipal level. The Bolivian participation law was conceived as a means of opening government to disenfranchised indigenous groups in rural areas. For most of Bolivia's history, rural settlements with strong ethnic identities have lived outside municipal jurisdictions in unincorporated areas governed by regional development agencies or by central government ministries. The National Participation Law was intended to incorporate the territorial gaps of municipal administration and to create a mechanism, the *comites de vigilancia,* as the bedrock of a system of accountability that included the rural poor and indigenous minorities. *Comites de vigilancia* were empowered to oversee all phases of municipal activities, from planning to implementation. Under the law, they were to report directly to the central government. They had the power to trigger suspension of revenue transfers when municipalities failed to carry out their functions.

The Popular Participation Law in Bolivia recognized and integrated grassroots groups into the political process as the collective eyes and ears of the central government. Perhaps as striking as the content of the law was the unprecedented manner in which it was taken to the public. The president, his cabinet, and party officials, accompanied by the press, embarked on a highly unusual U.S.-style public education and promotion campaign to "explain" the law to the electorate. The Bolivian law is an outstanding example of central government sponsoring legislation not only to strengthen local government, but also to create a system of accountability at the local level through the community-based organizations.

Legal recognition was given to selected community-based organizations to act as priority setters, promoters, developers, and supervisors of projects at the local level. Community-based organizations were designed to operate somewhat like the *comites de solidaridad* in Mexico, except the Bolivian versions are "standing" organizations. They were meant to operate continuously. The *comites de solidaridad* in Mexico are formed solely for the purpose of supervising the implementation of specific community civil works.

Detractors of the Bolivian law point out that it sets up a mechanism for the central government to be present in, and to have a controlling influence over, local affairs. It is possible to imagine many other arrangements to achieve local accountability without the sharp imprint of presidential control embodied in the law. For instance, democratic election of local groups, parent teachers associations, or local councils of broad representation could, with bipartisan recognition based on objective criteria, serve the same watchdog functions envisioned in the Bolivian law.

Alhough legislation in several other countries—Chile and Venezuela, to name two—defined and regulated local organizations, none had the bite of the Bolivian law. Chilean law (1990 Nueva Ley de Juntas de Vecinos, Law No. 18893), for example, distinguished local groups in terms of residency or function (i.e., the group's focus or the things groups engage in, such as mother's, sports, health, or community improvement clubs). The Chilean law created a regulatory framework governing such matters as dues, use of funds, and other rights and obligations. It also required groups to register with national authorities. Venezuelan law (Ley Organica de Regimen Municipal of 1990) detailed how grassroots groups were to be constituted and registered, and how they were to gain legal recognition. The law also stipulated procedures for bylaws (e.g., how officers are to be elected). In a further shift downward of decentralization in Venezuela, *parroquias* (the level of public administration below municipalities) were authorized to serve as formal channels of public input into policy and planning in local affairs. In 1990, Venezuelan *parroquias* began to hold national assemblies. Legislation in Colombia, (Ley 134 1994) called for widespread public participation in the conduct of local affairs (Fondo para la Participacion Ciudadana) "to develop and carry out campaigns to make citizen participation more effective." This law went hand in glove with Law 152 of 1994 that provided guidelines on the formulation of and participation in urban plans.

Beneficiary Contributions

Participation in the form of financial, material, or labor contributions is an acid test of participation, and decentralization in the region fostered many examples of direct contact with citizen groups to mobilize resources—known as counterpart contributions—for neighborhood improvement programs. Counterpart contributions from beneficiaries were not new. In some countries (Mexico, Honduras, Chile) they were customary, even a tradition, in community development. Housing and water-supply projects in these countries have for many decades been financed partly in this way. But with decentralization, beneficiary contributions have been institutionalized in new ways at the local level.

In the years subsequent to her first community consultations mentioned earlier, Mayor de Sa extended community involvement into the realm of cost sharing in Conchali, Chile. She first offered neighborhood juntas modest amounts of discretionary spending from the municipal budget. Later, she developed a series of matching grant programs financed entirely by the municipality to pave streets and to provide street lighting, working block by block. These grew into a major municipal program.[5] To participate, neighbors were obliged to form a progress committee. Each committee was responsible for one linear block of residential household units. The immediate objective was to obtain street paving by raising a minimum of 25 percent of the costs. The committee opened an account into which members deposited funds to cover their share of the cost. Committee members drummed up support in the neighborhood and organized contributions. The larger the percentage contribution the committee made, the greater the possibility of quick approval by the council and public works department. In five years, the municipality under mayor de Sa completed paving with forty-five different block groups and extended the program to street lighting, following the same principles (World Bank 1992). Similar cost-sharing programs have surfaced in a dozen cities.

In Monterrey, Mexico, the former mayor (and then governor) Socrates Rizo promised to invest increases in property tax revenues back into neighborhoods in proportion to revenue increases, rather than mingle them into the general fund. Rizo's main concern was to answer this question posed to his staff and visitors, "How do I know what the people want?" He felt that community guided investments from tax increases was the best way to answer his question. In Tamaulipas, a northeastern state in Mexico, a philosophical cousin of the mayor's fund is known as *hombro a hombro* (shoulder to shoulder). City works are financed on a fifty-fifty basis as neighborhoods raise their share of income. In Ecuador, more than 120 municipalities have signed "planning contracts" with barrio organizations. Most are tied to block-scale upgrading works. Others are more involved, aiming to bring an element of equity into the municipality's annual operational program in larger scale works for water, sewerage, drainage, and public lighting by adjusting downward the required advance contributions from poorer communities.

Condominial sewerage systems in Brazil took the principle of counterpart contribution one step further, combining it with appropriate technology by involving community residents in the operation of sewage disposal. A condominial system refers to ingenious design changes that reduce the need for excavation and scale down standards of service (fewer clean-out traps, smaller-bore pipes). These features reduced construction costs by as much as 75 percent in some circumstances. Reductions in operational costs were also possible. But to achieve these reductions, neighborhoods and families had to participate in maintenance by keeping waste traps clear of debris. This involved regular checking and, if necessary, unpleasant clearing of foreign objects—solid waste like rags, paper, sticks, weeds—that get washed into the system. One study (Serra 1993) showed that user contributions to routine maintenance brought down monthly tariffs by as much as 65 percent in some systems, as compared to the conventional system (see also Watson 1995).

This system required unusual involvement of communities in the identification, selection, and implementation of sewerage projects and to contribute 20 percent of the total cost of each project in kind—i.e., cash, labor, materials, or some combination of these. These participatory features made household sewerage connections affordable to low income households, and many municipalities sought to take advantage of this innovative approach to sanitation. While condominial sewerage was not invented because of decentralization, it embodied a technology which was suited to the participatory spirit that was building during the quiet revolution.

Citizen-Initiated Contact and Electoral Process

Some local groups—NGOs in Colombia, municipal associations in Central America and Chile—instituted ratings systems by which local governments were ranked or given public recognition for good performance. Another, purer form of Hirschman's "voice option" (Coulter 1988) allowed citizens to communicate a request or complaint directly to public officials. Many local governments in Latin America took the initiative to set up public relations offices. Some of the most sophisticated used computerized programs to characterize the source of complaint and track progress, summarize the nature of complaints and responses each month, and generate periodic reports. In the Venezuelan state of Lara, an experimental program (financed by German foreign assistance) set up a telephone hotline that allowed citizens to express a wide range of complaints and opinions about local government. A computerized tabulation system allowed the governor to quickly "read" the trend line in hundreds of calls recorded monthly. Other cities set up central complaint centers or instituted an ombudsman's office with much the same functions as the complaint centers. None of these contact points for feedback to government existed before decentralization.

The electoral system represents the most fundamental instrument available in democracies to tap into the public will, and more than half the countries in the Latin American region have reformed local elections in some way to enhance the power of this instrument. Although it is a definitive method of arriving at public choice, many problems remain to be addressed.[6]

Electoral regimes are complicated and costly to change. Voting to make public decisions is clumsy, involves lengthy feedback loops, often confront voters with "bulky" spending packages that mix many options, and sometimes these proposals are not clearly articulated (by mayors, parties, and politicians). In addition, an uninformed or lethargic electorate can make all of these factors worse. Most decision makers in local governments in the region are left without the benefit of fully functioning electoral systems.

Yet the ballot box has been used surprisingly frequently by enterprising mayors—sometimes without explicit authorization to do so—as a way to tap into community sentiment and even to consecrate spending proposals. For example, the electoral process became a part of political campaigning in Colombia. Law 387 in Colombia compelled candidates for local office to declare a spending program in advance of the elections so that the public has an opportunity to vote on alternative sets of preferences embodied in the proposals of competing candidates.

The voting process was also employed to gain support for borrowing and spending in Tijuana. Two stories illustrate how the envelope of participation was pushed into the voting domain. The first is from Las Condes—a rich suburban municipality on the edge of downtown Santiago—the second, from the fast-growing Mexican city of Tijuana on the border with California. In both cases, first-term mayors drew inspiration from outside their countries to successfully introduce change in the public decision-making process by submitting major proposals on the ballot for voters to decide directly.

Mayor Juaquin Lavin of Las Condes learned of Singapore's success with congestion pricing in managing traffic.[7] The mayor thought that similar techniques could be implemented in Las Condes to help smooth cross-town traffic moving from periurban neighborhoods through Las Condes to downtown Santiago during rush hour. The mayor proposed to charge fees for cross-town commuters and to place traffic barriers in strategic neighborhoods in order to reduce congestion. These actions were unusual, and for some neighborhoods, controversial, and the mayor decided to submit the ideas to the citizens of Las Condes for a vote. Although not permitted by law, referenda were also not prohibited, and the mayor received voter support for several of his proposals. Developing the proposal and educating the public involved substantial time, effort, and expense.

A newly elected mayor of Tijuana encountered greater obstacles. Mayor Hector Osuna proposed a $170 million works improvement program to protect the city from disastrous floods like those that hit Tijuana just weeks before he took office in 1992. Mayor Osuna developed a proposal that would require the municipality to borrow money. Since under Mexican law, the city must have state authorization to borrow, Osuna needed to demonstrate political support for his plan. He knew of California's extensive experience with initiatives and referenda, and thought that a public referendum would be a feasible way to demonstrate political support to the state legislature. A year of technical planning was followed by intensive public education and political debate involving hundreds of meetings and much media attention. The central question was whether property owners were willing to pay improvement levies. Again, as in Chile, referenda per se at the city level are not permitted in Mexico, so the mayor instead advertised the vote as a "public consultation." The city arranged to use voting records, special identification cards, and computerized systems of voting and vote counting. A storm of problems, including the assassination of presidential candidate Luis Donaldo Colosio immediately before the referendum, clouded the outcome of the vote.[8] More than anything, the story illustrates the determination to incorporate citizen inputs and the difficulties and high costs of traversing uncertain terrain in the use of the electoral processes to decide local issues.

The constitutional and electoral experiences of the countries in the region vary widely, but most elections are governed by national laws and held simultaneously with national elections, allowing nonlocal issues to influence local issues and outcomes (Molina and Hernandez 1995). Direct election of mayors is allowed in little more than half the countries in the region, but municipal councils are almost uniformly elected directly. Most countries allow the re-election of mayors and councils, but some require them to wait one term before running for re-election. Representativeness is another issue. Most cities elect councils "at large," meaning that councilors represent the entire city and not specific districts. Only three countries use single-member district voting (Belize, Mexico, and Venezuela for half of the legislature); Colombian law allows for single-member district voting but chooses not to use it. Only three countries in the world (Venezuela the only one in Latin America) use the "single-member district/plurality wins" voting method at the municipal level. Further reform is needed to strengthen democratic accountability.

Legal and Judicial System

Participation in public affairs by means of legal and judicial actions is in its infancy in the region, although decentralization has spawned new interest, and some action, in the courts. For example, local neighborhood groups in Mexico City have successfully sued contractors, and even the city, although the central government retains tight control over public spending programs (*Wall Street Journal* 1992).

In a different vein, a number of council-initiated actions have resulted in mayoral impeachments. For example, in the Brazilian state of Para, a mayor was removed from office by council vote even before President Collor was charged with impeachable offenses in 1992. After the Collor scandal, mayors were even more sensitive to public sentiment. Some local observers in the Parana state municipal association described the behavior of mayors in terms of "walking around on eggs," meaning that they were responsive to public outcry about Collor scandals and were being extraordinarily careful about their public image. A dozen mayors were charged with impeachable offenses in Colombia in the early 1990s, and corruption at the local level has become a more prominent feature in local Colombian politics.

The 1992 Bolivian participation law also demonstrated the unfortunate effects of provisions intended to strengthen accountability. An aberration of the impeachment process occurred annually in La Paz for several consecutive years due to a loophole in legislation that allowed city councils to vote on ratification of the mayor upon the one-year anniversary of his or her election to office. For several consecutive years after the passage of the enabling legislation, the city council in La Paz, in each case a council weighted in favor of the opposition party, voted not to ratify the administration of the mayor. The practice spread to other Bolivian cities. This lack of endorsement then triggered a succession process by which the democratically elected mayor was replaced by a member of the council (also in the opposition party). For the most part, however, actions against sitting mayors are rare, although the legal mechanisms for impeachment are included in many national constitutions or municipal laws.

To be effective, judicial mechanisms require a complex infrastructure of law, case history, local courts, and professional expertise, none of which can be found in the region. As a frame of reference, many judicial systems are already overwhelmed with criminal and high-stakes civil suits, and have no resources, financial or otherwise, to deal with municipal issues. Some countries (e.g., Venezuela) have no system of local courts, and in many countries the "standing" of citizens in courts is in question.[9] In still others (e.g., Mexico) there is no professional bar.

COMMON THREADS, LESSONS, AND CONCLUSIONS

The common denominator of the post-decentralization modes of participation is that officials at many levels of government believed it was in their interest to tap into existing grassroots groups and to mobilize new ones to expand the role of citizen participation in local government. Local authorities have been drawn into experimentation by a new system of incentives created with power sharing and the advent of larger resource flows in the form of shared revenues. For the first time in decades, the decisions of local governments have meaning. Local authorities could affect the futures of their communities and their constituents. Sensing this, grassroots organizations in what Carroll calls the civil sector breathed new life into planning, policy making, and project implementation of neighborhood works and services. What is more, citizen participation rejuvenated the character and the quality of local government. In the initial stages of decentralization, local leaders and ordinary citizens alike were quick to see the new possibilities citizen participation offered in a decentralized system of government.

Four main areas have been explored in this chapter, planning and policy, preference detection, implementation of small-scale projects, and accountability mechanisms. In these fundamental ways, the experience with participation in the quiet revolution is fundamentally different from those decentralized strategies promoted by development agencies over the past few decades, for instance, PIDER in Mexico and integrated rural development in Brazil. Though similar on the surface, these rural and integrated programs were applied by central authorities to broad geographic areas that had little or no governmental discretion. These stand in contrast to the decentralization of the quiet revolution that was promulgated with looser rules by central governments, allowing substantial discretion to local authorities to make arrangements and implement programs. The experience of municipal development in many countries shows that decentralization in the quiet revolution represented a distinct step toward allowing more autonomy and discretion to local governments.

The many forms of participation juxtapose the idea and practice of participation before and during the heat of decentralization. Moving the instruments of government closer to the people has not always resulted in more efficient selection or better governance. It may even lead to increased local corruption or cooptation by power elites.

Will local elites achieve local capture? Will they take advantage of decentralization, control the resource allocation process, and set up a rent-seeking system of corruption and kickbacks? Participation can be seen as a weapon against and as a tool that helps achieve local capture. In the United States, the problem of capture was documented by Verba and Nie (1987), who found that individual participation increases with socioeconomic status. Thus, the label "local elite" emerged from the speculation that groups with better education and income would come to dominate the participatory process and capture benefits. The potential problems of capture were confronted in the United States by encouraging more participation from individuals as well as from associations and interest groups. Since information is crucial to participation, an effective media is practically indispensable. Of course, many other tools are also important in order to improve access to information, as has been shown by the Freedom of Information Act in the United States.

A few additional points are worth noting about the circumstances of capture and control in Latin America as compared to the United States. First, national, not local, capture in Latin America has long been a far more important source of bias in the incidence of benefits and capture of rents. The lion's share of all public expenditure still takes place at the national level where focused interventions of organized political powers can influence the flow of large volumes of resources. Only small fractions are channeled through municipalities, and these are open to close scrutiny by the voting public.

The many examples of leading governments illustrated in this chapter reflect only a small fraction of the experience in deepening citizen participation in the region. We have no way of knowing whether these experiences—like advisory councils, participatory budgeting, and neighborhood funds of Conchali—might fall into disuse, only to become some decades hence the flash of inspiration that got smothered under the accumulated weight of administrative process, governmental structures, ordinary corruption, "capture" by local elites, and political opposition from central authorities.

At the same time, participatory experiences during the quiet revolution have important impact by demonstrating what is possible under new rules of the game. Elected officials and the governed have shown eagerness toward experiences and models that work. Conchali, Tijuana, and Porto Alegre offer concrete examples of moving decisions closer to the governed. The information generated with these experiments became a kind of coin of the realm in the region among city leaders and community organizations searching for new solutions during early stages of decentralization. Most of the cases cited in this chapter portray local governments as beholden to citizens in ways that were not possible under former centralized arrangements. Colombian and Bolivian participation laws began to cement these new relationships into the national matrix of political life in those countries. The National Solidarity Program (Programa Nacional de Solidaridad; PRONASOL) in Mexico, participatory budgeting in Brazil, and the effect of innovations elsewhere suggest that this process may continue with the expanding scope and spending in these programs.

Securing the sustainability of good governance through participation, and realizing other potential objectives—such as increasing efficiency in resource allocation and effectiveness in implementation—may depend critically on outside help. The direction of assistance by international development assistance agencies—the World Bank, the Inter-American Development Bank (IDB), and European and American bilateral agencies—are laying new emphasis at the local level. For instance, they are fostering horizontal linkages that have already begun to grow like crystals as the vertical ties to central governments begin to weaken. These new local and regional structures reinforce the process of rebuilding civil society.

Another, perhaps more important, political lesson emerges from this picture. Power sharing and democratic participation mean that the traditional measure of local government performance—whether local goods and services are delivered efficiently—is complemented to an important degree with the notion that local governments must also become mechanisms of accountability. In addition to delivering services, local democratic participation is becoming a potentially important underpinning in the responsible management of the financial system and, ultimately, part of the mechanism to guarantee macroeconomic stability.

The forms of participation discussed in this chapter are the most important in terms of recent practice in the region, but many issues have been left out, for example, voter registration, campaign and electoral financing, political parties, the media, and expert technical assistance to citizen groups. Accountability cannot be completely achieved in pluralistic societies without an integrated system of mechanisms working together. Most of the countries undergoing decentralization have not achieved this integration. And even though surprising progress has been made in incorporating citizen participation in governance, the long-term sustainability of decentralized governance depends to a great extent on a more complete set of democratic institutions.

6 □ Neighborhood Works, Poverty, and the Environment

If national authorities were ambivalent about local governments handling new moneys and new responsibilities, leading local authorities, buttressed by stronger inputs from citizens' groups, were themselves quite unambivalent about the two priority areas for spending: urban poverty and environmental decay at the local level. Of course, these two topics cover a wide gamut of issues, but for local leaders the focus was quite narrowly on livelihoods, income flow, and improvement in the environmental circumstances of low-income neighborhoods. From the perspective of city authorities, poverty and environmental issues merge into a single area of concern. Up until the quiet revolution, they were regarded as two separate domains. During and after the quiet revolution, the chief executives in leading cities began to focus on local issues, and because of rapid urban migration and the neglected infrastructure of past decades, local governments came to see and address these issues in tandem.

This view challenges the conventional wisdom and traditional developmental approaches taken by national and international authorities, a view that is often encouraged by NGOs. International groups identify two separate agendas. The first is a poverty agenda that is often linked to, but rarely integrated with, "brown" environmental issues. The poverty agenda focuses on short-term concerns that affect immediate human welfare (and sometimes survival itself) such as water, sewerage, and waste disposal. The second agenda involves a "green" environmental domain, and is focused on long-term sustainability of large ecosystems. The green issues—for instance, global warming and deforestation—get a lot of play in the press and tend to be handled by national authorities, supported by international NGOs. But the brown issues in cities—water supply, wastewater treatment, drainage, solid waste collection, citywide transport problems and accidents, smog, congestion—take a heavier toll on the poor than on the city population as a whole. An informal survey of mayors in the late 1990s showed that after job concerns, environmental issues at the local level, led by solid waste, were the top priority.[1]

Local actors, both public authorities and private entrepreneurs, working in concert with various not-for-profit groups, became increasingly willing to address environmental problems using small-scale actions with intensive doses of local participation. Cities of all sizes in Brazil, Colombia, Central America, and Mexico took actions to address poverty and the environment. Their experiences show that environmental and poverty issues were not policy and political issues left only to national authorities and international NGOs, even when they are concerned with brown issues. Leading cities after the quiet revolution were demonstrating that local participatory action could be effective in solving local problems.

The critical strategic lesson in these experiences is that the key to success is an informational advantage—an informational infrastructure—found only at the local level. These information resources of local knowledge about how and where to take actions lay dormant in every neighborhood and every city. The experiences described in this chapter show the enormous potential of tapping into this specialized knowledge. The experiences of the quiet revolution strongly suggest that, with the right guidance and skill, the informational infrastructure can be harnessed anywhere to help solve problems of the urban poor in the megacities of Asia, Africa, and Eastern Europe.

POVERTY AND THE URBAN ENVIRONMENT: CONVENTIONAL APPROACHES

The poor have been the largest single economic group of urban residents in the Latin American region (as well as in the developing world) for the past half-century. By relative dollar and index measures—that is, based on the distribution of income and a composite index developed by the United Nations to measure well-being—more poor households have been in cities than in rural areas from the turn of the century onwards. In past decades, the very largest cities were the major marshaling points for low-income households trying their luck in the city. Typically, a third or more of the urban populations in the 1970–80 period were composed of households living "under a poverty line," that is, having less income than they needed to buy minimum acceptable calories and proteins, shelter, clothing, and other necessities.

But at the dawn of decentralization, national and local officials faced a distinctly different set of conditions concerning urban development and the poor than was true only decades earlier. At least three changes were apparent. First, demographic circumstances had spread the burden of need for poverty assistance from the largest cities and rural areas to a new set of cities in the intermediate range. Recall that growth rates in the second tier of cities— those under a million or so in population—had, in nearly every case, risen half again as fast as those for the largest cities nearby. These largest cities, such as Mexico City, Santiago, and Buenos Aires, began growing more than 2 percent per year over the past decade. Leon, Puebla, Tijuana, Goiania, and other cities in the 100 thousand to 1 million range began growing at rates of 3 to 4 percent annually.

The second change was that local officials in leading cities learned they would have to cope with many dimensions of urban poverty. Helping the urban poor was not merely a matter of creating jobs and raising incomes. Most mayors who focused on the poor learned quickly that statistical measures of poverty were not very useful for understanding the environmental concomitants of being poor. Poverty in urban Latin America means not only that elemental necessities are often out of reach in economic terms. The largest fraction of people's daily lives is consumed by commuting to poorly paying jobs and low-quality schooling. Travel to jobs and schools often requires many hours of crosstown transit and, for the poor, high fares. The time and money costs rob many of the opportunity to obtain secondary education, especially young females. Compared to urban populations as a whole, the urban poor also have larger families, lower life expectancies—often by years or decades, again especially for females—and mortality and morbidity rates that annually kill hundreds of thousands of children under the age of five in the cities of Latin America. Moreover, despite the return to positive growth rates in most Latin American countries, recent new evidence suggests that the benefits of expanding economies have not been making an impact on the poor.[2]

The third reason that urban officials are challenged by poverty as never before is that the poor and cities everywhere were increasingly subjected to real and perceived violence of a kind that was not seen even in the largest cities two decades ago. Mayors in many cities began to address this issue. For example, former mayor Rodrigo Guerrero of Cali focused on violence in the city as the highest priority concern for his administration in the late 1980s.

Newly elected Martin Burt of Asuncion discovered in his interactions with citizens that violence, and a sense of insecurity, were increasing among ordinary citizens. Perhaps it is because drug trade and related violence have spread across the continent, bringing with it a growing visibility of personal assaults. Perhaps citizen concerns reflected a general sense that the state was shrinking back from traditional functions of security, law, and order. Whatever the cause and underlying dynamic, local officials began to voice a need to cope with violence that was not present in the decades before decentralization.

Shortcomings of National Efforts to Meet Community Needs

National programs have failed to solve the problems of poverty because the cost is high compared to conventional volume of investment, and because, with few exceptions, national efforts have been clumsy and blunt. In the first place, a full-scale solution to problems of poverty in Latin America's cities would require resources that have been and still are wildly out of proportion with public and private investment. The basic infrastructure and services for drinking water, sewerage, solid waste disposal, and direct health-care services are largely unmet. The total direct investment from all official sources in the region has been about US$12 billion per year. Meeting the few basic service needs would, by itself, eat up one-third of that total. In urban sanitation alone, at least a threefold increase in historical levels of annual investment would be required to reach targets set by the World Health Organization (WHO) for water and sanitation by the turn of the century. This would entail the expenditure of approximately US$50 billion to reach WHO service levels in the next several decades.[3]

Nations not only have insufficient resources for physical investments, but many national social programs are poorly designed. Poverty remains entrenched in part because of the inherent flaws in the system of social structure—poor education and job-training skills and poor delivery of services. Part of the problem is that national programs have been guided by principles of design and implementation that overlook the poor (see table 6-1). For instance, employment, education, credit programs, and social safety nets—typical components of national poverty programs—assume or require a certain level of literacy, employment in a tax-paying entity, or some kind of material collateral. Rarely can any of these conditions be met by poor urban households. Virtually no poor household can meet them all. For instance, poor households are often composed of parents and children who have had little more than a few years of formal education. Without literacy skills, parents cannot qualify for jobs that provide social security and insurance

Table 6-1. Programmatic Mismatches: National Strategies and
the Urban Poor

Objective of national assistance program	Assistance type	Program characteristics	Circumstances of the poor
Raise employment	Create jobs	Job targets often in the formal sector	Poor are usually in the informal sector
Improve job skills	Training	Literacy required	Illiterate
Primary education	Elementary school assistance	For designated age groups before entering labor market	Eligible age groups already in labor market
Credit	Loans for businesses, homes	Small holders with collateral	Possess no material collateral
Social security	Medical and unemployment insurance	Formal sector businesses and firms	Workers in the informal sector

Source: After Homi Kharas, World Bank, lecture at World Bank, November 21, 1996.

benefits. Instead they work in the informal sector, that is, they work as self-employed manual laborers or street vendors with none of the rudimentary benefits of a modern social welfare system.

National social programmers have long faced a dilemma. In order to reach poor households everywhere, a broad national program is needed to reach the poor in all cities, but at the same time, some objective sorting or selection criteria is needed to direct assistance to where it is most needed in each locale, and this requires detailed knowledge of circumstances on the ground. How is it possible to help the nation's poor without having detailed information about their needs, creditworthiness, and employment potential? The answer of course is that none of this information could be gathered and managed by a central program bureaucracy. It is not surprising then that with decentralization, a handful of national programs began to meet these needs by working with local intermediaries, such as community organizations, the church, housing cooperatives, and after decentralization, local governments.

National Assistance to Meet Local Need

Some interesting program examples illustrate the scale and complexity of mounting major alleviation efforts. They illustrate how the groundwork was laid for local governments to devise and implement their own assistance to the poor after the quiet revolution. During and after decentralization, leading cities devised strategies to address problems of poverty and the environment that they saw as inextricably linked. The programs are all national in scope and incorporate local counterparts as not only an explicit, but also an indispensable, feature of program implementation.

Mexico's National Solidarity Program, Brazil's efforts to improve water and sanitation, and programs by Brazil and Chile in primary education and health have been thoughtfully designed and effectively implemented. One of the keys to success is strong participation by some agent at the local level— the NGO, a cooperative, or a local government—to gauge the nature and scope of need and to help implement solutions. The basic formula for improving local environmental conditions in urban settings was invented by grassroots groups concerned with housing during the periods of most rapid urbanization in Latin America. During the 1960s many neighborhood organizations were formed to achieve a foothold for squatters in cities and to improve shelter and security of tenure.

The formula they used involved social organization by block and neighborhood units of low-income groups and the application of political pressure on local and national officials. This strategy was coupled with sweat equity and small-scale capital channeled over a long period of time into the construction and expansion of household and community facilities. Much of the core residential areas in the low-income neighborhoods of today's cities was created or improved in this way. These solutions also involved low-cost, and often locally manufactured, inputs, for instance, siding, door frames, hardware, electrical connections, sanitary sheds, concrete basins, and cover caps for pit latrines. These components were capable of being installed using labor-intensive techniques and gradually improved over time. Even though the outcomes—shelter and sanitation services—were substandard in a technical sense, they were affordable and had the great advantage of being upgradable over time.[4] Similar characteristics describe the features of successful national programs for the poor in the 1980s and 1990s.

Recall that PRONASOL was initiated by the Salinas administration in 1989 and was built on experience of the previous decade with matching grant arrangements in which federal, state, and local governments joined efforts to solve local problems. Salinas saw the matching grant program as an opportunity to address the nation's poverty, and to advance his party's political agenda, through the provision of social infrastructure and support for income-generating activities. PRONASOL focused on three major groups— peasants, indigenous peoples, and the urban poor. It was designed to replace top-down federal assistance with a participatory approach emphasizing community initiative, shared responsibility for implementation, transparency, and efficiency. Between 1989 and 1993, over US$8 billion in federal funding was channeled through PRONASOL, most of it matched by varying levels of state and local funds. Nearly every municipality in Mexico has participated in the program.

Approximately 11 percent of PRONASOL financing was earmarked as municipal funds, providing municipalities with annual grants amounting to approximately US$5 per inhabitant (Campbell and Freedheim 1994). Projects were selected by a municipal PRONASOL council after holding neighborhood assemblies to gauge demand. For selected projects, a PRO–NASOL committee was formed at the residential level and given budgeted resources for the project. These neighborhood groups were then responsible for procurement and implementation of the work and for mobilizing local contributions—in various blends of unskilled labor, materials, and cash— equal to at least 20 percent of the cost. Increasingly during the late 1980s and early 1990s, local governments all across the country were incorporated into the PRONASOL framework.

Social funds, known variously as social investment funds or social emergency funds, have grown increasingly popular since they were launched in the early 1980s. Originally, social funds were a vehicle to channel financial assistance quickly to help those thrown out of work by fiscal programs (as was the case of Bolivian tin miners in 1988) or to provide short-term assistance to the poor during and after the social and economic shocks that followed macroeconomic adjustment. Adjustment programs—which involved the sudden elimination of price and other subsidies and reduction of public sector payroll—were aimed at restoring fiscal stability and growth and were conditions of IMF assistance in many countries after the debt crisis of the 1980s. The funds were a kind of stopgap measure to absorb the worst shocks of price increases and unemployment that affected the poor. Over time, some funds began to involve local governments as a way to improve targeting as well as to handle administration.

Despite their uniform appearance and, in their first years in Latin America, nearly universal chief objective (absorbing the shock of adjustment), social funds commonly called social investment funds (SIFs) followed a wide variety of organizational and implementation routes to serve their purposes. The funds aimed mainly at palliative, and not developmental objectives. Bolivia targeted employment, infrastructure, and social programs; Honduras, basic infrastructure and poverty; Nicaragua, employment and infrastructure; Guayana, employment and social programs; Haiti, economic and social assistance; and similar objectives in Guatemala, Peru, and Ecuador. The goal was to stimulate employment and provide social services, although some sought to achieve this by building infrastructure. The social funds were inconsistent in giving attention to other developmental objectives, such as strengthening local institutions.

One common denominator to all of the cases is that municipalities served as a chief or collaborating partner in the execution of the funds. Guatemala's social investment fund, built on the pioneering experience in Bolivia, aimed to strengthen public sector management at the local level. A variety of buttressing mechanisms were built into the Guatemalan and Honduran social investment funds to help municipalities in key areas—to identify and prepare projects, budget counterpart financing, manage contracts (such as procurement), handle project implementation, and assume responsibility for operating costs. Some of these ideas, for instance, gauging and verifying demand, had been tested in the first Bolivian fund and in a Guatemalan pilot effort. The funds provided assistance to local governments to explore with city neighborhood groups the depth and nature of need, and these efforts revealed large pent-up demand for assistance for environmental sanitation in low-income neighborhoods and a local willingness to take responsibility for project implementation (Glaessner et al. 1994).

Grassroots groups and NGOs were recruited to play a facilitating role in social funds. These groups became integral players in the design and implementation of projects in Bolivia, Chile,[5] and Guatemala. An abundance of local committees and grassroots, issue-oriented groups emerged in Guatemala at about the same time as social funds and decentralization were being promulgated. Many groups already existed, and others were attracted to operate in Guatemala, stimulated in part by the sudden availability of new financial resources that came with automatic revenue sharing in the Guatemalan decentralization strategy. Grassroots groups organized for specific projects or general community improvement, and most often they were registered with the government in order to obtain legal standing (*personeria juridica*), which was needed to handle money, own property, and enter into contracts. These groups, along with nongovernmental and private voluntary organizations, were welcome because they were seen as a way to compensate for the absence of governmental authorities and the weakness of municipalities at the local level.

Sometimes social funds run the risk of undercutting efforts to strengthen local governments. Central programs that channel money to specifically targeted groups, even when funds flow through local governments, can impede one of the strongest aspects of decentralization—resource allocation decisions. For instance, authorities in Guatemala judged that national institutions were incapable of discharging all their responsibilities effectively. Recognizing the importance of institutional capacity in development assistance, the Guatemalan SIF sought to serve also as a ground-preparing mechanism designed to prepare institutions, national and local, for their service-delivery responsibilities. To do otherwise, social funds run the risk of "backdoor recentralization," meaning that they provide financing directly to local beneficiaries, circumventing the public sector institutions set up for those purposes. To strengthen the local public sector, the Guatemalan SIF required that municipalities be responsible for community inputs and that ministries be supportive of local efforts in specific ways, for instance, by promising to assign rural health promoters to clinics financed by the SIF with contributions from the municipality. The Guatemalan SIF also could not finance projects and services that were not consistent with ministry policy, standards, and norms. The principle of mutual support between levels of government might have been more effective had it been supported as a component in the government's national decentralization strategy.

The Guatemalan SIF aimed to take advantage of this auxiliary capacity and made many groups eligible to participate in projects, provided they worked directly with local governments, and provided they could demonstrate expertise and some kind of track record. For instance, a well-known NGO, Agua del Pueblo, had been working in rural water supply projects for many years in rural parts of Central America. Agua del Pueblo put forward many programs for financing under the Guatemalan SIF. Financing through the Guatemalan SIF was also available for activities related to deworming, feeder roads, school lunches, and nutrition for children.[6]

THE RISE OF THE SELF-SUPPORTING CITY

Mayors in leading cities began to harness NGO and grassroots groups with mayor's funds.[7] Many of these innovators found that the social fund was a welcome source of assistance to leverage their homegrown efforts. Mayors from Cuiaba to Cucuta began to participate actively in programs of this type, and these experiences reaffirmed the political and social advantages of doing so. Locally sponsored versions of social funds began to surface in many cities as city officials, grassroots groups, and private entrepreneurs recognized a change in the institutional environment that came with the quiet revolution. Even earlier, more emphasis on participation had been stimulated in part by shifts in national and international programs calling for increased input from user groups in the design and implementation of national programs for water, sanitation, and housing (e.g., an historical perspective on participation can be found in World Bank 1996). With the onset of social funds, leading cities moved forward to address high-priority concerns.

Four types of social programs, two of which involve local funds, illustrate actions taken by local authorities in specific areas of poverty and local environment. These are community facilities, low-cost shelter, primary education, and violence. In each of these representative cases, local officials mobilized community interests and local resources to become more responsive to the needs of low-income households.

First are the nearly ubiquitous municipal programs for neighborhood infrastructure and community facilities, most often run on general revenues from city tax income often supplemented by provincial and national grants. A homegrown program in Cuiaba, capital city of booming Matto Grosso, Brazil, is a good example. Second are homegrown, community-based efforts exemplified by El Mezquital, a squatter community on the edge of Guatemala city, where upgrading efforts were developed into a national program after a decade of careful nurturing by local grassroots and international assistance organizations. The grassroots organizations in Guatemala were convinced that the time was right for local action following a struggle with cholera, a decades-long civil war, and decentralization reforms. An important subset of this category was private-sector initiatives, such as Centro de Estudios y Promoción del Desarrollo (DESCO) in Peru and Argoz (a private company) in El Salvador, both of which specialized in financing land and home improvements. A third example was a dramatic turnaround in the administration of education, as exemplified by the community education program (Educación Comunal, EDUCO) in El Salvador. Fourth was the struggle for the return to a peaceful way of life in cities, exemplified by community mobilization in the city of Cali.

These cases exemplify scores, if not hundreds, of similar programs devised in the 1980s and 1990s by local governments and community leaders in the region. Each case illustrates a different feature—sponsorship, participation, finance, or management—of the many decentralized approaches to urban poverty. Above all, the cases illustrate a strong correspondence between problem and solution, a correspondence that reflects a better fit engineered at the local level than is possible in national programs discussed earlier. Of course, it should be remembered that these cases are successful solutions, and are intended to illustrate a point about mayors moving to achieve superior solutions to problems of the poor. Many more problems in the cities go unattended or are poorly handled by local authorities. But the programs that do work, such as those described here, share a precision and elegance that come with local inputs to design, and these features are indispensable to successful handling of the minutiae of detail that typifies local problems.

Neighborhood and Community Facilities

This class of programs is characterized as largely homegrown solutions to small-scale infrastructure in poor communities and neighborhoods. Included along with Cuiaba's are such programs as Tijuana's ¡Manos a la Obra! and Conchali's (Santiago) Fondo de Desarrollo Vecinal (Neighborhood Development Fund, FONDEVE), all neighborhood development funds sponsored by the city. These and other programs shared common traits, one of which was that they were conceived and launched by popular first-time elected leaders. The local efforts were patterned after other, usually national, programs, which made it a little easier for the local citizenry to understand. Also, they made funds available to community groups based on collective decisions and some cost recovery, even if only in the form of contributions by residents in the form of labor and materials. The programs were also extremely successful in terms of implementation, participation, and payback. A chief innovation was reliance on citizen demand measured in requests for works, consultations with organized community groups, structured surveys, and contributions in cash or in kind from the community. Gauging and verifying demand were tools deliberately used by city leaders to guide program spending on social infrastructure. In addition, the responsibility for contracting, oversight, and repayment of works was often placed directly in the hands of elected, single-purpose community organizations.

The Cuiaba experience is singled out because it emerged as one of the first efforts by newly elected mayors in Brazil following the end of the military years (1964–85). Recall that decentralization in Brazil came shortly after a period of political liberalization, known as the new "democratic opening." Political initiatives opened the country to democratic processes after more than two decades of military dictatorship. The sanitation program in Cuiaba was conceived during the mayoral campaign, during which neighborhood after neighborhood complained about the lack of water and sanitation. The outpouring of sentiment by low-income populations was a precursor of the energy and enthusiasm of popular participation that would emerge throughout the region in the decade to follow. The winning candidate for mayor, Dante Oliveira, was determined to respond to the clamor for sanitation improvements, particularly for the 60 percent of the city's residents who were poor and resided outside the service perimeter of the water and sewerage company. Mayor Oliveira immediately created a city program to serve the poor, a program that was separate from that of the state water company. The state company was technically responsible for providing new service connections, but was overwhelmed by the rapid growth of sprawling low-income settlements that had mushroomed around the city.

The mayor fit a familiar pattern of newly elected mayors in the quiet revolution. He consulted widely among community groups. He commissioned a survey of need. He recognized a vast disparity in the service levels of low-income communities arranged around the outskirts of Cuiaba in comparison to the average level of facilities for drainage, wastewater connections, and sewage treatment in the city center. Asked why the mayor selected this as a priority, the head of the project team answered, "The poor have as many votes as the rich."[8] The mayor had received strong support from the poor in his campaign, and he responded in much the same way as newly elected mayors in over thirty cities in Brazil by turning to the need to improve sanitation in low-income communities.

The mayor lobbied national agencies for financing and formed a team of young engineers, architects, and social workers to design and implement the program. It consisted of "condominial sewerage" (an alternative technology that requires less extensive excavation and standards of service that are below national levels). The program was financed by a federal loan to pay for civil works. Local citizens were mobilized (and paid) to carry out the unskilled labor. These and other significant inputs were made by the 45,000 residents in eight neighborhoods around the city. Once the system was in place, the state water company assumed responsibility for operation and maintenance.

Cuiaba's program cost under $1.5 million, and did not have the scope or the impact of programs like ¡Manos a la Obra! in Tijuana, which funded over 660 small-scale infrastructure projects for road paving, terracing, and drainage. Altogether, Manos projects totaled more than US$10 million, and had nearly 40 percent of their costs covered by beneficiaries through direct contribution. Municipal and state officials initiated the Manos program in September 1994 by holding a series of public forums—one in each of Tijuana's sixteen administrative districts—over a two-month period in which citizens were asked to submit proposals for small infrastructure projects via previously existing neighborhood committees. The enthusiastic response surprised even the project sponsors: over 6,000 citizens participated in the forums, submitting more than 2,400 requests for works. Two months later, the municipal and state governments hosted a Citizens' Participation Congress. Tijuana's community relations office reported that 15,000 people attended. The event was essentially a political rally in support of the new government's participatory programs. Mayor Hector Osuna used this opportunity to announce, together with the state governor, his commitment of $4.4 million for community works.

The list of requested works was narrowed down by the municipality based on technical feasibility, reducing the number of possible projects to around 1,300. In the early part of 1995, councils were established in each of the 16 delegations (municipal districts) to determine which works would be funded. To insulate the program from political influence, it was agreed that the councils would be dissolved at the end of each project cycle. Each council was composed of 32 members, divided evenly between community representatives elected in an open community assembly and officials appointed by the municipality. Once established, the municipality provided these councils with a list of project proposals and a budget. Municipal officials then worked with their elected counterparts to decide which projects deserved *Manos* funding. Communities were expected to elect a council to contract the works, oversee their construction, ensure that payments were made to contractors, and contribute to the cost of the works. Neighborhoods were divided into four classifications based on their ability to pay. The lowest income neighborhoods were responsible for 20 percent of project costs; those in the higher income brackets were expected to pay up to 80 percent.

In total, over $15.7 million was invested in community works through ¡Manos a la Obra!. Around 42 percent was paid by beneficiaries. The program was effective in targeting the poorer sectors of society, with 75 percent of its funding going to neighborhoods in the low- and medium-to-low income categories. Between 1991 and 1995, Conchali's FONDEVE financed over 270 projects worth nearly US$750,000. These cases are remarkable for the sharply proactive roles played by mayors and the equally vigorous response by organized community groups.[9]

These cases in Brazil, Chile, and Mexico represent but a few of the scores of communities with first-generation mayors elected during the quiet revolution who mobilized citizens to act. They organized neighborhood funds, mobilized local groups, and addressed poverty and environmental issues in local districts by paving streets, installing lighting, building community centers, and installing water systems, gas lines, and sewerage. Sometimes the presence of not-for-profit organizations, both domestic and international, was augmented by outside resources. These helped to mount the FONDEVE program by calling attention and bringing political clout to neighborhood and community causes. Independent forces in many communities became more effective than in the past because government at the national level began either to withdraw or because, as in Guatemala, local and national NGOs were attracted to resources being made available at the local level.

Financing Land and Shelter

Mayors working with local groups have also been instrumental in returning to issues of land and shelter for the poor. These have been, and still are, more difficult issues, long postponed as public policy matters until the quiet revolution. Acquisition of land and construction of shelter have been, on a per capita basis, much more expensive than providing community facilities. Both have been, strictly speaking, private goods, meaning in economic jargon that the benefits of the shelter projects were for consumption by individuals and families, not by the community. Therefore, land and shelter costs should be borne privately as well. Given the high price tag of land and shelter, little was done in Latin America during the decade of debt. Also, the issue of land aroused intense political interest because land tenure and property rights were often involved in the improvement of shelter for the poor. For these reasons, assistance for the poor for shelter was pushed off the list of government programs during the 1980s. With the quiet revolution, mayors were turning once again to the issue, drawn there by their constituents. But mayors rarely had the political clout and financial resources to address shelter and land problems alone. Because many decentralization laws gave municipalities shared responsibility for shelter, local governments could act unilaterally, but rarely comprehensively, as they did with mayors' funds. However, in each of the cases described briefly here, local governments did play an active role, taking the initiative to address issues that were important to the poor and bringing in or brokering well-organized local groups in a supporting role to find solutions.

Two cases are especially worthy of note, ARGOZ in El Salvador because it has lasted more than two decades, and El Mezquital in Guatemala City because it has managed to build strong local alliances from a grassroots base. In El Salvador, a long-standing program to help *colonias ilegales* (illegal neighborhoods) stresses the importance of public service delivery over new housing. In the past, illegal and sometimes so-called marginal neighborhoods sprang up outside the urban planning framework. Residential areas established in this way were not connected to public services such as water and sewerage. A solution, embodied in a 1992 national law, redefined marginal plots as rural plots, making them subject to lower standards and eligible for public services. The lots were offered by local government at a given price (at rural land value) or on a rent-to-buy option, allowing poorer families access to otherwise unattainable land. The ARGOZ case in El Salvador, like many before it (going back to Turner 1968 and Strassmann 1986) have shown that access to land titles in this way triggered new efforts in savings and investments by the households.

Mayors played a secondary but important coordinating and facilitating role in El Salvador and in Guatemala. Mayor Hector Silva, a medical doctor before turning to politics and winning office in San Salvador, was one of the reform mayors elected to power following decentralization. The civil war in El Salvador during the 1980s traumatized the nation and polarized factions in the political process. Mayor Silva's signal trait was his ability to convene representatives from many points on the political spectrum. This talent helped facilitate the effectiveness of ARGOZ by serving as an arbiter and broker of arrangements with local communities. Another example is El Mezquital, a sprawling squatter settlement of 50,000 people on the edge of Guatemala City. Like other examples in this category, El Mezquital exhibited well-organized local groups, with varying degrees of outside assistance. UNICEF was particularly important in gestating resident organizations in El Mezquital.

Though unable to solve the problems of low-income shelter on their own, mayors have often redirected attention to issues of the poor that had been lost during decades previous to decentralization. Moreover, mayors found strong allies in international agencies and NGOs. Programs like Programa para el Desarrollo Local (PRODEL, or Local Development Program) in Nicaragua, DESCO in Peru, Fundo para el Desarrollo Comunal (FONDA–COMUN, or Community Development Foundation) in Venezuela, and Fundación de Vivienda (FUPROVI, or Foundation for the Promotion of Housing) in Costa Rica are additional examples of institutional partnerships that were formed before decentralization, but came to have new partners and more potential after the quiet revolution.[10] These examples showed that so-called marginal communities had a significant resource base (in human, material, and monetary terms) and that mobilizing and coordinating available, but untapped, resources was the key to successful urbanization programs for poor neighborhoods. Demand-driven and participative programs involved many local actors. They aimed not merely to construct new homes, which had been the standard central government approach to shelter for the poor. Rather, local, participatory programs sought to build incrementally as income and circumstances of poor families allowed, to add rooms or facilities to existing housing or to contribute to public-service installations.

Primary Education

In education, as in other areas of public-sector services like health, newly decentralized government institutions allowed greater space for community-initiated and community-directed input. In almost every country of the region, primary health and education services were transferred in whole or in part to municipal governments or were privatized. For most countries, the transitions were difficult, as when Venezuelan states found teachers' unions to be an unforeseen challenge. But in many places, initiative from below sparked insight into new solutions. Again, as they did with providing shelter and land, mayors played a mobilizing, facilitating, and coordinating role. For instance, in El Salvador, a pilot program known originally as EDUCO grew into a national plan motivating community participation in several aspects of local education (see Winkler 1997).

EDUCO in El Salvador is a prime example of the grassroots process in motion. EDUCO involved local organized groups cooperating with the municipality's leadership and school officials. A pilot project begun in the early 1990s, EDUCO provided preschool and elementary education to impoverished and often isolated communities. Local officials and parents had to demonstrate interest and commitment to be a part of the program. It was designed to operate in a decentralized manner and make use of intensive community participation. EDUCO successfully reached more than 100,000 children in 3,300 districts, employing over 2,800 teachers (according to 1995 data from the World Bank) in areas where public education was previously inaccessible. EDUCO helped reopen schools once closed due to armed conflict. Based on its immediate impact, the original pilot project was adopted by the El Salvador government as a national model and subsequently reproduced in other parts of the country. At the local level, the EDUCO program strengthened teacher capacities and promoted the creation and organization of local associations for community education. These associations were composed of parents and other representatives at the local level, including municipal officials, who helped determine curriculum, hire teachers, distribute material resources, and manage funds to direct program activities. These arrangements effectively placed the management of education services in local hands. For their part, regional and national authorities helped plan the EDUCO program at a national level and provide material and financial resources.

The church too became involved in education service delivery, as illustrated by Fé y Alegría, a Jesuit NGO still in operation in Colombia. Fé y Alegría reaches more than half a million poor students in twelve Latin American countries. The NGO offers services to backstop teacher and administrator technical capacity and helps mobilize local community resources to build and maintain schools. The local government pays teachers' salaries. In Peru, parents actively generate local financing for education; in Mexico, parents verify that teachers are on the job; in Chile, parents may choose schools for their youngsters, including private schools subsidized by the state. Chilean municipalities work assiduously to compete with private schools to attract students. These examples illustrate programs that are not always led by mayors, but they have the active involvement and a new level of resources, energy, and commitment of their local governments.

Leading local government involvement in education, as with shelter and community facilities, reflects changing priorities of citizens. In return, the best mayors are asking for and making use of community involvement in educational programs, spurring parents on to participate in the resource management of their local schools or reacting to community pressure to give greater attention to education. Either way, citizen input and parent-teacher councils have played a role to directly influence resource management in the delivery of education services. Meanwhile, the local (or national) authority has taken a secondary role in terms of service delivery, focusing more on resource financing and regulatory responsibilities. These programs both mobilize support and instill ownership from beneficiaries of public services.

Violence and Security

Violence and a sense of personal insecurity in cities have risen quickly to the top of the list of concerns of both the poor and rich in many cities, but few local governments have been able to address this problem effectively. In part, insecurity in cities seems to arise from an objective reaction to facts: violence is increasing in cities. The UN and other bodies have begun to conduct cross-national studies in large cites to document violence.[11] Although data on these problems are not systematically collected—which makes it difficult to verify the objective basis of these concerns—homicide rates in Rio, Bogota, and other cities are now or have been at or near 90 per 100,000 population, putting them in the same range as the highest ranking cities in the United States (e.g., Washington, D.C.). But growing concerns about violence may also be another reflection of changed priorities. Violence may always have been an issue in cities, but was not previously accorded as high a priority for public action by national governments.

Certainly mayors have begun to voice concern and take action after the quiet revolution. For instance, Mayor Martin Burt, succeeding Carlos Filizola in Asuncion, ranked "insecurity and violence" near the top of his list of problems in the city, because "it is shared by a large segment of the population."[12] In his inaugural address to Mexico City, the first mayor ever to be elected to lead government in Mexico City, Cuauhtemoc Cardenas, received the strongest of many standing ovations in response to his call for "freedom from insecurity for every citizen" (*Wall Street Journal* 1998). Local leaders, not national ones, voiced these concerns first as a part of the quiet revolution. And in scores of cities—Cali, Leon (Mexico), Caracas, and others—the mayors have launched fresh, and often innovative, programs to address insecurity among residents.

In most cases, mayors have taken a multifaceted approach involving active input by community residents. One of the first and best known programs is Cali's DESEPAZ (Desarrollo, Seguidad y Paz—Development, Security, and Peace). DESEPAZ was the creation of Mayor Rodrigo Guerrero, a physician and Ph.D. in public health and Cali's second mayor elected under Colombia's decentralized system. Guerrero typified the new wave of mayors with professional backgrounds and fresh ideas about solving local problems. Guerrero saw violence as a preventable social disease, one caused by many factors and therefore one that required a multidimensional approach. Local leaders met regularly with their authorities to discuss and deal with neighborhood crime in public safety councils—the most effective element of the program. Law enforcement improvements focused on upgrading living and working conditions of beat officers. Microenterprise development extended NGO-financed credits for self-built housing, food marketing, primary health care, education, and other services for the community.

The approach integrated two mutually reinforcing components, community education and establishment of a culture of tolerance and peace. The programmatic elements comprised a wide array of actions: peace promoters in neighborhoods, district conciliation centers, the promotion of healthy family life by city departments, development of techniques in conflict resolution, social marketing using TV ads on tolerance, and a weapons reduction program. Organized councils at the community level anchored grassroots and citywide efforts. Councils maintained regular contact with authorities and each other. They participated in community education programs supported and sustained by networks of NGOs and municipal resources.

Programs in other cities employed many of these same elements. For instance, the mayor of Leon (Mexico) launched a comprehensive program for security and special programs for neighborhood gangs in the city. At bottom, Guerrero's programs, like those in Leon, Mexico City, and Rio, were built on the premise that peace is not provided by the government, but rather results from community efforts. Mayors have played the critical role in all of these programs, first in recognizing the problem, then in mobilizing the community to devise and implement solutions.

NEW RELATIONSHIPS IN GOVERNANCE

In the past, local leaders appointed by central government authorities may have cared about poverty and environmental issues, but they did not show the same energy and dedication to these issues at the local level that mayors have shown since the beginning of the quiet revolution. Local authorities over the past decade have also drawn very little distinction—as international NGOs once did—between poverty and environmental issues. Today, local governments across Latin America may still be weak and ineffective—their legacy of dependency over more than five decades—but some of the largest and most visible are becoming active, independent, and stronger in their posture toward a new set of issues about which their constituencies care very much. The views from city hall and the neighborhoods became more clearly focused on issues close to home and less influenced by global environmental issues. Mayors in leading cities began to reflect the concerns of their electorate and to strike a new balance in the intent of their programs and the content of their budgets. Environmental and poverty concerns are attracting the attention of local leaders as never before.

All of the new local approaches to problems of poverty and the environment discussed in this chapter share common traits that are emblematic of a new style of local government seen in various degrees in many cities. First, the approaches are triggered by a sense that new room to maneuver was opened in the decentralization process. Mayors have been listening more and reacting differently than in the past. Leading cities not only began to show new thinking, voice new rhetoric, and take new actions. They were also being led by a new caliber of officeholder. Above all, mayors have established new ties to neighborhood and community groups and have joined in new relationships with national and international NGOs. These circumstances affect poverty and environmental questions as much as any other because, relative to the past at least, local groups began to see results of the strength of their votes. At the same time, leading cities were reversing traditional circumstances of government by placing implementation responsibilities at the consumer end. The participatory nature of governance was being extended to phases of program implementation.

By accident or design, the new participatory approaches involved in the experiences discussed in this chapter all drew on a rich information infrastructure that characterizes urban life. The participatory approaches to helping the poor—in shelter and community facilities, education, and even community violence—are predicated upon common wisdom in the streets of community life. And yet, one of the least examined features of urban life for the poor is the informational character of their resource base. Cities are filled with information-intensive resources—interpersonal networks of exchange, chance encounters on the street, various forms of printed and electronic media—much of which comes at little or no monetary cost to the poor. Informational resources, like tips about sources of employment, locations of "squattable" land, the identity of someone who can clandestinely tap a water main to hook up to indoor water, can lead to concrete improvements in the quality of living and the environment of the urban poor. These informational resources constitute what Lomnitz (1974) once thought of in metaphorical terms as "hunting and gathering" grounds for the poor. More than three decades of ethnographic literature on urban settings have done little to strengthen our understanding of how civic, private, and public groups can work with the poor to gain access to informational resources and transform them into tangible gains or a means of making a living. Decentralized governance today adds a premium to information. Without it, participatory programs and democratic accountability cannot be fully effective.

The new approaches discussed here—local-sponsored solutions to infrastructure, services, shelter, education, and community peace—fundamentally changed the relationships governments have with citizens at the local level. Local, not national, leaders have been induced by political and electoral reforms to listen to local voices and act to meet local needs. This new dynamic has helped to engineer a new model of governance. In it, the relationship between government and the governed, the contract between elected official and voter-taxpayer, has fundamentally changed, at least in the leading cities. Mayors began to shift budgets and programs to pay attention to the problems of the poor and the environment. Leaders and bureaucrats from Conchali to Tijuana reaffirmed this new contract with each ribbon cutting and each collection of tax or fee. Citizens, including the poor, were getting more of what they wanted. The new dynamic has lead both the government and the governed to a fresh start at traditional democratic local government. At least in the short history of the quiet revolution, the feedback systems in political and fiscal accountability have begun to work.

7 □ Finances

Participation in the New Fiscal Bargain

TIM CAMPBELL AND MARCELA HUERTAS

Popular participation in the quiet revolution has been portrayed as a means of expressing opinions about municipal affairs, contributing resources toward local works, and serving as a watchdog mechanism to oversee the performance of municipal government. Leading local governments also found new ways to extend participation into the financial realm. Leading cities began to engage voters, taxpayers, and neighborhood groups in decisions over costs and spending. We refer to this form of participation as fiscal choice, that is, public affairs decision making by citizens who are informed about the costs of city investments and confer tacit approval to pay for them, either by increased taxes to finance large civil works or increased fees to cover added local services. In some cases, Tijuana for example, community choice was boiled down to a direct vote by property owners and taxpayers on a ballot measure. These and other examples show that leading cities in the quiet revolution have deepened the new compact of governance by extending it into the financial realm.

Note that the purpose of this discussion is not to review the principles and practices of local public finance during decentralization in the region nor to conclude with factors of success in participation in municipal finance. These are subjects covered in detail by others (Weisner 1994; Aghón 1997, 1996; Shah 1998; Fukasaku and Hausmann 1998; Campbell and Fuhr 2003). Rather, this chapter focuses on new understanding of fiscal issues and the application of new solutions during and after the quiet revolution. After decentralization, leading cities experimented with a wider range of objectives and new forms of finance than were found when central governments were in control. Above all, leading mayors have emphasized consent, often with public participation forming a direct link to the wishes of citizens in the public choice-making process. The quiet revolution has been a process of bringing government and the governed closer together around issues that can be illuminated or resolved through mechanisms of voice or choice.

In financial issues as well, fiscal choice has brought the beneficiaries of public works into an active relationship with their government. We call this relationship a fiscal bargain. It is the financial version of the compact in governance referred to in earlier chapters. Leading mayors made use of these tools, and voter-taxpayers responded positively, because both parties seem to learn from past experience that distance in governance—distance arising from bureaucracy, imperious attitudes, or misplaced loyalties—poisons the compact of trust that lies at the center of democratic regimes. Fiscal participation has been explored by leading cities as a way to reestablish this compact. The experiences gained in these cases can help to devise policy for stronger local governments in decentralized systems.

NEEDED: NEIGHBORHOOD CAPITAL AND FINANCE IN LATIN AMERICA

Finance is a key dimension in the quiet revolution because restoring growth in the region and generating jobs require filling in missing or decaying infrastructure. Recent studies in the United States, Brazil, and Asian countries demonstrate this (Altshauer 1989; World Bank 1993; Ferreira and Malliagros 1998). The World Bank estimated that in the late 1980s, Asian countries were producing one percentage point in economic growth for every percentage point of growth in the stock of infrastructure (World Bank 1993). Capital investment in Latin America's infrastructure has also been shown to be falling behind demand. Investment is vital not just for economic growth. Investment capital is needed for poverty reduction and for an improved environment as well. But investment needs are very large. The World Bank estimated that annual investment needs in the 1990s and the first decades of this century will be in the $60 billion range, not considering annual maintenance costs of about $3 billion (Ringskog 1995).

Moreover, small- and neighborhood-scale works are not taken into account in estimates like those made by the World Bank. Shelter, water, drainage, roads, solid waste, and other facilities at the neighborhood level are important components in moving the urban poor out of poverty and moving cities to increased productivity. No hard data are available to fully document these costs, but an estimate of around $2,500 per household for shelter, water, and sanitation for the ten million poor households in the region would add another $25 billion to total investment needs just to reach minimum standards in cities today.

Borrowing is an appropriate way to finance long-lived infrastructure, because debt repayment can be spread over a long period, making it possible for present and future generations to contribute to repayment. But for local governments, debt-financing options have been limited. When countries borrow, capital is often rationed to lower levels of government. Cities are sometimes completely blocked from borrowing. For example, Chile's municipalities are unable to pledge municipal assets as collateral. Unless the central government borrows on their behalf, they are effectively shut out of the credit market. When international capital markets began to grow in the late 1980s and early 1990s, inadequate knowledge about local management and the poor track record of many cities impeded the flow of capital to local governments. Private capital is by nature highly selective, favoring sectors rich in information flow, low in risk, and high in returns. These conditions are found in only a handful of cities and normally not found at all in poor urban communities. For these reasons, along with standard public welfare reasons (e.g., that shelter and sanitation are viewed as consumption goods rather than productive investments), the local infrastructure segment of the market has long been the purview of public sponsorship and thus low in investment priorities.

In short, massive flows of capital are still needed for city- and neighborhood-scale infrastructure, but many limitations and constraints block capital from reaching cities. And getting capital to low-income neighborhoods is even more difficult. As shown in the previous chapters, changing priorities began to emerge with the quiet revolution, and leading mayors in decentralizing systems began to search for new patterns of financing capital investment.

The Fiscal Bargain and the Paradox of Own-Source Revenue

One of the most striking features of the quiet revolution has been the direct linkage established between the improvements to works and services city residents say they want, and the tax or fee burdens authorities say residents would need to pay in order to finance them. Customary fiscal models of government take as axiomatic that this exchange—payments for goods and services—will be completed. In fact, four decades of centralized systems in Latin America effectively severed this linkage. And one of the signal features of the many innovations seen in the aftermath of decentralization in the region is an effort to restore this critical fiscal connection.

The balance of this chapter reviews the many ways civil society, governments, and even the private sector, worked to restore this fiscal relationship. A great deal of community participation was involved in the creation of assets at the neighborhood level in these changes. To some extent, the new model of governance did, and continues to, attract international capital. At the neighborhood scale, residents were willing not only to undertake the risks of credit as a collective, but to do so by reversing part of the traditional flow of capital, as illustrated in the case of Mendoza, Argentina. This and other examples show some of the ways to complete the succeeding stages of reforms in decentralization, particularly fiscal reforms that enable local governments to become more financially sustainable.

Conventional wisdom has always ranked local governments in Latin America as the weakest element in the governance system, and decentralization strategies tended to weaken them even further in fiscal terms. For these reasons, some observers (e.g., Shah 1998) worried that automatic revenue transfers would make it unnecessary for municipalities to take reform measures needed to raise their own local revenues. Yet paradoxically, local governments all across the region ran political risks of raising taxes and fees. They did this despite the perfect excuse—transferred revenues that were automatic—given them by central governments. Transfers put money in municipal coffers without any effort being required on their part. Yet a large number of cities raised taxes. How can this paradox, one of the most telling in the quiet revolution, be explained?

First, let us examine the fiscal system of local governments. Taxable sources of finance have been limited to property, commercial and business licenses, and automobile registrations, along with a few other minor sources of revenue, like fees for market stalls, building permits, and the like. None of these has ever produced much income at the local level. A brief glance at

Table 7-1. Revenues by Level of Government for Selected Countries

	Argentina		Brazil		Colombia		Chile	
Government level	1984	1991	1980	1991	1980	1990	1980	1991
National	54.3	59.7	55.7	54.7	65.8	67.2	90.7	88.3
Intermediate	43.0	40.3	32.5	29.5	22.7	18.3	0.8	1.0
Local	2.7	n.d.	11.8	15.8	11.5	14.5	8.5	10.7
Total	100.0	100.0	100.0	100.0	100.0	100.0	100.0	100.0

Source: Aghon, 1996

table 7-1 reveals the proportional share of revenues by level of government a decade ago. Local income—also known as "own source" revenues—accounted for only a few percentage points of total public sector income.

Weak political will and low administrative capacity are the usual explanations of why cities have produced so little revenue—perhaps a third, on average, of what they could produce given the potential embodied in property and other taxes assigned to them. All in all, most local governments in the 1980s raised perhaps 10 percentage points of their spending needs from their own sources (Dillinger 1995). Dillinger (1992) among others, has argued that property taxes are unlikely—even impossible politically—as a source for raising revenues because of the perverse incentives in the system. For instance, appointed authorities, drawn from the ranks of local property owners, see no self-interest in exerting effort to collect more tax. Besides, negotiating off-budget transfers in the form of special grants from the central government can be rewarding for officeholders who boast that income generated in this way amounts to spending "someone else's money" Consequently, local governments felt a perverse incentive to "game" the system by making special pleas to higher levels of government for additional financial resources.

The combination of transfers and grants after the policies of decentralization in the 1980s swelled municipal coffers—by a factor of three or four—sometimes overnight. Table 7-2 illustrates for key countries the degree to which spending by local governments reflected the sudden income from transfers.

Resolving the Paradox

Contrary to the predictions of fiscal finance experts, many local governments did increase the amounts of income that they could raise themselves, despite the revenues transferred automatically from central government. Table 7-3 records the real increases in own-source revenues raised by selected cities in

Table 7-2. Expenses by Level of Government (Percent) for Selected Countries

	Argentina		Brazil		Colombia		Chile	
Government level	1980	1991	1980	1991	1980	1990	1980	1991
National	66.3	55.6	64.8	51.8	67.7	69.5	96.1	87.6
Intermediate	28.3	35.7	26.2	30.7	22.8	18.2	1.1	1.0
Local	5.4	8.7	9.0	17.5	9.5	12.3	2.8	11.4
Total	100.0	100.0	100.0	100.0	100.0	100.0	100.0	100.0

Source: Aghon, 1996

the initial years after decentralization. It shows substantial increases in large and sophisticated cities like Porto Alegre, Brazil, and eye-opening increases in cities of less than 100,000, as in the case of Villanueva.

Why did so many cities run this political risk of raising taxes when money from transfers was, as one analyst characterizes it, "falling out of the sky into their laps"? This paradox can be explained in several ways.

First, the explanation for increased efforts has to do with the conditions and uncertainties in national systems of revenue sharing. Shared revenue was not always completely unconditional. In Colombia, for instance, strings were attached indirectly. Performance had to improve in a municipality's efficiency and service standards for it to sustain its share of revenues from year to year. In other countries, the flows of automatic transfers were not always regular, that is, not always received on time. Also, they were not always predictable because sharing formulas are usually based on total central government income. When total income falls, so too do shared revenues. In addition, formulas for sharing are often so complicated that few mayors can calculate their share of income in a given year. All of these imperfections in the system explain why mayors would want to raise more income on their own.

But another part of the explanation has to do with a desire of city authorities to be masters of their own destiny. According to many city officials, the new autonomy and responsibilities given to local governments with decentralization played a role in city efforts to raise revenues. One mayor, Marlon Lara of Villanueva, speaking at a conference on local government, summed up the sentiments of many by saying, "There is so much to do, so many things to fix, that even with shared revenues, resources are still insufficient." Still another reason for raising taxes, also voiced by many mayors, was articulated by Mayor Mauricio Arias of Manizales. In his words, "When taxpayers see they are getting new services, they are willing to pay." Taking greater control, being more autonomous in decisions over how money is spent, and delivering the goods all reflect the fiscal dimension—the fiscal bargain—of the new compact of governance being forged in the quiet revolution.

Large cities and small have found many ways to gather more income on their own. Most mayors, if they take the trouble to review property tax systems, as many did upon reaching office, recognized that simply by increasing coverage and updating property values, their present system of tax administration would yield substantial returns. For instance, in the early 1990s, the mayors of Merida in Mexico and La Paz in Bolivia sent out teams of city staff working under the supervision of the city tax office to the inner core of the city verifying and updating property records and property values. In both

Table 7-3. Recent Own Source Revenue Increases
(Real Terms, Selected Cities)

City	Years	Increase
Porto Alegre, Brazil	1991–95	22%
Tijuana, Mexico	1989–94	58%
Manizales, Colombia	1988–94	165%
La Paz, Bolivia	1990–95	218%
Valledupar, Colombia	1988–94	246%
Villanueva, Honduras	1991–93	373%

cities, only a fraction of the urban core was on the property tax records. In Merida, a little more than 40 percent of the urbanized area was covered, but total tax income jumped by 30 percent. Cadastre records in medium-sized cities like Merida were typically 10 and sometimes 20 years out of date, both in terms of the properties listed as well as in terms of property values on record. Many mayors have gone beyond mere updates. Leading mayors have simplified cadastres (La Paz), introduced self-assessments (Bogota), or both (Quito). Still others (Porto Alegre, Tijuana) simply raised property tax collections. Many, like Quito and Manizales, and scores of cities in Chile, have modernized their entire financial information system in the municipalities.

Own-source revenue increases are not merely anecdotal to a score of cities. A combination of national policies and local efforts made revenue increases a widespread phenomenon. Colombia is a good example. The rate of property tax increases doubled in the latter half of the 1990s, compared to the previous period, across the entire spectrum of Colombia's more than 1,000 municipalities. Increases in revenue raising in Colombia were partly due to legal requirements imposed on municipalities as a condition of revenue sharing. But in specific cities, mayors went much further. Some, as in Manizales, tied gasoline surcharges and betterment levies to specific improvements in service. Revenue increases by local government have been both systematic and marked over the past 10 years. Table 7-4 reflects this change for four countries.

Not all of the resources mobilized by local governments are captured in statistics presented here (that is, from data gathered by central governments). Much effort by local governments is ignored because cash and in-kind contributions from local neighborhoods are usually not counted as income in official statistics.

Table 7-4. Own Source Revenue Increases by Level of Government
for Selected Countries (percent GDP)

Local Government level	Argentina		Brazil		Colombia		Chile	
	1984	1988	1980	1991	1980	1990	1980	1991
Level of local income	0.6	0.9	2.4	5.6	2.5	4.3	3.1	3.1

Source: Aghon 1996

SIX PATHS TO CAPITAL: THE NEW FISCAL BARGAIN

Leading local governments invented new ways, based on a new fiscal bargain, to mobilize capital and manage risks more effectively than ever. Table 7-5 is a preview of the many ways local governments began to raise capital. The table illustrates six new ways that leading mayors and local leaders have devised to increase the openness and effectiveness of financing arrangements. The examples range from mobilizing capital from low-income communities to attracting private capital from outside the city, and even outside the country, to meet local needs. This mobilization did not result in massive flows of capital. Rather, the cases represent a sea change in the way the problem was approached.

The significance of these innovations can be more easily grasped by mapping them onto the conventional framework of intergovernmental and local finance. An earlier discussion of financial aspects of national decentralization strategies (chapter 4) spoke of a few cardinal rules, such as financial form follows spending responsibilities, meaning that the form of financing local works should be determined by the kind of facility being built and the primary beneficiaries of it. For example, individual households pay for their own garbage collection and water connections through user fees, but where benefits extend to the public at large, as in city parks, everyone pays a share through property taxes (Bahl and Linn 1992). For secondary education and health, superior levels of government also make a contribution because benefits flow well beyond the high school district or regional hospital. In other words, in the conventional framework of public finance, each kind of tax or fee should be linked to the purpose and the impact of the expenditure.

But in practice over the past 50 years in Latin America, a single source of revenue, the property tax, has been the standard form of raising revenue to finance most local infrastructure. Because it has been the conventional source, and arguably the most productive in terms of revenue, it has become the financing source of first resort.[1] In theory, property tax is appropriate to pay for services shared over a broad area, such as drainage works, major streets, city renewal. In some cities, property tax helps to pay for telephone

Table 7-5. Typology of Fiscal Bargains

Financial tool	Description	Example
1. Mortgage-backed credit	Formalizing title for the poor and engaging local banks in lending	Leon, Nicaragua
2. Social censure as guarantee	Beneficiary indebtedness for neighborhood works with cosigners at the neighborhood level	Mendoza, Argentina
3. Political contract and referendum	Betterment levy approved by citywide vote	Tijuana, Mexico
4. Property management: swaps and self-valuation	Property owners establish values of property within prescribed categories	Bogota, Colombia; La Paz, Bolivia
5. City bonds on capital markets	City bond issues on domestic and international markets	Guaymallen, Argentina; Rio de Janeiro, Brazil
6. Private cities	Privately financed new towns and financial partnerships with local governments	Curauma, Chile

service and public markets. In many cities, property tax covers the costs of general government services and administration. In other words, the property tax has been used to finance city needs that are sometimes a great distance, metaphorically and physically, from the taxpayer.

In contrast, leading mayors have begun to make a closer connection between services provided and the taxes or fees collected to pay for them. The fiscal bargain struck in the quiet revolution has focused on cutting the distance separating the source of payments from the actual services.

All of the practices reviewed in this chapter—small-scale contributions to improvements, user fees, referenda, social censure as collateral, and even domestic and international bonds—emphasize or rely on financial arrangements that draw beneficiaries and risk takers more closely into partnership with local government. In doing so, we find from this experience new insight into ways to overcome the risks of finance at the neighborhood and city levels. At the same time, we shall see that these new schemes have not addressed some of the most important developmental aspects of local government finance—deepening public awareness, achieving broad-based participation, and regulating excessive or irresponsible spending.

Mortgage-Backed Credit in Leon, Nicaragua

With the help of outside donors and NGOs, communities in Leon, Nicaragua, teamed up with local governments to transform investments by "property holders" into assets that can be valued, traded on the market, and mortgaged.[2] This has been achieved under the program known as PRODEL in

Nicaragua. PRODEL was established in 1993 with help from the Swedish International Development Agency (SIDA) to address urban poverty and community development. After a period of trial and error, PRODEL began to offer assistance to five urban centers where local authorities could show an interest and commitment to install infrastructure to accompany home improvement loans. Mayors in each city provided community services and infrastructure in neighborhoods where PRODEL, through a local bank, helped to arrange small, short-term home improvement loans to low-income families (Stein 1996).

PRODEL's main achievement was to use the commercial banking system to facilitate access to housing credit for the poor. In this scheme, PRODEL has helped local branches develop procedures, like techniques for appraising credit worthiness of the urban poor. As mentioned earlier in this and the previous chapter, the urban poor rarely if ever have collateral and regular incomes needed to guarantee loans. For these reasons, local banks do not have the expertise, nor the business appetite, to pursue a line of business in lending to low-income households for home improvements. The cost of doing business—of appraising the credit worthiness of borrowers—is too great. Yet the lending market represented by homeowners is large, and PRODEL's program aimed to fill this market niche.

After extensive background and community checks, home improvement loans were made on the basis of personal promissory note, equivalent to a signature loan. PRODEL's experience showed that monthly payments to retire a home loan should be no more than 15 to 20 percent of family monthly income. By keeping loans small, PRODEL found that this could be achieved. The Banco de Credito Popular, a local commercial bank, handled the background work and prepared documentation. The staff from PRODEL worked with municipalities in social programs and community outreach. PRODEL also set up a revolving fund to offer microcredits (averaging $400) to small business to improve jobs and income in the communities.

Securing Community Contributions in Mendoza's Poor Neighborhoods

The Mendoza Provincial Program on Basic Infrastructure (MENPROSIF) operated on a different principle—that of social censure—to secure loans (Campbell and Fuhr 2003). The MENPROSIF program financed basic sanitation and other services to low-income households at the neighborhood level in the province of Mendoza, Argentina. Under MENPROSIF, neighborhood projects began with a collective expression of need, together with a statement of willingness to pay, for local small-scale infrastructure like water connections, sewerage, gas lines, and the like. A team from the province would then document the project, verify community willingness to take part, and help with preliminary designs. Engineering estimates were converted into unit costs and reported back to the community in open meetings. Often, projects would have to be adjusted, scaled up or down, to match community willingness to pay. With a cost figure in hand, each of the member households—usually in yet another open assembly—would then agree to take a pro rata share in credit to cover the cost of proposed works. Each residence would then be obliged to identify two and sometimes three co-signers, often but not always from the neighborhood, to secure the credit risk. In practice, this process would take weeks or months to sort out. Residents in their senior years, or in other ways impeded from earning income sufficient to cover unit costs, were underwritten by third parties, sometimes the local government, and in some areas, even the contractors.

This basic model of social censure in lieu of physical capital has evolved since the program's inception in 1991. By 1996, MENPROSIF had implemented 274 small-scale projects averaging a little under US$100,000 each. By the end of the decade, more than 50,000 households in over half the municipalities in the province had benefited from the program. Many unexpected bonuses were discovered along the way. For instance, the costs of facilities grew progressively lower. After the project was formulated, contractors were invited to bid on the works. The bid prices were presented before yet another community meeting. The competitive effects of this process lowered the costs by 30 percent below the levels of comparable projects built in 1991. The competition between contractors grew in intensity, to the point that winning bids hinged not on price, but on timeliness of completion and even warranty of works. In addition the project enjoyed extremely high rates of repayment and project completion (in the 90 percent range).

MENPROSIF's key feature was its reliance on social censure, that is, the pressure of potential disapproval on the part of friends and neighbors in the face of default, as a way to secure loans. This system enabled the poor to access credit and be able to afford 70 to 80 percent of total project costs. The system greatly reduced state subsidies for works improvements of broad social interest. MENPROSIF offered credit to neighborhood residents at 15 percent interest with 24 months to pay, while local banks were lending at about 35 percent over shorter terms. For most low-income residents, the MENPROSIF program was their first experience with institutionalized credit, something they had avoided because of socioeconomic barriers like the detached and impersonal business environment of banks. The process of formulating the project—discussing designs and working out the pro rata share of debt—was undertaken with friends, kinship networks, and neighbors, and this helped participants to better understand the details of the project and the cost implications for each family. Moreover, deliberations were facilitated greatly by provincial authorities trained in community work. Their skills also eased the task of taking on debt and made the process more readily understood.

Residents of Mendoza's poor neighborhoods were willing not only to undertake the risks of credit, but to do so by reversing part of the traditional flow of public-sector capital investment. Poor residents would go into debt to build infrastructure normally financed entirely by the state. A bargain with neighborhoods consecrated this exchange. Mendoza's water and gas utilities would offer free services for a period of 6 to 12 months in exchange for the value created by the community's investment. The importance of these exchanges is that they show one way toward a future stage of decentralization, one in which both community and municipality are engaged in achieving financially sustainable investments.

Political Contract for Public Financing of Infrastructure in Tijuana

Tijuana invented yet another distinct form of fiscal bargain, this one in the form of a community vote on whether and how the city should go into debt in order to build emergency drainage and flood control works (Campbell and Katz 2003). In contrast to the earlier cases, the Tijuana experience involved an entire city in a collective decision over whether to go ahead with the program. At the center of this case was a $170 million emergency urban rehabilitation and construction program known as the Programa de Activacion Urbana, or PAU (Urban Action Program). PAU consisted of a package of civil works designed to rehabilitate the city following disastrous floods in 1993. A deluge dumped more water in January of that year than the city would normally get in 12 months. Flash floods ravaged the arid and highly urbanized landscape, killing 60 persons, creating rivers of mud two meters deep in some city streets, and causing several hundred million dollars in damage. The floods traumatized the city. Assistance from state and federal authorities and across the border from California helped in emergency efforts, but much long-term damage was done. PAU was conceived as a way to refurbish parts of the city and prevent such a disaster from happening again.

A team of planners and engineers retained by the city set about drawing up plans to fix the major transport and drainage bottlenecks. The team was fortunate to have data from the recently updated cadastre system. Using this information on land use and values, the team was able to devise and cost out various schemes for reconstruction. The city settled on a plan that could achieve a reasonably complete integration of its transport and drainage networks. The resulting blueprint was the basis for PAU to fill in disconnected and incomplete networks of infrastructure, including roads, bridges, culverts, drainage systems, and other works that affected many of the most densely urbanized portions of the city. But the cost was far beyond the city's means.

To finance PAU, the city would have to mobilize financing from several sources. Besides the city's own investment budget, grant assistance was sought from the state, increased tax revenues from citizens, and borrowing from banks. Two parts of the plan required broad citizen support. First was a betterment levy on all properties directly affected by PAU. The city's computerized cadastre records again were an indispensable source of information needed to calculate levies and communicate the plan to the public. Second, in order to incur indebtedness, the city was obliged by law to obtain authorization by the state legislature. Mayor Hector Osuna felt that a public vote would be the most persuasive method of demonstrating popular support for PAU.

In preparation for the referendum, the city launched a campaign of public education and debate. Hundreds of community meetings and scores of press conferences were held. The mayor and his team made many presentations to community meetings, detailing the proposals, explaining financing arrangements, and pointing out the benefits. Many segments of the population supported the plan. Critics attacked PAU as too expensive, unfair, and unnecessary. City officials concentrated on educating the public about the betterment levy as a way to spread the cost burden equitably to those whose properties would appreciate because of PAU. After nearly a year of debate, the vote was held, and although turnout at the polls was light, voting ran two to one in favor of the PAU.[3] With an opinion poll to verify the results, legislative approval for indebtedness was gained in a close vote.

The vote on PAU was a climax to a long succession of public events and innovations that began to change the character of governance in the city. The innovations included property tax reform, restraint in public spending, cadastre modernization, a small-scale public works program for the poor, and long-term strategic planning with the private sector. Each of the innovations in the city built upon previous measures, each added something new to city government, for instance, becoming more modern and transparent in handling property tax and more participatory in decision making and planning for both the poor and the rich. Each of these changes extended the climate of expectations of citizens about their government. A new climate of openness and believability was introduced in Tijuana (Guillen 1995). At the center of this was a new, closer relationship between executive and electorate forged by the PAU debate and vote. This qualitative change, the transformation in the character of governance, is one of the clearest reflections of the new political contract forged in the quiet revolution.

Managing Municipal Property

Decentralization opened up new room to maneuver for mayors, and leading cities took advantage of this new autonomy by finding new ways to handle the key asset under their control—property. Two examples are selected here—swapping land between public and private holders and a technique known as self-evaluation, used to establish the value of land for tax purposes. Both cases illustrate how leading cities began to experiment in an environment that would not have been possible or as easily arranged before the quiet revolution.

Land swapping—known variously as land readjustment (as in Japan) or collaborative intervention zones, and land trades—is a way for a city to achieve a public purpose (establish a right of way or needed public facility like a park) without having to put forward a capital outlay to buy up and hold property. This technique has been used effectively in Bogota to re-develop peripheral areas where urban infrastructure was inadequate. In the Bogota case, the city and its water authority worked in collaboration over the past decade to implement the city's urban reorganization plan by upgrading whole city blocks in low-income neighborhoods by means of property swaps. Water and sewerage improvements were made on groups of lots belonging to low-income individuals. The improvements were made at little or no financial cost to the families, and costs of investments were recovered by reapportioning each family's holdings to smaller lots in proportion to the value of the land contributed. The surplus urbanized lots remain municipal property for later sale at market prices or for other purposes (Marino 1997).

Still another form of participation in local finance—self-evaluation of property—is neither entirely new nor as demanding of community organization and commitment as, say, was required in the Tijuana referendum. Self-evaluations have been employed in centralized and decentralized regimes in many cities, even before decentralization. The novelty in the cases of Bogotá and La Paz, is that property owners and local governments collaborated on the setting of tax burdens (Piza 1996 and Cuevas 1996).

In the Bogotá case, Mayor Jaime Castro began work on property reform soon after his election into office under the new election laws enacted during Colombia's decentralization. The mayor sought to modernize reform and modernize property management, that is, to verify measurement, fix location on maps, and update registration. But reforms proceeded very slowly. New legal and institutional frameworks were also needed in order to establish a special tax regime for the city. By 1994, a broader reform of local taxes was well underway, and self-appraisal was adopted within these reforms. A set of procedural norms for its administration were also put into place.

Under self-appraisal, the taxpayer would declare the value of his or her property, but the declared amount must exceed a minimum set by the city. The limit was defined either by the value recorded at that time on the property records or half the market value (as estimated by the city). Property owners were constrained by a penalty if the value declared by the owner of the property differed from that recorded at the time of sale. In other words, a property taxpayer assumes the burden of gauging tax-related value and making payments accordingly. By setting the value too low, taxpayers would be hit with a large penalty at the time of sale. Too high a valuation would lead to excessive yearly payments. Taxpayers were protected from having to pay more than double the previous year's tax. The benefit of self-appraisal from the city's point of view was that it decentralized the burden of setting values, transferring this responsibility to the taxpayer.

Significant increases in collections were recorded immediately. The change in revenues to the city was due more to an increase in the number of lots that paid the tax than to a substantive increase in per capita collections, bringing about a "better distribution of the tax load and a significant reduction in evasion" (Piza 1996). The success in this case—with its chaotic records and hopelessly out-of-date information—offered hope as a feasible, if second best, solution for streamlining property tax management. Compared to conventional systems, self-evaluation required a less rigorous system for valuation and reduced administrative efforts, oversight, collection, information systems, and sanctions.

The city of La Paz met with similar success under slightly different technical arrangements.[4] The city's level of collections increased during 1994. In Bolivia, the Law on Popular Participation eliminated the direct involvement in local taxation by central government, and defined property tax as a municipal revenue. Under that law, those localities that so requested could collect tax directly, provided they could demonstrate administrative capabilities to do so. Municipal efforts to modernize the collection process, which included the implementation of an integrated computerized system for taxpayer records (Cuevas 1996), helped greatly to increase the volume of revenue in La Paz.

Capital Markets

Further along the scale of local finance are capital markets. Many municipalities sought financing from domestic and international sources on the capital markets. Instead of neighborhood groups and property owners making extra contributions for city improvements, institutional investors, some from the city, others from far away, buy city paper in search for high returns. A dozen big-city mayors sought financing from capital markets, and a half-dozen successfully floated bond issues in the past few years (Freire, Huertas, and Darche 1998). Many more hopeful mayors visited multilateral lending institutions seeking help in accessing capital markets. They come with strong proposals in hand, demonstrable credit-worthiness, and the backing of their national government. However, with a few exceptions, city bond issues were not generally familiar to city residents, and if average citizens were aware, they had a limited understanding of city bonds. Further, some city bonds were developed by private international bond banks and other institutions with a strong financial interest in the outcome. Still, cities were seeking to sell their good names, and the onset of proactive mayors after decentralization brought an increase in interest by local governments in capital markets finance.

The combination of willing helpers from Wall Street and eager cities produced a remarkable surge in bond issues. Table 7-6 records those issues for 1995 and 1996, up from no more than a handful in the earlier 1990s. Freire, Huertas, and Darche (1998) report 28 city bond issues between 1991 and 1997. Two cases are described briefly to illustrate a range of experiences. Guaymallen, a small, well-managed city in Argentina, sold paper to local interests close to the city, buyers who knew city leaders and who could understand the purposes and risks of the bond issue. Rio de Janeiro sold to international investors for city debt restructuring, a market and a purpose distinct from those of Guaymallen.

Guaymallen (population 220,000) was considered one of the most progressive and best governed cities in the province of Mendoza, Argentina. Up until the 1980s, Guaymallen was surrounded by rural and small urban centers that collectively had a population of one million inhabitants engaged mainly in agricultural processing. The city's economic base in agriculture—including viniculture, olive and olive oil production, and livestock—began to transform in the mid-1980s with private investment in industry, reflecting the city's strategic location as a transshipment point on routes connecting Mendoza's most important cities.

Table 7-6. Selected Regional and Local Government Bond Issues,
Latin America, 1995–96

Issue date	Subnational government	Rating by S&P	Amount in millions (US$)	Currency	Maturity (years)
10/2/94	Minas Gerais (state)	N/R	200	US	6
10/4/95	Buenos Aires (province)	BB–	100	US	3
11/23/95	Buenos Aires (province)	BB–	150	DM	3
5/27/96	Bogota (city)	BBB–	116	US	15
7/2/96	Rio de Janeiro (city)	B+	125	US	3
8/2/96	Mendoza (province)	N/R	150	US	6
9/18/96	Buenos Aires (province)	BB–	150	CHF	7
9/27/96	Buenos Aires (province)	BB–	200	CHF	7
4/3/97	Buenos Aires (city)	BB–	250	US	10
4/16/97	Cali (City)	BBB–	165	US	17
5/12/97	Buenos Aires (City)	BB–	150	ARP	7

Source: Standard & Poor's

The high degree of urbanization and the change in economic base created serious obstacles to the city's development. Output and population grew, and new infrastructure projects in streets, water, and power were undertaken in an attempt to support industrial development and contend with the increased urban population. Improved delivery of municipal services—water, drainage, and paving—became one of the priorities for the city. But the city had a small share of revenues from the province. National revenue transfer systems also imposed constraints on the city's capacity to make the needed capital investments. Leaders in Guaymallen began to search for alternatives to finance its infrastructure projects, and capital markets was one favored alternative because of the relatively low cost of finance.

Mayor Jorge Pardal and his secretary of finance saw borrowing on the capital markets as an option for financing that could be developed for greater use in the future. But their lack of experience and credibility stood as obstacles. Initially, the city council was reluctant to authorize capital markets borrowing, fearing among other things that one administration would reap political benefits from investments only to saddle the next administration with unpayable debts. But the finance secretary, who had served four successive terms under mayors from different parties, had a strong reputation for fiscal responsibility, which helped to influence council thinking. The council enacted "sunset" legislation that allowed the city to issue bonds, but only under the condition that their maturity period be limited to the mayor's term in office. Mayors in Argentina may be elected to only one four-year term in office (although they may be reelected in nonconsecutive years). The municipal law meant that any debt instrument, like the city bond, would need to mature quickly before the end of any incumbent's period in office.

With this sunset arrangement in hand, the mayor moved ahead with a small bond designed for the local market as a way to finance capital works and to gain experience and credibility in the local market. A revenue bond was issued in March 1996 to build gutters in city streets. Special assessments on property taxes were pledged to redeem the bonds. The bond was issued in hard currency (in contrast to many other examples from Argentina and other Latin American countries) for a total value of $3 million to be divided in three equal series of $1million. The first series was issued in December 1996 with a maturity of 31 months. The bond had an interest rate of 10 percent payable in five installments, each one being equivalent to 20 percent of the total issue. The bond was listed on the Mendoza Commercial Exchange, underwritten by the Mercado de Valores de Mendoza, a private finance house in the province. The transaction was guaranteed by treasury bonds to a value of $1.9 million. These were deposited in Caja de Valores de Mendoza, a private bank in the city. The Guaymallen bond was quickly oversubscribed.

The second series soon followed. Because of the sunset law, the second series had a very short maturity, just one year, with 50 percent of the interest payable by the end of January 1999 and the remainder at the end of July 1999. The interest rate was fixed at 9.5 percent and was well below that of the previous series. This was a very low rate, reflecting awareness in the market of the good performance by the city and of the city's capacity for repayment. The federal treasury bonds that had been originally deposited with the municipality served once again as a guarantee for the second series.

The two series were rated AAA by Magister/Bankwatch Ratings and by Standard and Poor's. The rating agencies based their assessments on the image and credibility of the municipality, the capacity to meet the financial requirements of the bond issue, the municipality's level of indebtedness, the information systems, and the state of intergovernmental relations. Other factors encouraged private sector interest in the bonds. For instance, central government contributions were channeled directly into a private bank account to which the municipality had no access. Investors could see in advance that the funds were available to make the bond interest repayments. As a result the bond had a rate of subscription from the private sector of 79 percent, very high by Latin American standards.

The case of Rio de Janeiro's bond issue is a contrast to that of Guaymallen in terms of the size and structure of the issue, as well as the terms and conditions. Whereas the Guaymallen issue was a revenue bond intended to finance small capital works and was sold to investors close to the city, Rio's bond was a general obligation issue, intended to refinance the city's debt, and was offered in much larger denominations on international capital markets.

The bond issue in Rio took place amidst public sector restructuring—of finances, decentralization of responsibilities, and a national deficit reduction program. Mayor Paulo Conde was also leading a dedicated effort to revitalize Rio's economy. Decentralization policies in Brazil transferred many new responsibilities for services to cities—primary health and education are two good examples—without commensurate increases in funding. Rio, like many Brazilian cities, was struggling to achieve a new balance in revenue and spending. City officials made a strategic decision to issue city paper, in this case a Eurobond, in part to catch the attention of the international community. The bond, in turn, was part of a package of financial reform and debt refinancing for the city.

This scheme fit well with the purposes of the central government. The most distinct feature of the Rio issue was the explicit backing by the central government to allow the transaction to be placed on the international market. But several major conditions were set. First, no sovereign guarantee was to be provided from the national government. This was announced publicly and intended to create a separation of liability (although most bond traders sharply discount such proclamations). Second, the bond proceeds could only be used to refinance debt. In addition, the federal government insisted on enacting federal reforms regarding privatization and foreign capital before allowing the city to issue its bond. This last condition effectively required the city to modernize and reform city finances, especially to restructure arrears in debt left over from the previous administration. The city was also obliged to limit operational deficits. Mayor Conde knew that clearing the city's balance sheet was in the self-interest of the city, and his municipal secretary of finance undertook the task successfully. The city's commitment was buttressed by a federal program designed to achieve greater liquidity and solvency of the intergovernmental system of finance.

The $125 million face value of the bond was sold to a small handful of investors. The underwriter, Merrill Lynch & Co., purchased $101 million, and eight international investment banks purchased the remainder. Despite proclamations to the contrary, investors in these bonds acted on an implicit sovereign guarantee, knowing that the central government would be very reluctant to allow the city to default. Nevertheless, the case illustrates how sharply the international financial community responded to the substantial fiscal and financial reforms undertaken by the city and federal governments. In turn, the city's efforts to achieve financial strength reflected in part a growing sensitivity to the aversion by foreign investors to fiscal irresponsibility and lack of transparency.

Although many characteristics of these two cases are contrasting—the size, market, and purposes—the cases illustrate key features of the new fiscal bargain. Both cities embarked on a new and largely unexplored path to capital markets in order to gain credibility, visibility, and experience. They did so with national and local backing, and this support, in comparison to times before decentralization, marks the sharp change in attitude between central and local governments in Latin America. Further, both cities had very strong credibility in the city's finances, and in particular, the municipal secretaries of finance. This factor also reflects a key ingredient in the new fiscal bargain. Cities sought to earn new degrees of trust and confidence after the quiet revolution.

Private Roles: Contributions, Contracts, and New Towns

Private contributions to local finance have appeared in many new forms. Much has already been written about straight privatization of municipal utilities and various variations on this theme, such as building, transferring, operating, managing, and leasing utilities.[5] But much less has been said about local legislation throughout Latin America which allows municipalities to incorporate private sector capital and resources into public business. Many experiments have been tried, ranging from mobilizing private capital in public works, to capital gains taxes, to property swaps, and even to private provision of whole municipal functions, as in new towns.[6] Several examples are described here which show the extent to which the effects of the quiet revolution are influencing public private arrangements in the provision of local services.

Resources have also been mobilized outside the formal fiscal-financial framework. For instance, private sector involvement has been incorporated in public sector business deals through so-called agreements ("convenios") or social pacts ("pactos sociales") for such local programs as employment generation, provision of health care, and other services. Under these arrangements, public resources from different levels of government are complemented with contributions from business and industry in negotiated agreements, commonly called a bargaining table ("mesa de concertación"). Rojas (1996) has documented examples from Bolivia, Colombia, Chile, and Peru where governments have explored the potential role for municipalities in large national infrastructure programs (highways, bridges, ports, telecommunications, electrical energy).[7]

Still another form of contract is the privately financed new town. Seen frequently in Europe and the United States, towns completely financed with private capital are, except for company towns, almost completely absent in Latin America. One exception is Curauma, near Valparaiso in Chile. A subsidiary of Cruz Blanca, a life insurance holding corporation, began financing the design and initial construction for a complete settlement, including commercial areas, schools, and fire and police stations. Facilities and services for a population of 200,000, are to be entirely privately financed and privately run. The development is somewhat like that of the new towns of Columbia, Maryland, and Reston, Virginia. Cruz Blanca faces problems similar to those of their financing counterparts in the United States. For instance, Cruz Blanca's main problem is arranging intermediate financing to bridge the 7- to 25-year span between conventional lending and long-term bonds. The Curauma prototype may pave the way for a wider set of solutions for urban development in Latin America by which private, and often long-term institutional funds from pensions and life insurance can be tapped as a source of finance for local development. As in the cases of Guaymallen and Rio bond issues, the backers of Curauma must balance many forces: community interest, political opposition, and government regulation. Obtaining the faith and credit of local government—in the city and region of Valparaiso, for instance—was a major requirement for launching the Curauma project. Without backing and cooperative agreements with municipal, provincial, and national governments, developers of Curauma could not hope to launch their enterprise.

In each of these examples, local governments and the private sector were exploring new ties based on a shift in assumptions about what is public and what is in the private domain. Leading cities were much more inclined than before the quiet revolution to follow through with the private sector on the logical consequences of opening up government decisions to the public and mobilizing their energies and resources. The small handful of cases here illustrate the spirit and direction of new connections in the quiet revolution.

BIG-TIME LESSONS FOR SMALL-SCALE BORROWERS AND SECRETS FROM SMALL CAPITALISTS FOR WORLD CAPITAL MARKETS

The new forms of participation set in motion by the quiet revolution have reached into many new areas of municipal finance. Leading cities have launched experiments with, and many are still working on, a wider range of objectives and new forms of finance than seen before decentralization. Wider and more meaningful participation by the public, including the private sector, in financing local public goods and services has been made possible by, and in turn helps to deepen, the compact of governance. The quiet revolution is not responsible for the sudden onset of capital markets finance, but it has helped to some degree. It has also helped to re-energize the revival of city-sponsored neighborhood upgrading programs for the poor. Techniques for providing shelter and community improvements were devised many decades ago by local groups working in tandem with local officials, the church, and other actors. But the quiet revolution has produced a new institutional environment and created the conditions for a new fiscal bargain in which these techniques are not only being mobilized once again, but they are leading to the invention of new forms of finance. The cases in this chapter were drawn to illustrate this fiscal bargain at several scales, neighborhood, city, national, and international.

Each case reflects deeper ties and increased degrees of trust between citizens and government. The citizens of León, Nicaragua, began to understand the power of financial leverage once government accorded legitimacy to their endeavors. The secret of MENPROSIF in Mendoza was collectivizing risk and debt, but again, local authorities, in this case the provincial government, played an important role in creating trust that made a difference not only to low-income residents inexperienced in institutional indebtedness, but also to contractors. In Tijuana, the voting mechanism was used on a citywide scale to test willingness of citizens to buy into the improvement scheme. In each of these cases, emphasis was placed on knowledge and understanding of community need and government intent. The cases of Mendoza and Tijuana also show extraordinary efforts by local authorities to educate the public about the choices open to them. The quality of information and the extent to which it was spread in public education campaigns in Mendoza and Tijuana hold lessons for a future generation of bond issues by cities. An informed public strengthens accountability and enhances a city's creditworthiness.

Second, a great deal of community input—participation, sweat equity, and money—is involved in the creation of assets at the neighborhood scale, some to the point of reversing the customary flow of services and infrastructure from government to citizens. Squatters in León and Guatemala City are learning, along with government authorities and local banks, that property rights and improvements have capital value that can be reflected, and traded, on a local market. Neighborhoods in Mendoza were willing not only to undertake the risks of credit, but to do so by reversing part of the traditional flow of community assets. Poor residents go into debt, rather than the state, in order to build capital stock of the state. Some compensation is offered to participants by public-sector utilities. Tijuana's referendum was another way to validate this exchange. The importance of these fiscal bargains is that they show the way toward completing the second stage of reforms in decentralization. Fiscal reforms that result in transparent exchanges of money for value are the central path to financial sustainability for governments everywhere.

A third issue concerns information exchange between citizen and government. Trust between government and civil society depends on understanding, and this, in turn, depends on information and knowledge about citizens and government. Mutual trust has been increased in the quiet revolution and has triggered new information flow and a self-perpetuating system opening up possibilities for all levels of city finance. Poor residents and rich bond buyers alike were more willing to take a stake in local government. The experience at the grassroots scale, exemplified by neighborhoods and individual home owners or squatters like those in León, was that trust and shared knowledge were fundamental ingredients in transforming the willingness of an individual to risk sweat equity, just as it was indispensable for market traders of subsovereign bonds. Widespread awareness of government intentions by the community is important for local government to be effective. At the other, international scale of finance, a limited awareness on the part of outsiders about the risks of buying city bonds will soon defeat deepening of the market.

At both extremes on the scale of city finance—from the household and neighborhood end to international capital markets—investors in cities need financial and institutional information to buttress their fundamental trust in the systems they are asked to finance. The extent to which this knowledge is shared governs the depth of the market, whether for the poor in Mendoza or traders of Eurobonds. At the same time, capital markets traders understand and institutionalize ways to gauge risk, for instance through ratings and interest premiums. Here, the big-time borrowers have a lesson for small-scale operators. The purpose and some of the methods of ranking city performance can be transferred to the neighborhood scale. Grassroots organizations could play an effective role in keeping track of city hall, publishing promises and performance in finance and many other areas. Thus, the big-time lessons for small-scale operators is to achieve, at least to emulate, "comfort" and "securitization," commonly used terms in the financial world, to contribute to better government at the local level.

PART IV □ □ □ □ □ □ □ □

Prospects for Sustained
Reform

8 □ Creating a New Model of Government
Contests, Competition, and Civil Markets

The change in political environment all across the Latin American region produced behavioral responses among leading governments at the local level. A large number of cities led by motivated mayors began to incorporate the participation of citizens in local affairs, to alter their priorities to fight poverty, and to mobilize finance. These changes have added up to a quiet revolution, one that in effect changed the nature of local government. During the period 1985–1995, the quiet revolution produced a qualitative transformation in governance—the structure and use of power by authorities in government—in leading cities. Leading local governments became more self-reliant and self-guided. They began to show elements of fiscal discipline, internal competition, and efficiency in resource allocation. Above all, local governments were more participatory in character. By contrasting these behavioral changes with the older, predecen–tralization model, it is possible to see that they constitute a new model of governance.

The evidence from previous chapters shows that local government reform was precipitated by decentralization policies but not consolidated with follow-up actions and support. Furthermore, the emergence of the new model is far from complete. After nearly two decades of decentralization policies, reforms are still only partially implemented in some places and are far from penetrating to the bulk of the 14,000 units of local government in the region. Meanwhile, some local governments have reverted to old traditions of clientelistic relations. Others, in Venezuela and Argentina for instance, have been subjected or succumbed to pressures or failed policy changes at the national level, making governance at the local level even more difficult. In effect, municipal governments in the region are in a cross current of national and international influences such as fiscal and political stability that complicate consolidation at the local levels.

For these and other reasons, it is all the more important to scrutinize leading governments that established a new trend in good governance. A very large number of municipalities discovered or invented ways to be more efficient, more responsive, more accountable, and more sustainable than in the past. Furthermore, these changes have been for the most part indigenous to the local political systems in which they occurred, and not a result of deliberate policy promulgated by central governments. By and large national governments, NGOs, and international assistance organizations followed, rather than led, in the first stages of the quiet revolution. It is true that reforms were triggered by national laws and that most nations intended to reform their intergovernmental system. But there is no evidence that any of the nations had a clear vision of the outcomes of their policies, nor is there evidence that they could foresee the scope and depth of change that was to be brought about by the new set of incentives embodied in decentralization. The aim of this chapter is to explore some of the institutional impacts of decentralization in order to better understand how the energies and inventiveness seen in many cities might be replicated with proper policies. The exploration starts with the emergence of new incentives.

NEW INCENTIVES AND THE TRANSFORMATION TO A NEW MODEL OF GOVERNANCE

The new political and institutional environment that was created with decentralization policies set in motion a transformation of the very idea of local government. A brief overview of the evolution triggered by decentralization policies will help guide the ensuing discussion. The sequence of events, in brief, was as follows.

Power-sharing arrangements in most government strategies gave to local governments much more authority over local services and infrastructure than ever before. Along with this power sharing came revenue transfers that handed to local governments an increased and largely secure flow of revenue. The guarantee of income meant that decisions by municipal governments would have real meaning because executive spending decisions could change local circumstances in a material way.

Decentralized decision making and spending powers were given in combination with another key element in the new set of incentives—democratization.[1] As the choice of mayor was made subject to democratic processes, the system of local government in Latin America became not only an open competition. It also became a system in which local government decisions involved much more directly than before the stakes and outcomes for participants in the decision making. Elected leaders had the means to make good on promises and to propose new programs. With financing to back them up, local authorities could improve their cities and the lives of voters. These factors in turn created new incentives for holding local office. Evidence shows that a new generation of pretenders to offices of the local chief executive were attracted into political races. The rising importance of local government also enhanced the status of the office itself, transforming it into a launching platform for higher office.

Under the new set of incentives created by decentralization, democratization, and fiscal reform, mayors in leading cities needed, and worked assiduously to achieve, a clear reading of wants and preferences in the community. Mayors also sought to obtain strong support from the electorate in order to succeed. This move closer to the electorate was a critical factor in creating a new model of governance. It represents the relocation of the political reference point, from higher authorities in the pre-decentralization system, to the electorate under decentralization. The shift in focus had more impact than any other single factor in creating the new model of governance. Participation in turn led to closing the distance between electorate and the governed and increased accountability in governance in scores of leading cities.

The new model of governance emerged from the changes triggered by decentralization. The model is characterized by six features—leadership, participation and focus on client, professionalism, fiscal bargain, competitiveness, and innovation—that illustrate the many ways cities might have failed to achieve leading status. First, in almost all cases of leading cities leadership itself was a pronounced factor. More highly qualified candidates sought and won office and were finding new pathways to political careers and higher office. Not all cities were blessed with visionary and energetic candidates. Second, policies and spending became much more oriented toward the voter-taxpayer by means of participatory mechanisms introduced in order to improve the selection and delivery of public goods and services. Incorporating the public and organized civil society into the political process was alien to some cities and, in any case, requires special skill. Leading cities that were able to meet this second test then had to deliver on their promises. Leaders improved governance in several ways. Mayors had to bring in more highly qualified personnel (third feature) to run the key posts in government, particularly finance, planning, and public works. In addition, (and fourth in the features of the new model) mayors found, through consultation and other forms of participation, that voters and taxpayers were reconnected to the essential business of local government: spending and taxation. Many cities preferred not to aim for larger capital investments nor run the political risks of tax increases. The fiscal bargain reestablished the linkage between the works and services improvements neighborhood residents say they want, and the payment burdens authorities say residents must bear to achieve cost recovery. The acid test of this fiscal bargain is the increase in own-source revenues across a broad range of municipalities (see chapter 7). Leading cities accomplished this shift, and it is one of the signal features of the new style of governance.

The fifth feature of the new model of governance is competitiveness. With leadership, mandates, finance, and closer connections to their constituents, local governments began to show a competitive spirit in several spheres of management and policy. Many cities were unwilling or were not in a position to formulate public policy in a competitive framework. Circumstances in leading cities drew neighboring or opposition forces into competition, which began to frame the terms of political debate around delivery of better services, even efficiency, and transparency in government. Alternative programs and policies were also made increasingly subject to public debate and decision. In addition, recruitment for key posts in many leading cities was put on a competitive footing. Finally, a sixth feature is that mayors proved not only to be prepared to make changes, they were innovative in many areas of city life. They tried many new schemes in delivering services, finding and training staff, probing community wishes, mobilizing resources, managing finances, and educating voters.

It is not surprising that with these many features, only a minority of cities were able to take advantage of new incentives and construct the elements of a new model of governance. Moreover, it is surprising that cities were able to create a new model of governance at all, given the political, managerial, and technical challenges confronting city executives. Perhaps the biggest reason that most cities were unable to achieve reform after decentralization is that subnational governments operate under a complex mantle of constraints. City leaders must be master politicians to show vision, leadership, and attract support. They must be master technicians to handle the complex array of sectoral concerns such as land use, infrastructure, taxation, and finance. Added to this are the managerial tasks to coordinate technical teams and guide participatory approaches to decision making. Finally, local executives must do this all in four years. Half of the local governments in Latin America cannot be reelected. It is hard to imagine a more difficult public sector challenge and amazing that so many fresh candidates with skill, experience, and qualification were attracted to city offices in the first place.

Leadership

Perhaps the most startling change in local government was that more qualified people began to seek local public office after decentralization policies were put in place. Separate surveys of officeholders elected over the latter half of the 1990s in Central America, Paraguay, and Colombia revealed that the ratio of professionals to total staff jumped from around 10 percent in the early 1980s to more than 40 percent in the 1990s. Engineers, physicians, business people, and academics were being drafted into local contests and winning mayoral positions. They sought public office for entirely different reasons compared to before decentralization. Fernando Chumaceiro, a popular figure from a wealthy family in the state of Zulia in Venezuela is a good example. Chumaceiro was easily elected mayor of Maracaibo following the decentralization reforms in the late 1980s. Asked why he chose to grapple with the tangle of problems in the city—a mounting backlog in infrastructure coupled with severe environmental pollution related to the state oil refinery complex nearby—his response was simple: "All my life, I dreamt of an opportunity to serve my country in a democratic system." Venezuela had been ruled by despotic governments and a centralized system of government for decades, and decentralization offered new leadership a chance to serve.

Others in Venezuela and elsewhere, especially those elected toward the middle of the 1990s, began to see local office as more important than before in terms of a political career. Anecdotal evidence suggests that local executive office became more important than the legislature, and, depending on the size and importance of the city, more important than a governorship in relation to moving up the political ladder of higher office. In the past, the career pathway to more powerful office in most of Latin America was through the governorship or national legislature, and in fewer cases, state assemblies. The quiet revolution changed that pattern. The opportunities created by decentralization have made it possible for local officeholders to establish a record as doers. Local office has become a platform for action. By the late 1990s, a half-dozen former mayors moved into higher office. Several are presidents, and many more—for instance Cardenas in Mexico, Lavin and Ravinet in Santiago, Andrade in Lima, Silva in El Salvador, Berger in Guatemala, de la Rua in Argentina, McLean in Bolivia—have entered the arena for national political office. Jaime Ravinet of Santiago assumed new and visible responsibilities as president of the International Union of Local Authorities, a position that gives him a platform with national and international visibility from which to speak about city issues.

Opinion surveys verify this new status. Surveys in Central America and Colombia have shown consistently that mayors were more trusted by voters and were more responsive than ever to their constituents. The Central American survey (Selligson 1994) showed that citizen confidence in municipal governments changed dramatically after the quiet revolution. In the late 1980s, local government institutions (mayors and councils) ranked just ahead of the national government, but were below religious institutions and community organizations. At the same time, local governments were ranked far ahead of labor unions and political parties. Within only a few years, these numbers had changed substantially. Favorable opinions about municipal governments rose to the 70 percent range. These findings reflected the results of similar polls taken in Colombia.[2]

The weakest link in the local power system is the legislative branch. In some cities where contracting is approved by council vote, councilors often have been suspected of being involved in corruption. Moreover, mayors in many cities became indebted to municipal council members because members are normally allotted a number of guaranteed patronage jobs based on the number of votes they can "deliver." Allotments of staff positions or other municipal jobs are so common that they have a name: cupos burocráticos (literally, bureaucratic places). Indebtedness is expressed in terms of patronage jobs, noncompetitive public contracts, and other practices that reduce the efficiency of local services and impede politically unconnected groups from expressing their preferences effectively. The situation is changing in some places with the onset of political competition, even at the local level, but the fact remains that most local governments in the region do not operate fully under a system of checks and balances.

Another problem is that neither the executive nor the legislative branch of local government have access to even rudimentary technical expertise—much less objective policy analysis—to illuminate the tradeoffs of public choices. Opposition gains in Mexico and Colombia, and increasing competition in Brazil and Argentina, have suggested that a new phase of political discourse may be on the horizon in some cities in those countries. More attention must be paid in the future to areas of leadership, capacity strengthening, transparent government, and division of labor among local branches.

Participation and Focus on Client

The increased emphasis placed on participation by leading mayors during and after the quiet revolution was also a factor in changing the nature of governance. Chapter 5 described the many ways public opinion was sought and citizen participation incorporated into the decision-making process of local government. These new practices—in voice and choice—began to transform municipal business into a more bilateral mode of transaction, meaning that municipalities, especially the leading cities, set up regular dialogues with the community. Dialogues included many forms of structured interactions, such as opinion polls, surveys, citizen consultations, and the like. Municipalities in leading cities began to take on some attributes of private businesses attending to the needs of customers. No practice is more illustrative of this change than participatory budgeting in Porto Alegre. There, voter-taxpayers have become participants in making resource allocation decisions. In effect they, not city technocrats, have become the final arbiters of how investment moneys of the city are to be spent.

This growing communication between city and citizen has begun to kindle interest in the measurement of city performance and publication of information systems and performance indicators so that cities can rate their progress in relation to citizen expectations and their own historical performance. National and regional associations of local governments, in addition to UN agencies, NGOs, and local community groups, have taken part in fostering report cards, publishing spending records, and focusing attention on the importance of community involvement and accountability in municipal affairs.

Professionalism of Staff

Recall that municipalities in Chile quadrupled professional staff members while reducing the total numbers of municipal employees between 1975 and 1988, a dramatic change that was attributable to the strong hand of a military dictatorship. But as the quiet revolution unfolded in the 1990s, many new mayors found that the municipal bureaucracy they encountered upon taking office was not up to the tasks their constituents had in mind for them, nor up to their own aspirations. Many mayors spoke of wholesale reform or of creating an executive unit capable of getting the job done. The Colombia study cited earlier reflected results strikingly similar to those found in Central America and elsewhere (table 8-1).

Table 8-1. Professionalism in Selected Colombian Municipalities

City	Population	Number of professionals		Ratio of employees/ professionals	
		1988	1994	1988	1994
Valledupar	240,000	29	118	12.2	4.8
Ipiales	70,000	3	30	62.3	7.3
Piedecuesta	60,000	3	15	28.7	12.1
Pensilvania	30,000	1	8	52.0	5.2
La Mesa	20,000	1	11	50.0	8.4
Cucunuba	8,000	0	2	–	8.5

Local governments across the gamut of population size increased the proportion of professionals among municipal staff. Professionals are defined as personnel having at least a university degree in their field of employment. In eight municipalities studied in depth by a World Bank team, the ratio of professionals to total staff improved dramatically. This improvement in staff professionalism resulted from both downsizing the total number of municipal employees and increasing the number of professionals. In effect, mayors were upgrading professional staff because it was in their interests to do so. In the words of many mayors, dropped professionalism was needed in order to meet the expectations of voters.

One of the most popular mayors of La Paz illustrated this trend among leading cities. As a four-term mayor (elected in nonconsecutive administrations), Ronald McLean twice sought to shrink the municipal bureaucracy. He was opposed by organized labor unions in his second term, but still managed to reduce the city staff by a third. In his fourth term, McLean proposed to reduce the number of municipal employees once again, this time by privatizing the services and then hiring the former municipal employees as private firms. Similar efforts are reported by mayors in cities around the region. Tarso Genero reduced Porto Alegre's staff by one fourth. The first mayor to be elected in Tumero, Venezuela, Efren Rodriguez, offered still another approach to professionalism.[3]

Manizales, a city of 347,000 in central Colombia, followed Chile's lead in systematic reform. A tailor-made training facility was set up with assistance from Cites Unies, an international NGO based in Paris whose members are European cities. Member cities offer staff professionals to provide technical expertise financed through bilateral assistance programs of European nations. Cites Unies helped to organize the Manizales Training Institute (Instituto de Capacitacion de Manizales—ICAM). ICAM reinforced the process of decentralization by improving skills and capacity of municipal employees. Salaries and promotions in rank were tied to the training regime. Although ICAM drew on similar experiences in Ecuador and Venezuela, Colombian law required municipalities to earmark a certain fraction of revenue transfers for training of local staff, and ICAM's budget was allocated under this legal provision. ICAM's training budget grew from US$70,000 in 1994 to around $614,000 in 1996. The program affected more than 6,500 local civil servants in its first five years of operation, but since then ICAM's effectiveness has been diluted.[4]

Fiscal Bargain and Own Source Revenues

The new model of governance includes an important structural shift involving taxpayers and government (see chapter 7). The fiscal bargain—the willingness of taxpayers to be taxed in exchange for services and infrastructure and, correlatively, the willingness of mayors to raise taxes in order to deliver services—also changed governance at the local level. The increases in own-source revenues is perhaps the most striking feature of the new model of governance.

Ironically, the "premature" transfer of revenues in decentralization policies in Latin America might well explain the unprecedented levels of participation by voter-taxpayers at the local level. Had the conventional formulation of reforms been followed—implementing revenue sharing after agreement was reached on what services local governments would supply and how much they would cost—the outcome in terms of accountability of decentralized government in the region might well have been different. Instead, the presence of shared revenues, together with democratic elections and power sharing, helped to fuel participation. Popular participation was both encouraged by leaders and forced on local governments by rising expectations among voter-taxpayers. The combination of increased participation and expanded autonomy in decision making led to stronger connections between city leaders and voter-taxpayers.

Policy and Program Competition

In the most advanced cities where the new generation of mayors entered second and third rounds of elections, candidates and some sitting mayors began to put their policies and spending programs forward for explicit inputs by the electorate. Heightened interest in local affairs, accompanied by such things as report cards and published records of city administrations, increased the importance of spending and investment programs. These are debated in open meetings, such as cabildos abiertos organized by Mayor Clemente Scotto in Puerto Ordaz, Venezuela. The mayor learned that his constituents were increasingly concerned with housing and jobs, two areas that are only indirectly or partially under municipal control. The mayor shaped a spending program aimed at supporting shelter improvements and local economic development as part of his campaign for re-election.

Political parties have played a central role in this competition in Mexico and Brazil. In these two countries, the parties began to groom local governments to offer a distinct identity and clear-cut choices to the electorate. For instance, Mexico's National Action Party, PAN, recognized that it could not compete on financial terms with the then dominant Institutional Revolutionary Party (Partido Institucional Revolucionario, PRI). PAN's strategy for local governments was to offer "clean and efficient government" and began to fashion an ideology about local government. The party used an association of local governments to educate its member municipalities and to project the image more broadly to the voting public. In Brazil the Brazilian Labor Party (PTB), published handbooks about managing public participation, and compiled a manual on how to organize participatory budgeting in the style of Porto Alegre.

In other countries, new generation mayors have made a point in local campaigns to set themselves apart from routine party politics in an attempt to demonstrate a fresh start. The new civic coalitions seen in Colombia in the first few rounds of municipal elections campaigned successfully against established interests of traditional parties in more than a third of Colombia's one thousand municipalities. Colombia's programmatic campaign legislation fostered this competition at the local level. By law, candidates for mayoral posts in Colombia are obliged to publish in advance of the elections the principal features of their spending program so that the voters can make more informed decisions. Other factors have stepped up competition, including associations of local governments and prizes for excellence in local government offered by NGOs such as the Gertulio Vargas Foundation in Brazil.

Innovations

Spending powers, transferred revenues, and increased competition for office have fueled innovation at the local level and created an environment there that has liberated new energies in local reform (Campbell and Fuhr 2003). Many in the new generation of leaders, fresh with mandates and ideas of reform, not only began to rejuvenate municipal institutions, they also began to launch innovations in many areas of municipal affairs. City leaders in Quito, for instance, built up a financial management system on par with many in the United States and Europe.[5] The mayor of Juarez, Mexico, began to strengthen the city's environmental enforcement efforts, because citizens asked for a cleaner environment. The mayor took action on many fronts, in part by mobilizing support from across the border in El Paso, Texas, where pollution-monitoring equipment was made available for air quality measurements. The city of Valledupar, Colombia, began to elect rural district police after many complaints were voiced over corruption and malfeasance. These cases, and many others mentioned in previous chapters (participatory budgeting, urban public transit in Curitiba, and social censure in Mendoza) are all examples of innovative new practices appearing all around the region.

Mayors chose to innovate in part because they came into office with a drive to deliver better or different government. With little help from outside, many local leaders responded to fresh political mandates to make changes, deliver better services, and lead their cities in a new direction. This made them eager consumers of new ideas and techniques. As one city invented new financial management or personnel reform, others took note, exchanged ideas, and began circulating them in a system of exchange. Innovations in running the corporate machinery of local government was made possible first by the fiscal, federal, and democratic reforms, and then by the new generation of leaders.

A World Bank study (Campbell and Fuhr 2003) discovered that some of the mechanics behind innovation in general are similar to those seen in various institutions, for instance, in industry (Leeuw and Sonnichsen 1994) and in government (Hopkins 1995). For example, a champion or visionary is considered in all of these cases as indispensable. Exceptionally strong leadership is found in virtually every innovation investigated in the study. A champion—a mayor or city leader—was able to "read" what was possible at a given historical moment, to understand what the public wanted, and to visualize a new way of doing things. Above all, the champion was able to convert this vision into reality. Another important factor in the innovations of local governments was the organized community, grassroots groups, NGOs, civic organizations, business associations, and others. These appeared to be indispensable to implanting innovations for the same reasons that participation was so important in the quiet revolution. Local groups articulated needs, offered feedback and counterproposals to leaders, and were then instrumental in ensuring that governments were held accountable.

Correlatively, the architects of the innovations were acutely aware of the importance of the organized community, and project implementers exhibited skill and experience in communicating with and promoting organization and managing community relations. In fact, communication with and education of the public were common factors in all innovations. Champions used various devices of public communication to define their ideas, provide them an identity, reduce uncertainties raised by the opposition, and persuade or convince the public and other political leaders that the innovations were a good idea. Private firms that market products understand the value of advertising and consumer awareness, and city leaders in the quiet revolution were quick to realize the importance of public education as well.

BUILDING A COMPETITIVE MODEL OF GOVERNANCE

After several decades of decentralization, the excitement about greater local autonomy has been overcome by the hard sledding of implementation. Many local governments continued, or soon reverted to, old traditions of clientelistic relations. How can the elements seen in the creation of this new model of governance be fostered to achieve a stronger system of local governments in the region? For starters, the systemic changes in the framework of local government require an entirely new approach to capacity strengthening. Sustaining and deepening the reform cannot be done at the local level alone, and cannot be achieved by piecemeal approaches that focus only on reform in civil service, finance, electoral system, or participation. All of these factors and more need to be addressed. Moreover, electoral regimes, like fiscal reform, professionalization, and changing mandates of councils, are governed by and patterned after national systems. This means that for additional reform to occur, a more systemic approach is needed to address the mechanics of governance and the structure of local and national relations (Molina and Hernandez 1995). Finally, not all local governments are alike.[6] Constitutions, national laws, and policies for most of the countries in Latin America treat all local governments alike, largely ignoring their intrinsic qualities, complexity of size, explicit or latent wealth, or role in national development. This is neither practical nor cost effective for assigning functions, setting standards, or designing accountability.[7]

A contrast with pre-decentralization efforts to strengthen capacity illustrates a central tenet in the new approach: self-interest as an incentive for change. The illustration is provided by experience with World Bank-financed institutional strengthening of local governments. Campbell and Frankenhoff reviewed strengthening efforts in 10 major municipal development loans during the period 1981–91 worth more than US$2 billion in investments (Campbell and Frankenhoff 1994). Strengthening efforts, a customary part of all investment loans, represented around 11 percent of the total, about US$200 million. Because local governments had only limited incentives to take advantage of these resources, limited use was made of training for personnel, computer software, cadastre systems, and other assistance. Even when constraints were relaxed to make resources more easily available for capacity strengthening, local governments simply had little incentive to make use of strengthening funds. Capital investments, not quality government, had a higher payoff for most mayors before decentralization.

In contrast, after decentralization, strengthening components in World Bank projects have been received more eagerly, and utilized with greater effectiveness. For instance, World Bank audits of several of its projects in Brazil, including two that were just getting under way at the time of the Campbell and Frankenhoff study, showed that the institutional strengthening parts of Bank lending had an impact on more than 90 percent of the target municipalities, that own-source revenues had been increased, and costs of on-lending (from state governments to municipalities) had been recovered. Virtually the entire set of municipalities in one state (Parana), were connected to a computerized information network (World Bank 1997).

No record of institutional change financed by overseas development assistance can claim to have made this kind of impact before decentralization. Few development projects anywhere have effected such widespread fiscal reform and own-source revenue increases, and few technical assistance and training programs have ever financed a sustainable strengthening of professional staff. More important, many cities have not been blessed with visionary, energetic, and reform-minded leaders such as those who were attracted into government and moved to make their cities leaders in the quiet revolution.

Ironically, the improvements and reforms made in many leading cities were for the most part indigenous to the political systems in which they were produced, and not a result of deliberate interventions by national governments. Neither did NGOs nor international assistance organizations offer much help to get things started. By and large, outside agencies like NGOs and international assistance agencies arrived on the scene after the revolution was well under way. The national reforms that triggered the changes in local government are therefore a potentially important source of lessons and insights about how to replicate and sustain the reform process, even as it must be recognized that not everything can be steered from the center.

AGENDA OF REFORMS

The reform agenda for local governments starts with the core structure of local governments. The executive and legislative branches of municipalities have not been given the attention they deserve by nations and agencies. The quiet revolution has demonstrated that for local government to work, the executive and legislative branches must operate with greater focus and must respect division of labor. Certain skills also need to be professionalized, particularly in posts of confidence. Further, new terms of engagement must be defined for civil society.

Many city executives, especially in larger cities, have an exceedingly difficult job. They must be the seers, the salespersons, the executive decision makers, the fundraisers, and the cheerleaders. Because of these complex and often conflicting roles, some cities have turned to the professional manager system as a way to separate the political from the technical issues in managing cities. Whether adopting a professional city manager or making greater use of specialized professional training and qualifications for analysts in the executive branch, new means of gauging and reaching qualification would help executives run cities. Executives and their staffs could benefit also from more rigorous training in program and budget analysis, decision making, and contracting. Lengthening terms of office would also help to afford city leaders more time to organize development programs.

Leadership is another area largely ignored. Few countries have national community leadership programs to spotlight the importance of leadership and focus policy, community action, and programs on the potential for young community leaders to make a difference in civil society and public affairs. Incentives might be offered to reward outstanding practice. Prizes, national service awards, scholarships and fellowships, internships, and other forms of national recognition could be offered to provide more explicit recognition of good practice. Additional actions could include collection and publication of information on the performance of public-sector executives in civic life and public information campaigns to educate and inform the public about the responsibilities of local governments and the rights of citizens.

In the legislative category, councilors are too often perceived as clientelistic intermediaries with job seekers, rather than advancing the public interests of the community they represent. The mayor and council members in one Colombian city illustrated the difficulties of overcoming the factors that close out public interest and lead to ineffective choice making in local government. Speaking at a round table on governance in their city, Colombian officials saw clearly the problems before them. The next challenge along the path of reform was to change the role of councilors from one of allocating municipal jobs and favors to political supporters to one of deliberating policy and holding the municipal executive accountable for his or her actions. The same can be said of many cities in the region. Leadership and the new model of government has proven to make a difference in many cities, and although it is not possible to dictate these changes, proper policies and good practices can make a difference in facilitating them.

Much more emphasis also needs to be given to the representative dimension of the councilor position. Beginning with the nominations process, greater accountability can be obtained (and more progress made against corruption) by focusing on individual links to electors, for instance, by using uninominal elections rather than party slates. Another area of change is to introduce elements of geographic representation along with at-large councilors who represent the entire city. Training in policy analysis techniques and in methods of detecting community needs and preferences (surveys, community meetings, problem solving) would add to councilor effectiveness.

Fostering civic involvement is another strategy to engage citizens. Participation in voicing demands, making choices, and being involved in projects proved to be as important in sustaining capacity as leadership was in launching it. Future strength of local governments, and the quality of public choices, could be improved by drawing on the analytic capacity in civil society to review and clarify choices. Universities and research organizations have not played the honest broker role in public choice and policy analysis that they might. Nations could also foster watchdog groups and sponsor the publication and dissemination of performance records by city governments

SECONDARY EFFECTS AND INSTITUTIONAL CAPACITY

The power sharing in decentralization and revenue sharing set in motion a virtuous sequence of events that led not only to a new model of governance, but also generated secondary effects that will help to strengthen local government. New agents and linkages that were not possible before decentralization have been stimulated. Four key secondary effects may also help to accelerate the creation and consolidation of the new model of governance: new channels of diffusion and help, new roles for local government, a system of higher expectations, and horizontal linkages.

In the past five years or so, an entirely new level of organization has come into being, created by the needs of local governments and by the financing available to them. NGOs and, most notably, associations of local governments, have been formed in countries where none had existed before. In some countries, new associations were being formed by region of the country, and sometimes by political party affiliation. For example, in northern Mexico, the National Action Party has organized its own association of local governments. Today, the Mexican Association of Local Governments (Asociacion Mexicana de Municipalidades) embraces all six of the main political parties. In Chile, the association of local governments operates on a web-based system that handles inquiries and assistance to virtually all of its more than 300 members. Similar web-based tools have been launched in other countries. Also in Chile, an association specifically for cities with professional city managers has appeared, and in still other countries, most notably in Central America, a confederation of local government associations (FEMICA) has grown steadily in influence and effectiveness.

Local leaders are asserting a stronger role in areas such as interregional trade, job creation, local economic development, and the national agenda. Increasingly, in international fora like Habitat II, Inter-American Development Bank annual meetings in Barcelona, and international conferences on local government and economic development (e.g., World Bank Conference on Competitiveness, Chihuahua, Mexico, 1997), local governments have taken a proactive approach, asserting themselves as new players with a legitimate role and important contribution to make in national and regional affairs. At the United Nations Conference on Human Settlements held in Istanbul in 1996, local governments were recognized as bona fide participants in conference deliberations. In the globalized economy, cities are increasingly aware of competition for trade and deal making, and leading cities are moving to improve their competitive positions.

The relatively intensive use of citizen and community participation in the new model of government, for instance, in participatory budgeting and advisory councils, has created a new standard of performance by local governments and set up a new level of expectations by citizens, particularly in key cities. Promotion of participation by mayors seeking inputs about community need attracted more attention to public affairs at the local level. This was accompanied by a subtle shift in expectations.

Several countries exhibit robust horizontal linkages, that is, ties and affiliations between and among business, political, and economic interests at the city and regional level. Before decentralization, when power was centralized, business interests and actors in civic affairs looked vertically, so to speak, up to central authorities for direction, help, and power. After decentralization, local and regional alliances have been formed around common interests, such as trade, political alliances, and community organization at the local level. Cooperation among municipalities is also emerging at managerial levels. As a result of this, countries throughout the region have set up associations to resolve concrete problems, and to that end, the joint execution of investment projects in sectors such as intermunicipal highways, promotion of productivity, marketplaces, environmental management of water catchment basins, and health posts, among others. The *mesas de concertacion* and *pactos sociales* discussed in the previous chapter are good examples of these horizontal linkages.

For national governments and international assistance agencies, these secondary effects—together with the new model of governance—constitute a new environment for change that allows distinctly different approaches to institutional strengthening. The quiet revolution has resulted in a more variegated landscape, institutionally speaking, at the local level. In one sense, greater capacity has been created with the development of horizontal alliances and the formation of new organizations, like municipal associations and confederations. Above all, a powerful incentive system was set into motion almost unwittingly by the decentralization strategies in the region.

However, the many machinations needed to create the new model of governance suggest the great distance still to be covered in order to capture a full-fledged movement toward good governance in the region. By comparison to the "good government" movement in the United States, it is possible to gauge the level of effort needed to accomplish a permanent shift to a new standard of practice. The good government movement can be traced in two distinct periods over 70 years, beginning in the late nineteenth century. Stronger local institutions were needed then for the same technical, economic, and political reasons they are needed now in Latin America—the ability to make better public choices, to allocate resources efficiently, to manage local fiscal affairs, to harness and regulate private-sector participation in delivering public services, and to be open to outside scrutiny (Campbell et al. 1993). This historical perspective supports the conclusion that a fundamentally new approach is needed to strengthen local institutions in Latin America today.

9 ▫ Banking on Decentralization in Continents of Cities
Looking Back on Assistance and Looking Forward to Reform

Decentralization and other reforms in finance and democracy resulted in a new model of governance in leading cities, and this model, in turn, emerged from a new system of incentives put in place almost by accident during the course of decentralization and democratization. But the new model of governance has not taken hold everywhere. Worse still, in many cities, old practices of clientelism and corruption have crept (back) into local government, threatening to spoil the gains produced by the quiet revolution.

The purpose here is to harvest the broader, systemic lessons of the Latin American experience and convert these lessons into policy recommendations for nations and development assistance agencies. First, we shall turn to the question of how the good practices of leading cities can be sustained and promoted in order to consolidate and expand improvements in professionalism, participation, fiscal management, and services to the poor in cities of Latin America. Although many of the lessons from Latin America's recent past may have relevance to other countries, a separate set of considerations is aimed specifically at initial conditions in countries that have embarked relatively recently on decentralization and democratic reforms. Neither set of lessons can be transferred indiscriminately. They must be tested and verified in each national context. But many issues from the quiet revolution are relevant to countries now embarking, or already engaged in, decentralization of the state.

All of the lessons from the quiet revolution run counter to the conventional policy wisdom about decentralization, not only in Latin America, but also in many other regions. Institutions like the World Bank and Inter American Development Bank in Washington promulgate policies that emphasize greater regulatory powers by central governments over the subnational system in the interests of maintaining fiscal stability. But political and institutional actions are needed to strengthen the system of incentives put into place by the quiet revolution, and these actions lead to shared responsibilities and a more important role for cities, not to greater control and suppression of innovation. Clearly more effective regulations are needed, but excessive central government controls can smother the embers of innovation and renewal that were produced in the quiet revolution. Furthermore, major changes in the external environment—changes in the conduct of international business and finance, and changes in the assumptions on the part of city leaders about their own role in their nations' fortunes—mean that a broader approach is needed, one more suited to the emerging environment for cities in international business. This chapter will outline the directions of this new approach and summarize the lessons for cities and nations now facing decentralization in a globalized environment.

THE RISING FORTUNES OF CITIES

The quiet revolution accounts for much of the change in behavior in leading local governments in the region, but other economic and political factors—such as globalization and the speed of international trade—are coming into play. The combined effects of the quiet revolution and emerging conditions brighten the prospects of cities in the region and raise the stakes for development.

First, despite the recent setbacks in Argentina and elsewhere, long-term growth in the region is expected to increase by a significant fraction over the coming decades. These prospects present the best opportunity in decades to improve the lives of the more than 100 million urban residents living in poverty. If the region were to follow an Asian pattern, the growth prospects for the region could signify a US$3 billion annual increase in investment in social areas. The World Bank and the Inter-American Development Bank have been laying the groundwork for addressing these needs, and cities can play a key role in this expansion. Many of the 50 medium-sized cities in the region are capable of helping to produce growth, and helping to channel assistance to the poorest urban areas.

Second, cities all around the world are showing a much stronger inclination to and have revealed an ability to address developmental issues, and local leaders are seeking help to do more. Cities sense the historic opportunity to attract investments, to expand trade, and to address poverty and make reforms, all against a backdrop of competition with other cities. Scores of mayors in Latin America have increased their own-source revenues, and leading cities have also reformed management and are moving on privatization. Mayors have sought capital market finance and pursued national level political office. These changes mean that development assistance agencies and governments alike can expect more pressure for attention to urban agendas and more demand for assistance in the future.

Third, big cities with the right incentives can and must act to advance, not retard, the development agenda by improving efficiency. The sheer size of the region's largest cities translates into large multiplier effects of improvements in city efficiency. Marginal increments of 5 to 10 percent in efficiency of local spending—spending that amounts to between US$100 to US$300 per capita—could, in cities with an aggregate population of 300 million urban residents, generate savings equivalent to a significant fraction of total official assistance already going to the region.

Fourth, cities now, more than ever, are growth engines that can increase their contributions to national development. The economies of the cities of Sao Paulo and Rio de Janeiro alone account for about 40 percent of Brazil's US$800 billion gross domestic product, making the size of these two city economies equivalent to the combined size of the economies of Colombia, Peru, Ecuador, and Bolivia. More focused attention on those factors that impede efficiency—poor coordination in policy and investment and poor investment choices—together with steps to speed up the sluggish interaction between private and civil groups and to improve in management skill—can make better use of resources, help attract private investment, facilitate trade and investment transactions, and stimulate local job creation.

Fifth, the organization of assistance to cities often does not match up with city needs. Many issues important to national development come into focus only at the city level and represent a complex agenda for city officials. For example, mayors and councils must deal with most of the same problems affecting national governments—transportation, water, poverty, and economic development, among others. Yet most governments and development assistance agencies treat each of these topics as a separate sector. National governments have a ministry for each one. Taken one by one, each of these sectors presents a major challenge to comprehend the complexity of issues, to gather data, to formulate policy options, and to devise programs. Managing this complex of issues together, as city leaders must do, is even more difficult.

What is more, the customary approach of financial and technical assistance agencies organizes assistance by sector rather than from the point of view of the executive or legislative branch of government, and this diffuses the policy attention of city leaders and blurs the focus needed to see clearly the tradeoffs between and among them. Rarely is it possible to achieve the benefits that can be enjoyed by linking several sectoral approaches together. Often, neither sector nor comprehensive approaches observe the temporal and territorial boundaries of city government. Increasingly, many cities in the region find they are dealing with large spillovers in congestion, pollution, and economies. They are effectively metropolitan areas, but few have the institutional machinery to deal with metropolitan affairs. The growing role of subnational units of government in spending and decision making threatens to make the current sectoral approach increasingly obsolete and its knowledge base incomplete.

With the rising role of cities in the developmental picture and concerns about reversion to clientelism, local corruption, and return to centralized control, urban centers need to follow the good practices already adopted by leading cities in the region. The urban system needs to reflect some of the features of an open, competitive system like that of Europe. A stronger public and private institutional environment would be needed if the business of cities becomes free from the many arbitrary external constraints and internal distortions created by regulatory, trade, and other barriers to investment. Also, the impositions of centrally mandated programs like health, education, and welfare would be less burdensome. As these administrative and political constraints recede, more objective market factors will become increasingly important in the pace and spread of urban growth.

Much is at stake for local and national leaders. Cities are a major part of their nation's fortunes and have shown over the past decade that they hold great promise to advance the interests of national development. Leading cities have already shown that they have the keys to unlock developmental potential. But much of what the leading cities have accomplished was done in spite of, rather than as a result of, the accepted policy wisdom. What can be done now to harness and advance the generative interests of cities?

A PATHWAY TO CITY RENEWAL IN LATIN AMERICA

Despite the growing potential of cities, and the rapidly changing external environment of global trade, prevailing policy wisdom is predicated on containing damage rather than fostering creativity and reform at the local level. This containment model is out of step with natural instincts of cities operating as decentralized democracies, and out of step with the growing role of cities in the international economy. Rather than enhancing the many incentives created by decentralization, national policymakers and international experts focus on mechanisms to balance and control fiscal relationships. Instead of fostering the spread of reformers and proactive city leadership, policies blunt the creative edge that leading cities have shown during and after the quiet revolution. Policy prescriptions focus on balance in functional assignments and revenue sharing and recommend that refinements in revenue and spending responsibilities be promulgated more or less simultaneously. This orthodoxy is spelled out in the World Bank's World Development Report and in other policy discussion documents (for instance, Burki et al. 2000; Burki, Perry, and Dillinger 1999; and Tanzi 1996).

This conventional view holds that the value of decentralization is undercut by weakness at the local level and by risk of instability. Without strict controls, decentralization can lead to increased fiscal pressures brought on by excessive borrowing and spending by subnational units of government. Moreover, decentralization, according to Prud'homme (1994), risks jeopardizing the equal treatment of regions and of the poor. Those places and groups that have fewer natural resources—or less fortunate histories—risk being harmed even further by decentralization because with it the equilibrating forces of centralized power would be weakened. Others (Hommes 1996; and Litvack, Ahmad, and Bird 1998) see a stronger political dimension to strategies of decentralization, but none of these authors builds a strong case for working in the political system as a means to buttress local public choice making or to strengthen local governments.

The lessons from the quiet revolution after more than a decade suggest that this prevailing wisdom overlooks the many political imperatives in decentralization. This is not to say that political rationale for decentralization is ignored. On the contrary, many authors (Hommes 1996 and Willis, Garman, and Haggard 1999 are good examples) are explicit about recognizing the political nature of decentralization. Precisely because the political imperatives are acknowledged widely the political means of implementing decentralization are ignored. Litvack and others (1998) take extra pains to point to the absence of markets as one reason why it is difficult to achieve political accountability (through such mechanisms as "voting with ones feet"). But virtually no attention is accorded to the corollary to Hommes's observation that decentralization is difficult for development agencies because it mixes economic tools with political objectives.

Yet many features of the quiet revolution, for example, the emergence of vehicles to build on local self-interest, offer fertile ground for cultivation. Leading cities have proved that a high payoff can be expected from the right combination of strategy and tactics aimed at inducing cities and their leadership into good behaviors. Incentives already built into the system of democratic local governance—direct election, possibility of re-election, financial effectiveness of local governments, popular participation—have proven to be effective in developing an entirely new generation of leaders. The same or similar incentives—positive ones like grants and prizes and negative inducements like credit and spending restrictions—can be tailored to achieve responsible autonomy and a balanced federalism. New strategic directions are needed now to allow leading cities to further develop their advantage and to encourage others to follow. Furthermore, the gradual elimination of national boundaries in trade and deal making, coupled with an increase in velocity of transactions—changes that can be captured by the term *globalization*—add to the appeal of a strategy of stimulation as opposed to containment. In the globalized world, cities become more important as distinguishing factors in business decisions about production and trade.

As cities grow more proactive, cities, regions, and nations need a comprehensive policy to send a fresh set of signals to encourage productive growth and coordinate public and private investments, not only to meet the ends of national policymakers, but also to meet the needs of local businesses and investors in search of productive returns. There are four main areas of such a policy, which offer alternative or complementary measures drawn from the experience of the quiet revolution (table 9-1).

Managing Fiscal Federalism

Macroeconomic stability was the chief concern for national and international policymakers even before decentralization, and new freedoms during the quiet revolution only heightened the importance of fiscal discipline. Central governments are invariably caught in a squeeze trying to ensure macroeconomic stabilization. They must address the inevitable pressures to reduce their own spending on the one hand and, on the other, to maintain or even increase the levels of transferred revenues to local governments. Many countries in the region have experienced increased costs to the public sector by not cutting back or by not holding to agreed-upon spending limits. Presidential promises and favorite capital spending projects of ministries are not the only sources of this spending. Many countries still allow discretionary

Table 9-1. Four Strategic Elements in Local Governments of LAC

Strategic Area	Policy of Conventional Wisdom	New Pathways to City Reform
1. Managing fiscal federalism	• Match functions and finance • Strengthen spending controls • Control or regulate borrowing • Clarify assignment of functions	• Fiscal rewards for good performance • Strengthen public accountability • More flexibility in assignment • Stabilize flow of transfers
2. Efficient local government	• Ceilings on costs of personnel and/or limits on revenue transfers • Privatization • Assistance on contracting and cutting personnel costs	• Competitiveness in management and production; contracting • Support local public choice (e.g., in preferences, decision-making, budgeting)
3. Good Governance	• Anticorruption and transparency • Capacity strengthening through training and TA • Strengthen external controls • Create internal reforms • Strengthen "intelligence" inputs for local decisionmakers • Public policy education	• Leadership programs • Strengthen branches of government • Electoral reform • Introduce competition among alternative spending proposals
4. Economic Development	• Few or sporadic actions; no programs, strategies • Link city growth to national economy	• Focus on local economic development; city development • Regional perspectives

spending by nationally elected representatives eager to help their home districts. Until these sources of fiscal pressure are closed, local governments will see no logic in keeping their own fiscal houses in order.

However, the methods for reducing risks and sustaining macroeconomic conditions for growth have involved mainly the placement of stronger central controls on local borrowing and spending. Many policymakers at the national and local levels alike are surprised to discover that financial autonomy in local governments in Europe and the United States means that, at the most, cities on their own can finance less than half of their spending needs. Successful decentralized systems in Europe and Latin America exhibit elements of local risk sharing, in which local governments are left exposed to feel political penalties from below—from voters, taxpayers, and the press—when they fail to deliver. Enduring democracies incorporate these strong voices, both for accountability purposes and to cement the legitimacy of governance itself. Stringent controls are sometimes necessary, as in Colombia and Brazil, where many local governments have overspent their income and sought refuge with the national treasury. But the experience of the quiet revolution suggests that controls on local governments need to be complemented by fiscal restraint at the national level and by economic, financial, and political incentives for local governments to act responsibly in their own interests.

Partly because of the push and pull from center and periphery, most countries need to create a period of stability in fiscal relationships as much as they need fine-tuning. Local governments are kept in the dark concerning intergovernmental transfers. Peterson (1997) points out that the flows of transfers to local governments are continually interrupted both by the uncertainties of public revenues as a whole, which rise and fall with the fortunes of the national economy, and by the vagaries of national politics. National governments are often tempted to tinker with formulas and policies, interrupting the continuity in income flow and making it virtually impossible for cities to plan for long-term capital investments. These variations in the income stream encourage local governments to think in the short term exactly when central governments should want them to be taking a longer view of local development, commensurate with their role in long-term capital investments.

Governments with donor help should be preparing the public for a stronger watchdog role in borrowing and spending. One of the most useful lessons of the quiet revolution is that power sharing and democratic participation can complement other, more traditional measures of inducing responsible fiscal behavior by local governments. Ultimately, local democratic participation must become a permanent underpinning of responsibility in the financial system and part of the mechanism to guarantee macroeconomic stability. The focus on technical solutions to finance and function has overlooked, or pretended not to need, the political process and more fully functioning civil responsibilities at the local level.

Less progress has been made in confronting voters and users of services with the cost burdens of supplying them. A few outstanding examples in previous chapters have shown how innovative local leaders have reconstructed a new fiscal bargain at the local level. Cities like Tijuana, Las Condes, and Manizales, and intermediate levels of government like the province of Mendoza and the state of Ceara, have essentially said that the government will provide the services that voter-taxpayers say they want, but that taxpayers must help pay for them. In some cases, referenda or opinion polls have been used to help local leaders commit to new taxes. In all these and many other cases, the bargain has been consecrated with the construction of physical, concrete, and verifiable works that citizens can connect to their new tax burdens or levies. Local fiscal responsibility is the most promising and highest priority area for further reform. Central governments, with state partners in federated systems, can help by constructing or improving a system of intergovernmental finance to induce fiscal reforms at the local level.

The division of labor among governments—the so-called assignment of functions—for the delivery of public goods and services is not a one-time formulation, but an evolving arrangement that changes over time. The goods and services that governments deliver depend on technology, economies of scale, service area coverage, and other technical factors that are subject to change. Water supply, for instance, is increasingly open to private provision. Technologies for traffic control, policing and security, environmental quality monitoring, telephone service, and welfare assistance are changing quickly with computerization. These technology changes affect the decision about which level of government should be responsible for these services. Functional assignments also need to be designed in accordance with local preferences to help bring financing in line with functions. These decisions cannot be made quickly, nor are the arrangements liable to be long lasting. It is helpful to recall that Spain's functional assignments are still being adjusted after nearly 30 years of experience. Moreover, they will be refined again as national monetary and communication barriers continue to fall in the European Union.

Many countries have made progress in defining local and national functions and are ready to move to the next step: incorporating promising local governments into the delivery of services by setting up matching conditional grant programs to help local governments pay for high-priority goods and services and integrating these grants with automatic revenue transfers. The conditions on grants should be aimed at attracting more local spending to meet national targets in coverage, and sometimes to achieve cost recovery, for programs of highest priority—for example, assistance to the poor, primary education, and environmental improvements. Although Mexico's PRONASOL program has many flaws, its design and execution provide excellent illustrations of how nations and states can induce local governments to shift spending patterns on, and recover costs for, programs of broad national interest, such as in primary health, primary education, and water and sanitation. Many excellent examples are also provided by U.S., German, and Canadian matching grant programs. The secret is to start small and be selective. Not all cities should take part, and matching grants should not aim to cover all services and all of the poor. The quiet revolution showed that spending made available for small works—defined and implemented at the local level—proved to be effective for establishing a reliable process for providing local infrastructure and services.

Efficient Local Government: Making Way for Productive Cities

Policymakers discuss two kinds of efficiency in local government, production and allocation, but governments and helping institutions have misplaced policy attention in two ways. First, policy has tended to focus only or mainly on production efficiency, and policymakers have ignored the potential of greater participation as a mechanism to exert downward pressure on costs in local government.

In production efficiency, all public-sector entities aim to deliver services at a lower cost (or deliver more services at the same cost). Measurements of efficiency are surprisingly elusive, and little direct evidence has been produced to demonstrate conclusive improvements in efficiency in one kind or mode of service delivery over another. Allocation efficiency is another matter. Efficiency in allocation refers to how closely public investment reflects the true demand of voter taxpayers for facilities and services. This is easier to show because it is self-referential. The proof of the best allocation of resources—for instance, the mix and amounts of capital investment or services at the local level—is voiced by opinion of voters and taxpayers. The chief argument for decentralization has always rested on the assumption that decisions closer to the people achieve a more efficient use of resources.

The strategy to achieve efficiency in local governments has followed two routes: privatization of services and cutting personnel costs in city hall. Although progress has been made in many leading cities on one or both fronts, the great majority of cities still operate most public services as public enterprises. Many impediments block progress in privatization, for instance, a weak regulatory system, insufficient data for valuation of assets and setting prices, and absence of remedies in cases of breach of contract. Private utility operators and financial backers do not invest where rules are not transparent and remedies are vague or undefined. Clearing these obstacles requires reform at the national level. Cities can also do much to enhance the potential to privatize services, but they cannot achieve this on their own.

On the cost-cutting side, ample evidence has shown that leading local governments at least are willing and able to streamline bureaucracies and cut costs. But in the vast majority of cities, reform measures, like any in the public sector, involve tradeoffs and sacrifices that make it too easy for local leaders to remain locked in, or soon return to, a "low-level service trap." Local governments cannot deliver better services even if they wanted to change because they do not have strong professional capacity to do so. Leading cities like Manizales, La Paz, Tumero, and others cited in previous chapters, responded quickly to changed incentives, cutting wage bills and reducing other recurrent costs after decentralization reforms. But successive administrations in those cities were not always able to sustain efficient practices.

Many tools are needed for both privatization and cost cutting. Stronger involvement of citizens has not yet been adopted as a strategic direction in national policy. It is asking a lot of local leaders to cut costs when this is scarcely achievable in the three or four years they have in office. Successive terms of office will help. But new policies to induce or require participation will also help to build incentives for continuity of reforms and programs. Creating a friendly competition among cities—to activate constituencies and pressure groups—will help to improve awareness and demand for more efficient government.

Citizen participation is the critical factor in allocation efficiency as well. We have seen that some of the most effective changes in leading cities during the quiet revolution have been made in participation. Many city leaders have followed an inexorable logic, produced under reforms that gave greater weight to executive responsibility, of seeking out voter preference and demand. This mechanism tightened the connection between effective demand for local goods and services and the budgetary process that leads to investments. No city has carried this farther or with more effectiveness than Porto Alegre, where participatory budgeting is the quintessential mechanism to translate demand into city spending programs. A body of experience is beginning to form that strengthens ties of communication between community preference and city actions.

In short, past policies aimed directly at cost cutting as a way to achieve efficiency in local government have had limited effect. A complementary strategy to get local governments operating more effectively is to generate pressure to reduce costs through deeper awareness and stronger involvement by citizens in public affairs. Central governments have the role of helping to build a framework for participation in local public choice making. Central and state governments can help foster competition for efficiency between and among local governments. An informed public is also better able to gauge strategies of city growth and to weigh alternative spending proposals. Central governments can help to finance a build-up of analytical capacity at the local level, to foster and publish results of policy analysis at the local level, and to help educate the public.

Good Governance and Accountability

National agencies and international institutions continue to promote conventional approaches to good governance that feature institutional capacity strengthening, such as increased technical proficiency and professional depth of municipal employees and external audits (as mentioned in chapter 8). More recently, even during the time of decentralization, new themes, like governance, were added to the idea of capacity strengthening (World Bank 1991). The idea of good governance came into vogue at about the time of the fall of the central state model in the mid 1980s (but not necessarily because of decentralization). Governance in development institutions focused on anticorruption, transparency, and democratic choice making, and these elements were added to the scope of work of institutional reform. However, these topics were infrequently extended to the local level. Good governance, based on accountability of local leaders, must be applied to the local level and, at the same time, extended in scope. A promising pathway forward is for governments and assistance agencies to strengthen local government, including supporting leadership programs for the young, prizes and awards, dissemination of good practices, and educational campaigns for the public. These improvements can be complemented by more effective auditing by national agencies.

This multidimensional approach should be seen as a complement to more conventional institutional strengthening in the slow and laborious models that have been utilized up until now. A "civic market" model will not work everywhere nor address all needs for local management, such as regulatory frameworks and development of career schemes for professionals. Neither will the model be applicable to the vast range of municipal capacities seen in some countries. However, the in-depth study in Colombia showed that capacity can be homegrown without outside help, in both small places and large (World Bank 1995).

Economic Development: Restoring Cities as Engines

None of the four main issues outlined in this chapter is more strongly affected by the current shift in fiscal balance or has more promise than the role cities and regions might play in economic development. The new leaders produced by the quiet revolution are searching for new spaces in policy and developmental terms. Mayors sense that they have scope to exert pressure and make changes to affect local economic development, and that this will help them solve problems of unemployment, poverty, and environmental decay. But to take action in this area means adopting a change in mindset about cities. In the past, conventional policy has seen municipalities as units of government, not as urban places that are also economic actors.

Most countries and development institutions blur the distinction between urban and municipal or fail to discriminate between them at all. The simplest distinction is this: urban, like nation or country, refers to a geographical space where populations live, transactions take place, and problems arise. Municipal refers to administration and governance of urban space and to reforms that may be necessary to make public business more efficient. In the past 10 years, with decentralization and reform of the state, the focus of World Bank attention has been on municipal governance—reform of the state, modernization, privatization, and fiscal effort. Before decentralization, national and Bank attention focused more on urban dimensions—productivity and growth, labor markets, transportation, shelter, and infrastructure. In the future, both urban and municipal focuses will be important, because local governments have been given a more prominent role and are becoming more aware of their potential as economic engines as well as trade- and deal-makers. Many cities are beginning to take actions by conducting city development strategies. For instance, Bombay, India, and many cities in Latin America are following the lead of Melbourne, Australia, and Bilbao, Spain, with the marshaling of key actors in civic alliances to agree on strategic plans (Campbell 2002).

Local leaders have new reasons to be hopeful. For one thing, the public and private sectors are not so distant from each other as in the past. Also, trade regimes like NAFTA, MERCOSUR (common market agreement of the Southern Cone countries), and the Andean Pact—not to mention the great promise of the European Union—are increasingly significant as mechanisms for trade making and job creation. MERCOSUR has advanced so quickly in the past 10 years that an association of cities already has been formed (Mercociudades) to work on the city-level regulatory, administrative, and planning tasks needed to take advantage of inter-regional trade.

Nearly 30 years ago, the World Bank published its first position papers on urban development designed to address the pressing needs of rapidly growing cities. Two decades ago, the Bank sponsored "The City Study" (published a decade later as Mohan 1994) a multidisciplinary effort with extensive cooperation from the government of Colombia to plumb the connections between cities and growth. Only a decade ago, a new urban policy paper (World Bank 1990) focused on cities as engines of growth, stalled by low institutional capacity, widespread poverty, environmental pollution, and a paucity of data. Much of the value of these efforts—not to mention the momentum to implement the Bank's urban policy—has been lost through the decade of debt, the onset of decentralization, and the Bank's own reorganization. In 1999, the Bank developed a strategy for urban development and local government (World Bank 1999). This strategy emphasizes national policies, city strategies, squatter upgrading, and capacity building.

The Bank and its borrowers have new reasons to resuscitate the idea of an urban strategy to foster an appropriate role for cities, to gauge their potential contribution to speeding or enhancing growth, to address problems of large agglomerations, and to steer them away from self-defeating ventures like city-sponsored enterprises of several decades ago. Trade-induced growth is itself a reason to coordinate city efforts in planning and coordinating infrastructure to link urban markets and manufacturing with intraregional investments such as railways, highways, and ports. New evidence is being added to the negative externalities of large city growth.

APPLYING THE LESSONS OF THE QUIET REVOLUTION

Much of the agenda to sustain decentralization is applicable to newly decentralizing countries, but a separate set of concerns is relevant to countries designing a strategy. What can we learn from the Latin American experience that might be of use to newly decentralizing nations? A review of decentralization problems and issues in the quiet revolution shows a surprisingly large overlap with those found in many countries now undergoing, or about to embark upon, decentralization. Issues of power sharing, fiscal reform, and participation in governance that has occupied so much of city policy in Latin America are surprisingly similar to those reported in other countries. A brief review of World Bank experience and documents on Armenia, Bangladesh, Georgia, India, Philippines, Poland, Hungary, Vietnam, the West Bank and Gaza, and Zimbabwe suggest that the experiences in the Latin American region may be helpful in finding a pathway and a pace of reform.

More caution and selective devolution of power sharing may be advisable in active urbanizing regions like Asia and Africa, as well as in those currently undergoing transition as in Eastern Europe and Central Asia. The Latin American experience may have handed over the instruments of power before local governments were ready. Central governments might do well to set performance standards by which local governments can demonstrate graduation before assigning increased levels of responsibility. Many standards have been suggested in the leading cities of the quiet revolution, for instance, the degree of public participation in choice making, internal mechanisms of accountability and control, generation of own-source revenues, and progress in strengthening institutional capacity. All of these are areas where local readiness can be tested. Another option might be to classify cities by readiness for devolution, based on their size and administrative capability. The process of handing over decision making and spending powers could be staged so that nations could manage better the devolution of power to the wide range of capacity typically found among local authorities.

Irresponsible borrowing and excessive spending by national and local authorities alike were key factors many decades ago when a swing toward decentralization set the stage for the quiet revolution. According to some accounts, governments may be ready for another swing back to more centralized control, at least in fiscal matters. Dillinger and Webb (1999) have traced the course of uncontrolled borrowing in Argentina, Brazil, Colombia, and Mexico, and suggest that stronger administrative and fiscal controls were advisable in the earlier stages of decentralization in Latin America. Restrictions on borrowing can help to maintain fiscal balance in Asia, Africa, and Eastern Europe, but restrictions should not smother the creative energies of cities that show promise to achieve creditworthiness. Colombia and Philippines have both devised systems to complement financial market forces by rationing credit to subnational governments based on categories of municipal capacity. But it does little good to set rationing systems in place only to have central governments break a fiscal accord by irresponsible spending of their own, as Colombia did in 1996.

Most central governments shared revenues with local governments faster than they spelled out local spending responsibilities. This practice of devolving functions and finance might have contributed to excesses in spending, but it also consecrated power-sharing arrangements and made local governments real partners in national systems of government. In the long run, this finance-first strategy may prove to have been a wiser strategy than the rational finance-should-follow-function dictum often espoused by international financial assistance agencies like the World Bank, since ready access to shared finances breathed real life into the new spending powers given to local governments. Newly decentralizing governments might wish to look for more controlled, more measured, ways to achieve a similar "buy-in" from local governments. For example, governments that can meet eligibility criteria like those suggested earlier, or those in the upper tiers of size, responsibility, and capacity, might be rewarded with greater discretionary income from transfers, as a step in the transition to full devolution.

Just as political leaders in Latin America drew inspiration from Europe, the Soviet Union, and each other in charting out the shifts in power that have led to a quiet revolution, newly decentralizing countries will have much to learn from Latin America. The strategy is to focus on a few and spread the message widely, giving more emphasis to spreading the word and demonstrating support for good performers while implying a threat of withholding support unless local governments show good behavior. Latin American ministers of finance had few formalized channels and virtually no systematic way to share lessons of reform and change. A fresh focus on leadership and the mechanisms of learning by local authorities is one way in which the speed of learning might be increased. Authorities in the new vanguard of decentralizing nations would be well served to exchange ideas with their counterparts in other countries. International lending and technical assistance organizations could play a very useful role by organizing a system of learning for local and national authorities in the lessons and good practices in decentralization.

Local leaders have emerged from political and electoral reforms to produce myriad innovations in governance. These paralleled—and even exceeded—the breadth of change espoused in the reinvention of government in the United States. For instance, scores of mayors invented or borrowed ideas for new, more effective ways to mobilize local finance, to foster institutional change, and to mobilize popular participation in local public decision making. Many mechanisms can encourage innovation, ranging from basic tools of planning to more sophisticated incubation of ideas, leadership, and education of the public.

The most striking of these innovations is the reconstruction of a contract of governance between elected officials and voter-taxpayers. In this reconstruction, the contract of governance has been renewed and reinvigorated by voter-taxpayers who have shown willingness to allow local elected leaders to take actions on their behalf in areas of public life in which the same voters show much less trust in national officials. In cities all across the region, voter-taxpayers have generally agreed to new tax burdens when elected officials can demonstrate through concrete improvements that tax revenues are at work in visible and verifiable ways. The essence of this governance innovation is fiscal decision making through participatory democracy at the lowest level. Engineering this change could not have been accomplished without the quiet revolution. But it can be encouraged and started by allowing local governments in newly decentralizing states to take part in the dynamic process of laying plans and spending money to implement change on a small scale in carefully selected places. Mechanisms of control and staging will need to be tailored in each institutional setting to discourage or control irresponsible spending. Implementing local spending will require careful accounting of the cultural factors that determine the nature of government and pace of change. But the value of spending first is taking part in the governance process, in generating the pride and enthusiasm this can bring to see palpable change, and this process can be started with small steps.

For decades, central governments have been coaxed and wheedled by agencies like the IMF and the World Bank to reform the public sector in order to restore growth. These efforts have met with mixed success. The quiet revolution suggests that the arena for the next stage of reforms in the Latin American region has shifted to the local level, where new models of governance are being invented. These models are marked by innovation in the governance contract, by widespread participation, and by new forms of accountability in spending. But can local reform be undertaken faster in transitional and newly urbanizing countries where distrust with governance has characterized many generations? There remains an important empirical question in many countries about the sequencing of reform and about the extent to which local governments can play a role in national affairs.

International lending and technical assistance organizations need not be only followers in the process of decentralization, as they were in Latin America. International organizations of financial and technical assistance are learning how to play a stronger role in the area of public choice making, the arena of political action that lays at the heart of the quiet revolution. International agencies are learning that they can be effective in structuring public choice through elections, public education, and stronger analysis of options and tradeoffs. They are also learning that assistance in these areas need not be tainted by partisan political concerns of agencies and analysts.

Contextual factors are decisive in how much or how little of the Latin American experience is transferable to other countries. The scope of these considerations stretches beyond this book, but some of the more important factors are worth mentioning. In the first place, traditions and past experience with government influence the environment of governance, and ideas such as governance contract and fiscal bargain will not be recognizable to citizens or policymakers in most countries. But local leaders, elected and community based alike, recognize the power of control over spending and the value of fitting infrastructure and services to local needs. This common ground is the starting place for decentralized democratic government.

Another contextual factor is the transition to market-based economies. Many former centrally planned economies are in transition away from central planning. The move away from the central state involves shedding political ideology and ways of life much starker than any seen in the Latin Ameri-

can experience. Albania, Armenia, Georgia, Hungary, and Vietnam are decentralizing as they move to market economies, and each has found a way to
begin recasting the idea of governance.

In Vietnam, for example, national and local officials began the "Doi Moi"
reform process in 1993 (Campbell et al. 1999). Reforms were intended to liberalize the economy and make it more subject to market forces. But even
before the Asian economic crisis of 1997, these reforms were out of sync with
the processes of urban development in Vietnam, particularly in the largest
cities. As liberalization of trade is deepened and state-owned enterprises are
converted to private market-oriented principles of operation, private sector
investors are breaking free from national constraints, only to be hampered by
city bureaucracies still operating under obsolete regulations like having to
pay unauthorized fees and charges in order to do business. Many regulations
originate with national policy or administrative requirements. Administrative regulations and political controls make local governments sluggish and
penalize them in comparison to their competitors in the region. Thus the
transition to free market economy is difficult to separate from the logic of
cities acting as more autonomous players in a decentralized system of government.

In still other countries decentralization policies are being promulgated as,
or after, globalization is taking effect. Unlike Latin America, where decentralization was launched before globalization, most of the countries in Asia,
Africa, and the former Soviet Union have additional policy complexity introduced with the opening of trade and the rise of cities in international arenas.
To the extent that cities start with weak institutional capacity, globalization
will make the stakes of decentralization much greater. Responsibility for economic development, trade, and infrastructure needed for local development
may be harder to leave to cities.

BANKING ON THE FUTURE

In key areas of development—fiscal responsibility, efficiency, good governance, and economic development—the leading cities of Latin America have
demonstrated a systematic response to new incentives generated during decentralization. The quiet revolution is essentially a change in the extent and
impact of participation in government at the local level. The conventional
wisdom of policy and practice in managing urban and municipal development is constrained in many ways and may be blocking important sources of
growth.

It is constrained in the way governance is conceived because local governments have not yet reached the status of fully responsible partners in national systems of governance. In the past, local governments had been kept weak because it was in the interest of the central government to maintain strong controls. Now, with decentralization, it is in the nation's interest to strengthen local governments. Nations need to exercise restraints, but also offer encouragement and incentives, and to build in a discipline that only the public can effect if it is actively engaged in affairs. Coping with these tensions in Latin America has been a struggle that has ebbed and flowed, where gains in the local arena have been achieved only with increased risks of national fiscal stability.

Decentralization has swung the strategic balance of power decisively away from the center, but the direction and force of this pendular moment is now in question. We have seen some evidence suggesting that the new energies and new approaches of leading local governments may only be temporary. In effect, for most of the 1990s, the quiet revolution has been marked by a tonic effect that might now recede with time as the seesaw battle of fiscal federalism swings back toward the center. Continued commitment to reform and local government renewal may be needed to sustain strong participatory democracy and participatory social programs at the local level.

Part of the tension in the region is caused by an intergovernmental impasse. To go further with decentralization means that municipal voter-taxpayers and national governments must trust local officials to succeed in their duties. By and large, national governments have not given local governments either the political space or the financial resources to discharge new functions, even when they have shown promise to do so. If anything, more reticence is being shown by governments in newly decentralizing nations.

To break this impasse requires that the system of governance—national and local governments and their electorates—must reach a new level of mutual trust. Local governments must be encouraged, and allowed, to manage their affairs. This autonomy must be buttressed by a partnership with central authorities. Creating these assurances by improving choice making, managerial skills, professional capacity, and strengthened political and economic incentives for officeholders, among other items is the highest priority on the agenda of decentralization in the region. The present conditions—short terms of political office, fluctuating revenues, restrictions on spending—may succeed in limiting fiscal mischief, but they also propel the revolving door of municipal leadership and personnel. They also leave in place the many constraints that keep local governments from entering the leading class.

New overtures in international lending and technical assistance organizations are beginning to direct more attention to issues of urban and municipal development. The World Bank's Strategy for Urban Development and Local Governance and the City's Alliance are two institutional overtures that seek to achieve a coherence of effort among donor institutions and to focus attention on cities. But much remains to be done with partner institutions in client countries in order to make efforts like these effective. The lessons of the quiet revolution suggest a strategy—selective loosening of controls at the national level and tightening civic linkages at the local level—that runs contrary to that presently being promulgated by nations and development assistance agencies.

NOTES

Chapter 1

1. For simplicity, I here refer to all states in Central and South America as well as the Caribbean nations as "the region" or "Latin America," unless otherwise specified in the text. Also, unless otherwise noted, the term "decentralization" denotes the shift of spending, decision-making, and sometimes revenue-raising powers from central to local governments, mainly municipalities. This definition is distinct from deconcentration, delegation, and other terms sometimes used in connection with administrative reform. See, for instance, Rondonelli, 1981.

2. The Tupamaros was a left-wing, revolutionary group organized around Marxism-Leninism and dedicated to the overthrow of the state. The organization was active in Uruguay in the 1960s and 1970s and carried out campaigns of guerrilla warfare, sabotage, and kidnapping of military officials.

3. I employ this term, drawing on ideas of Thomas Hobbes and John Locke, to describe the implicit agreement between the state and its subjects in which powers are voluntarily given over to elected leaders to act on behalf of voters and taxpayers.

Chapter 2

1. Of course, the great waves of migration to cities in Latin America was also an urbanization of poverty, and this began in the late 1950s.

2. I am indebted to Fernando Rojas, personal communication, for much of the information about Spain's role during this period.

3. Personal communication with Carlos Hugo Molina, Deputy Minister for Decentralization in Bolivia from 1992 to 1996.

Chapter 3

1. I am indebted to George Peterson of the Urban Institute, as well as to Scott Quehl (formerly of the World Bank) and Ken Davey, University of Birmingham, for many of the ideas and some of the text—drafted as part of earlier World Bank reports (e.g., Campbell et al., 1991)—which is included here. Many of the observations in this section are also attributable to World Bank 1994.

2. The terms "*comuna*" and "municipality" are, for most purposes, interchangeable in Chile. Technically, however, *comuna* is based on the French term for population settlement; municipality refers to the apparatus governing the settlement, i.e., the mayor, the economic and social development council, and the municipal bureaucracy.

3. For a fuller discussion of this period, see Friedmann (1976).

4. Even though the 1925 constitution called for provincial assemblies, these were never implemented. Instead, according to Friedmann (1979), the powers of regulation of municipalities and control of municipal fiscal affairs were, in 1942, passed on to *intendentes*.

5. Note that this definition of subsidiarity differs sharply from standard European usage which stresses that public services and functions should be assigned to the lowest feasible level of government (Council of Europe, 1985).

6. Patricio Aylwin Azocar won the presidential election held on 14 December 1989 standing on behalf of Concertación de los Partidos (CUP) a center left alliance of 17 parties. He won with 55.2 percent of the vote and took office in January 1990.

7. The term *spontaneous deconcentration* was invoked by Roberto Eibenshutz, then the Dean of Social Sciences, University of Mexico at Xochimilco.

8. In-bond refers to licensed foreign firms that are allowed to import duty-free component parts needed for manufactured items that are then exported as Mexican products. In-bond production, known commonly as "*maquiladoras*" grew along the border for many years at nearly double-digit rates starting in the 1970s.

9. Mexico floated the peso in late August 1976, and this resulted in a devaluation of 40 percent. At the same time, trade deficits were running at over $3 billion and capital flight was reaching $200 million per month. Oil discoveries in the late 1970s triggered expansion. External lending was leveraged on this expansion, and when the downturn in oil prices came in the late 1970s, Mexico was exposed to enormous debt, with little alternative other than to devalue the currency.

10. PIDER (Programa Integral para el Desarrollo Rural) was created to coordinate federal agencies implementing integrated rural development projects.

11. State planning committees (*Comites Estatales de Planeacion para el Desarrollo*, or COPLADEs), manage the process of identifying investment options and taking decisions.

12. In 1987, 431 COPLADEMSs were counted along with 165 special sectoral or regional subcommittees (Aspe 1988).

13. As an example of the "horizontal influences" mentioned in chapter 2, the first administrator of the Colombian funds organized a special study tour in Mexico to study the CUD system.

14. In respect to failures of the state in economic matters, and the strategy of shifting responsibility to local levels, Venezuela seems to have followed a similar strategic shift as did Brazil, Argentina, and Mexico.

15. The Comision Presidencial para la Reforma del Estado was established by Decree 403 of December 17, 1984, to elaborate proposals for integrated reform of the state. An executive summary of its work was published as *La Reforma del Estado* (COPRE 1988).

16. Personal communication.

17. *Ley Organica de Descentralizacion, Delimitacion y Transferencia de Competencias del Poder Publico, 1989.*

18. *Gubernatorial Election and Removal Act (Ley Sobre Eleccion y Remocion de los Gobernadores de Estado) of 1989.* G.O. No. 4.086 Extraordinario de 14-4-89.

19. "National government should keep and strengthen its competencies in the areas of planning, elaboration, and execution of programs of national interest. At the same time, *states and municipalities will receive powers to formulate and carry out sectoral policies as well as budgetary management in all those areas in which its contact with local communities in-*

creases the administrative capacity to respond efficiently to demands of the population" (my translation and emphasis, p. 38).

20. The governor, in personal communication, said that central government control over education homogenized the richness of the many regions and left no room for the unique cultural and historical richness of Lara.

Chapter 4

1. Many studies and reports have covered specific countries and specific sectors affected by decentralization, for example, Aghón, 1996; Campbell et al, 1991; de la Cruz, 1998; Haas and Rosenfeld, 1995; Fukasaku and Hausmann, 1998; Rojas 1995; Weisner 1994; World Bank 1990, 1991, 1992, and 1995.

2. This section draws heavily on Campbell, Peterson, and Brakarz (1991) and benefits greatly from analysis and written input from George Peterson of the Urban Institute.

Chapter 5

I am very grateful to David Gow, John Frankenhoff, and Scott Quehl who helped develop ideas discussed in this chapter.

1. The term NGO covers a broad range of organizations. As a whole, NGOs might be thought of in terms of a hierarchy, the base of which is formed by primary support organizations (PSOs) whose cohesive force arises from some common territorial interest or shared problem, for instance, neighborhood improvement. Grassroots and member support organizations (GSOs and MSOs) are aggregates of PSOs. GSOs and MSOs can be thought of as second- and third-level groups (local and national confederations) that represent the interests of PSOs before official functions, such as city council hearings or the central government legislature. MSOs are distinguished by a membership, and the political or financial clout this can bring. NGOs = GSOs + MSOs = PSOs + e (e refers to other groups not fitting neatly into the other categories).

2. Personal communication.

3. This topic, like several other major innovations touched upon in this chapter, is covered in greater detail in Campbell and Fuhr, 2003. Other innovations include the mayor's fund in Chile (FONDEVE) and the referenda in Tijuana.

4. Tarso Genero, speaking at the Third Inter-American Conference of Mayors in May, 1996, Miami, Florida.

5. The program, known as FONDEVE, is described in the next chapter.

6. Several remarkable campaigns have been sponsored by UNICEF and national institutions during mayoral campaigns in Colombia to focus voters' and candidates' attention on children's health issues. The UNICEF programs made use of effective radio, TV, and poster ads designed to shape debate and foster commitment among local government officials during mayoral campaign seasons. For instance, the ads stressed the importance of reaching targets for immunization and that these objectives should be associated with the programs of candidates running for mayor. The UNICEF ad campaign infused the political debate among mayoral candidates with the issue of immunization and triggered a competition among the candidates over who could the most for childhood immunization. (UNICEF, 1993)

7. Singapore is one of the leading cities in the world in relation to what is known as congestion pricing. The city reduces demand for roadways by raising parking charges, provid-

ing public transport, and reducing demand during peak demand, such as rush hours, by imposing fees using high technology tracking systems to identify motorists using city streets during those times.

8. The experiment with the referendum in Tijuana is described in detail in Campbell and Fuhr, 2003.

9. Citizen involvement in the judicial process in the United States over local government issues arose out of concerns quite similar to those of present-day Latin America. One major issue about local government concerned the capacity of government agencies to regulate individual and corporate behavior (DeSario and Langton, 1987). Federal laws such as the Federal Register Act of 1936, the Administrative Procedure Act of 1946, and the National Environmental Policy Act (NEPA) of 1969 forced procedural and substantive limitations on government actions. These laws were then used as a basis for judicial review. One key step was the achievement of "standing" by citizens, meaning the legal right to participate as affected parties in judicial proceedings. Judicial rulings in U.S. courts over the past 20 years have resulted in standing not only for individuals with "pecuniary" interests, but also for those with "aesthetic, conservation, or recreational" interests (Anderson, 1973 p. 27). As a result, local groups have brought numerous lawsuits challenging growth ordinances and county or area development plans. Citizens have also sought judicial recourse over perceived unfairness of public decisions (Boots, et al. 1972, p. 2). Prior to 1978, municipalities and their officials had enjoyed broad immunity from federal statutes (Lee 1987, p. 160).

Chapter 6

1. An informal survey of mayors conducted by Alexandra Ortiz of the World Bank at the Fourth Inter-American Conference of Mayors in 1998 revealed that poverty and employment issues ranked as the top priorities among mayors in all sizes of cities.

2. In a unique study sponsored by the World Bank, Janice Perlman and a team from the University of Rio de Janeiro located a significant fraction of the 750 households she interviewed originally in 1968–69. The preliminary findings are that families are better off in some material circumstances, but in many cases the second and third generations are locked into the same conditions of poverty that Perlman reported about their parents and grandparents (Perlman 1976, 1999).

3. These gross estimates probably undercount the effects of rapid household formation. In Brazil, household formation in the 1990s was growing 20 percent faster than urban populations as a whole. The bulk of the young in Brazil's population pyramid was moving into the age range of marriage, and this cohort generated a demand for 800,000 connections in water and sanitation per year, just to keep up with prevailing levels of service.

4. Low-income communities often take decades to reach the level of services that modern residential developers provide as customary features of a residential development of finished houses. Middle-class buyers purchase all these services on credit and pay back a mortgage over several decades. Low-income households make small improvements in a stepwise fashion, often over many decades, sometimes using windfall gains or family savings, gradually upgrading the quality of shelter and services.

5. For further detail on the unusually large role of Chilean municipalities in poverty assistance, see Campbell et al. 1990.

6. These kinds of activities were eligible for SIF financing for communities that fell within a "poverty map" drawn up to indicate the poorest districts of the Guatemalan western highlands. These criteria, interpreted with the assistance of operational manuals, small

seed grants to inexperienced villages, and SIF field staff, proved to be sufficient to guide municipalities and to partner nongovernmental and grassroots groups in project identification, development, implementation, and—in some cases—maintenance.

7. Recall that mayor's funds are small discretionary amounts of money put aside by mayors in many cities to finance local improvement projects in neighborhoods (street paving, drainage, lighting, etc.), usually on a matching basis.

8. Personal communication, July, 1986.

9. Documentation of these and other cases can be found in Campbell and Fuhr 2003.

10. Unlike many other development programs, PRODEL, a program financed by Swedish development assistance, does not directly execute activities itself. Rather, it provides technical assistance and financial and human resources to support and strengthen agencies already providing lending and technical support to householders and communities. PRODEL provides incentives to communities by giving them a challenge grant, based on a self-proposal for neighborhood improvement. The grant must be matched by no less than 35 percent of the total cost of the project by resources mobilized by the community. Matching funds can come from the municipality, private groups, or community members themselves. PRODEL also finances a maximum of US$25,000 per project (or no more than 65 percent of the value of a single project) in a community. The funds are administered either by the mayor or the town council. Both must sign off to verify that a community's proposals meet conditions of eligibility before project implementation can begin.

11. United Nations Interregional Crime and Justice Research and the International Crime Prevention Center (Montreal). The Center conducts research, provides technical assistance, and carries out international education programs.

12. Personal communication, January, 1996.

Chapter 7

1. I use the term "arguably" because many fiscal financial analysts argue that a local government income tax, piggybacked onto national income tax, would be the most equitable and administratively easiest method of raising local revenue.

2. The cases of Leon, Nicaragua, Mendoza, and Tijuana are all explored in greater detail in Campbell and Fuhr 2003.

3. In fact, tragedy nearly obliterated Tijuana's decision over the PAU. Two days before the scheduled referendum, presidential candidate Luis Donaldo Colosio was assassinated in Tijuana. Shaken by the trauma and because the nation was in mourning, city officials rescheduled the date of the vote. When the vote was finally held more than a month later, the momentum and interest in PAU had been dissipated. Less than seven per cent of the electorate cast a ballot. For this reason, Mayor Osuna commissioned a public opinion poll several months later and obtained virtually the same result as returned in the referendum.

4. As in the case of Bogota, La Paz is divided up into zones for purposes of taxation. However, a substantially undervalued tax is applied (values below 50 percent of current market values); this low starting base results in severe underestimation of appraisals as rated by the taxpayers.

5. Refer to the World Bank's Private Sector "Viewpoint" Series, which compiles discussion papers on different aspects of privatization and publishes them in its quarterly journal *Public Policy for the Private Sector*.

6. Generating revenues under capital gains tax has been used for certain local goods and services in Colombia. Although capital gains taxes have been contemplated in several coun-

tries (e.g., Peru and Bolivia) they have not been implemented, either because of a lack of political will or because of insufficient technical capacity on the part of local administrations. Cost recovery by means of capital gains tax not only promotes greater financial autonomy, but may also generate strong incentives for efficiency in production in those services that have to be self-financed.

7. The municipality in Miraflores explored ways to concession public services, following discussions in the Peruvian national Congress to modify the municipal law system.

Chapter 8

1. Since the onset of democratic choice making of municipal authorities in the mid-1980s, eight of twenty-three nations surveyed by Bland (1994) rewrote national constitutions, and even more passed electoral reforms. Since 1985, changes in the timing or nature of municipal elections have been effected in Bolivia, Brazil, Chile, Colombia, Ecuador, Honduras, Panama, Paraguay, Mexico, and Venezuela. These changes tended to narrow the focus of electoral choice, for example, by making local elections separate from national contests, by identifying candidates by name rather than just by party, by directly electing a municipal executive, and by allowing re-election. Further reforms are under way in many countries.

In Colombia, for instance, an informal agreement was reached at the time of the constitutional assembly in 1990–91 to gradually reform electoral processes so as to move toward a uninominal system and away from the slate ballot quota system in effect before then. A compromise intermediate agreement put individual names on ballots, so candidates were identified by name but still classified by, and representative of, a party slate. Also, district elections were introduced for the lower house of congress. Studies were launched to extend districts to smaller jurisdictions within municipal boundaries. Eventually, uninominal district elections were to be extended to the municipal level.

2. An in-depth study of 16 municipalities in Colombia showed that leadership was a key factor, not only in innovation, but in at least five other areas as well: (1) political skill, where negotiation, vision, and handling of conflicting forces were important; (2) breaking the inertia that tends to hold back local governments, because the bureaucracy and the public are locked into old beliefs and assumptions about how things should work; (3) expanding horizons with a vision that involves others and recruiting the public to become part of the vision; (4) managing complex organizations and showing how to delegate; and (5) managing conflict, particularly within the councils, the legislative branch of local governments, which is perhaps the most resistant to change.

3. Tumero (population 190,000) is the county seat of the municipality of Marino, situated in the Maracay Valley 100 kilometers southeast of Caracas. The valley is one of the most fertile and diversified intensive agricultural producers in the country. Tumero won a number of investments in agro-industrial installations for storage, processing oils, food canning, livestock feed, and shipping, including food exports. The first mayor to be elected after state reforms in 1989, Efren Rodriguez, was a native son and political independent. He ran on a platform of good government ("to rescue credibility") and distinguished his first actions in office by not acceding to customary practices of partisan favoritism in the appointment of his cabinet and staff. He selected most personnel on the basis of merit, finding some candidates by placing want ads in local newspapers.

4. Successive administrations reduced financial support to ICAM and the number of trainees was reduced. Incentives to attend ICAM courses were further weakened when ICAM training ceased to be a criterion for salary increases and job promotions.

5. Personal communication from James Westbury, Public Administration Specialist, World Bank.

6. Although the region has nearly 14,000 municipalities, the small sample reviewed in this study suggests that size is not necessarily a predictor of capacity. We have seen skillful innovations in the very small and serious shortcomings in the very large. The important factor is political will at the local level. This strategic dimension is predicated on motivation to improve performance. Nevertheless, economies of scale need to be taken into account. All countries have a wide range of local governments, and neither central governments nor helping institutions are able to handle this diversity very well. Broadly speaking, about a third of the total number of municipalities in any country are either large, strong administratively, or rich. These should be managed differently from the small, weak, or poor. All local governments need help to improve their core business functions: planning, revenue raising, spending, and management. But delivering the assistance to the two groups of governments should be treated very differently. Policymakers in countries and development institutions need to develop intermediaries like states, NGOs, and associations of local governments (this last as in the case of Hungary) to broker and help deliver technical assistance. Help for smaller and weaker communities should be largely more forgiving fiscally and supportive socially.

7. Very few countries make any discrimination about intrinsic capacity. Two notable exceptions are Philippines and the West Bank and Gaza.

REFERENCES

Affonso, Rui de Britto A. 1997. *Os estados e a descentralizaçáo no Brasil*. Serie Política Fiscal, no. 93. CEPAL/GTZ.

Aghón, Gabriel. 1996. *Descentralización fiscal en América Latina : Balance y principales desafíos*. Santiago de Chile: Proyecto Regional de Descentralización CEPAL/GTZ.

————. 1997. *Descentralización fiscal en América Latina : Nuevos desafios y agenda de trabajo*. Santiago de Chile: Proyecto Regional de Descentralización CEPAL/GTZ.

Altshauer, D. 1989. Is public expenditure productive? *Journal of Monetary Economics* 23:177–200.

Alvarez, Claudia. 1996. *La asignación de funciones a nivel local en Argentina: El caso del municipio de Santiago del estero*. Serie Política Fiscal, no. 89. CEPAL/GTZ.

Anderson, F. 1973. *NEPA in the courts*. Washington, DC: Resources for the Future.

Araujo, María del Carmen. 1996. *Descentralización fiscal: El Caso de Ecuador*. Serie Política Fiscal, no 90. CEPAL/GTZ.

Aspe, Pedro Armella. 1988. *Descentralizacion*. Mexico City: Cuadernos de Renovación Nacional.

Bahl, Roy, and Johannes Linn. 1992. *Urban public finance in developing countries*. Oxford: Oxford University Press.

Bailey, J. 1994. "Centralism and political change in Mexico: The case of national solidarity." In Wayne A. Cornelius, Ann L. Craig, and Jonathon Fox (eds.). *Transforming state-society relations in Mexico: The national solidarity strategy*. San Diego, CA: UC San Diego, Center for Mexican Studies.

Barrios, Armando. 1997. *Descentralización fiscal y estabilidad macroeconómica en Venezuela*. Serie Política Fiscal, no. 94. CEPAL/GTZ.

Bird, Richard. 1978. *Intergovernmental fiscal relations in developing countries*. Working paper 304, Development Economics Department, World Bank

Bird, Richard, R. Ebel, and C. Wallich, eds. 1995. *Decentralization of the socialist state: Intergovernmental finance in transition economies*. World Bank Regional and Sectoral Studies. Washington, DC: World Bank.

Bland, Gary. 1994. "Local and intermediate level electoral policy in Latin America and the Caribbean." Prepared for the Latin America and the Caribbean Technical Department, World Bank. August.

Bonfim, A., and A. Shah, 1991. *Macroeconomic management and the division of powers in Brazil perspectives for the nineties."* Working paper 567, Country Economics Department, World Bank.

Boots, A. J., et al. 1972. "Inequality in local government services:" A case study of neighborhood roads.

Borja, Jordi. 1988. *Estado y Ciudad. Descentralizacion politica y participacion.* Promociones y Publicaciones Universitarias, S. A. Barcelona, Spain.

Brewer Carias, Allan-Randolphe, Carlos Ayala Corao, Jorge Sánchez Melean, Gustavo Linares, and Humberto Romero. 1990. *Leyes para la descentralización political de la federación.* Caracas: Jurídica Venezolana.

Burki, J., et al. editors, 2000. *Annual World Bank Conference on Development in Latin America and the Caribbean 1999: Decentralization and accountability of the public sector.* World Bank. Latin American and Caribbean Studies. May. Stock number 14709.

Burki, Shahid Javed, and Guillermo E. Perry. 1997. *The long march, a reform agenda for Latin America and the Caribbean in the next decade.* Washington, DC: World Bank

Burki, S. Javed, Guillermo Perry, and William Dillinger. 1999. *Beyond the center: Decentralizing the state.* Washington, DC: World Bank.

Campbell, Tim. 1981. *Resource flows in the urban ecosystem: Fuel, water, and food in Mexico City.* Working paper 360, Institute of Urban and Regional Development, University of California–Berkeley.

———. 1996. *Banking on decentralization in a continent of cities—looking back on lending and forward to reform in the urban sector of LAC.* LACTD dissemination note.

———. 1997. *Innovations and risk taking: The engine of reform of local governments in Latin America and the Caribbean.* Discussion paper 357, World Bank, Washington, DC.

———. 2002.*City development strategies: Review of progress and policy framework.* Transportation and Urban Development Department. Washington, DC: World Bank.

Campbell, T., et al. 1999. "A tale of two cities in Vietnam: Towards a strategy for growth, poverty and environment in the cities and regions of Vietnam." Washington, DC: World Bank.

Campbell, Tim, and John Frankenhoff. 1994. "Institutional development (ID) and decentralized governance." Draft discussion paper. LATAD, March 31.

Campbell, Tim, and Sara Freedheim. 1994. "Basic features and significance of PRONASOL, Mexico's national solidarity program." *Decentralization to local government in LAC: Source book on policies and practices that work.* Source book note 2. LATAD, July.

Campbell, Tim, and Harald Fuhr. 2003. *Leadership and innovation: Risk-taking in local government of Latin America and the Caribbean.* Washington, DC: World Bank Institute.

Campbell, Tim, with assistance of E. Muñoz and M. Morgan. 1993. *Participation, choice, and accountability in local government: LAC and the US.* LACTD Dissemination Note. May.

Campbell, Tim, and T. Katz. 2003. "The politics of participation in Tijuana, Mexico: Inventing a new style of governance." Chap. 5 in Campbell and Fuhr, 2003.

Campbell, Tim, G. Peterson, and Jose Brakarz. 1990. *Decentralization in Chile. A case study.* Latin America and the Caribbean Technical Department. World Bank.

Campbell, Tim, with George Peterson and Jose Brakarz. 1991. *Decentralization in LAC: National strategies and local response in planning, spending, and management.* Technical Note No. 5. Latin America and the Caribbean Technical Department, World Bank.

Carroll, Thomas. 1992. *Intermediary NGOs: The supporting link in grassroots development.* Hartford: Kumarian Press.

Castaneda, T. 1990. *Para combatir la pobreza politica social y descentralización en Chile durante los 80s.* Santiago: Centro de Estudios Publicos.

Casas, Carlos. 1997. *Descentalización fiscal : El caso de Perú.* Serie Política Fiscal, no 92. CEPAL/GTZ.

Castells, M. 1983. *The city and the grassroots.* Berkeley: University of California Press.

Clark, Terry N., ed. 1994. *Urban innovation: creative strategies for turbulent times.* London: Sage Publications.

Collier, David, ed. 1979. *The new authoritarianism in Latin America.* Princeton: Princeton University Press.

Comisión Presidencial para la Reforma del Estado (COPRE). 1988. *La reforma del estado.* Caracas: Editorial Arte.

Cornelius, Wayne A., Ann L. Craig, and Jonathon Fox, eds. 1994. *Transforming state-society relations in Mexico: The national solidarity strategy.* San Diego: University of California–San Diego, Center for Mexican Studies.

Coulter, P. B. 1988. *Citizen demand for urban public services.* Tuscaloosa: University of Alabama Press.

Council of Europe. 1985. *European charter of local self-government.* European Treaty Series, no. 122. Strasbourg: Council of Europe.

Cuevas, J. 1996. *El impuesto a la propiedad inmueble: el case de la ciudad de La Paz.* Documento presentado al III Seminario del Proyecto Regional CEPAL/GTZ de Descentraliazciojn Fiscal en America Latina. Octubre.

Cumby, R., and R. Levich. 1987. *On the definition and magnitude of recent capital flight.* NBER working paper 2275. Cambridge, Mass.: National Bureau of Economic Research.

de la Cruz, Rafael, and Armando Barrios, eds. 1994. *Federalismo fiscal: el costo de la descentralización en Venezuela.* Caracas: Nueva Sociedad.

de la Cruz, Rafael, et al. 1998. *Descentralizacion en perspectiva. Fundacion Escuela de Gerencia Social.* Ministerio de la Familia. Caracas: Ediciones IESA

Davey, Kenneth J. 1993. *Elements of urban management.* Urban Management Program discussion paper 11, World Bank, Washington, DC.

DeSario, J., and S. Langton. 1987. *Citizen participation in public decision making.* Westport: Greenwood Press.

Dillinger, William. 1995. *Better urban services: Finding the right incentives.* Development in Practice Series. Washington, DC: World Bank.

———. 1992. *Urban property tax reform, guidelines and recommendations.* Washington, DC: UNDP/The World Bank/UNHCS).

Dillinger, William, and Steven B. Webb. 1999. "Macroeconomic management in decentralized democracies: The quest for hard budget constraints in Latin America." Poverty Reduction and Economic Management in Latin America. Processed. World Bank.

Edwards, Sebastian. 1993. *Latin America and the Caribbean a decade after the debt crisis.* Washington, DC: World Bank.

Epstein, P. D. 1984. *Using performance measurement in local government.* New York: Van Nostrand Reinhold.

Estache, Antonio. 1995. *Decentralizing infrastructure: Advantages and limitations.* Discussion Paper 290. Washington, DC: Infrastructure Operations Division, World

Bank.

Ferreira, P. C., and T. G. Malliagros. 1998. "Impactos produtivos da infra-estrutura no Brasil: 19950/1995." *Pesquisa de Planajemiento Economico* 28(2):315–337.

Fox, Jonathan. 1994. Latin America's emerging local politics. *Journal of Democracy* 5, 2:105–16.

Foxley, Alejandro. 1984. *Paradigmas de desarrollo y democratización: temas de investigación.* Working paper 17, Kellog Institute, University of Notre Dame, Notre Dame, IN.

Freire, Mila, M. Huertas, and B. Darche. 1998. *Subnational access to the capital markets: The Latin American experience.* Regional paper, Global Program in Capital Markets Finance, World Bank.

Frieden, Jeffrey. 1991. *Debt, development, and democracy: Modern political economy and Latin America, 1965–1985.* Princeton: Princeton University Press.

Friedmann, John. 1976. *The urban transition: Comparative studies of newly industrializing societies.* London: E. Arnold.

Friedmann, John, and William Alonso, eds. 1975. *Regional policy: Readings in theory and applications.* Cambridge: MIT Press.

Fukasaku, Kiichiro, and Ricardo Hausmann, eds. 1998. *Democracy, decentralisation and deficits in Latin America.* Paris: OECD.

Fundaçao do desenvolvimento administrativo (FUNDAP). 1995. *A federacao em perspectiva, ensaios selecionados.* Sao Paulo: FUNDAP.

Gage, Robert W., and Myrna P. Mandell, eds. 1990. *Strategies for managing intergovernmental policies and networks.* New York: Praeger.

Galindo, Mario, y Fernando Medina. 1995. *Descentralización fiscal en Bolivia.* Serie Política Fiscal, no 72. CEPAL/GTZ.

Gillespie, Charles. 1989. Democratic consolidation in the Southern Cone and Brazil: Beyond political disarticulation? *Third World Quarterly* 11, no. 2:92–113.

Glading, A. 1992. Time to fine-tune Mexico's solidarity program. *Wall Street Journal,* 18 December, eastern edition.

Glaessner, Phillip, Kye Woo Lee, Anna Maria Sant'Anna, Jean-Jacques de St. Antoine. 1994. "World Bank discussion papers poverty alleviation and social investment funds: The Latin American experience." Discussion paper 261, World Bank.

González, Edgar, e Iván Jaramillo. 1996. *El nivel intermedio en el arreglo institucional: Diagnóstico y perspectivas en el Ámbito Latinoamericano.* Serie Polítca Fiscal, no 86. CEPAL/GTZ.

Guillen, Tonatiuh. 1995. *Innovaciones y conflicto—Sociedad civil y gobierno local.* Tijuana: Colegio de la Frontera Norte.

Graham, P. 1976. *Petaluma, the California growth control plan: A bibliography.* San Luis Obispo: The Council of Planning Librarians.

Grindle, Merilee, and Charles Thomas. 1991. *Public choices and policy change: the political economy of reform in developing countries.* Baltimore: Johns Hopkins University Press.

Haas, Jorg-Werner, and Alex Rosenfeld, eds. 1995. *Descentrilizar en America Latina?* Quito: Programa de Gestion Urbana (PGU).Hirschman, A. O. 1970. *Exit, voice, and loyalty: Responses to decline in firms, organizations, and states.* Cambridge: Harvard University Press.

Hatry, H. et al. 1981. *Practical program evaluation for state and local governments.* Washington, DC: The Urban Institute.

Hommes, Rudolf. 1996. "Conflicts and dilemmas of decentralization." In Bruno, M., and B. Pleskovic. *Annual World Bank Conference on Development Economics, 1995.* Washington, DC: World Bank.

Hopkins, Elwood. 1995. *The life cycle of urban innovations.* Urban Management Program Working Paper Series. Washington, DC: World Bank.

Hull, Terence H. 1999. *Striking a most delicate balance: The implications of Otonomi Daerah for the planning and implementation of development cooperation projects.* Demography Program, RSSS. Canberra: Australian National University.

Kelly, A., and J. Williamson. 1984. *What drives Third World city growth?* Princeton: Princeton University Press.

Kwitny, Jonathan. 1997, *Man of the century: The life and times of Pope John Paul II.* New York: Henry Holt and Co.

Lee, Y. S. 1987. "Civil liability of state and local governments: Myth and reality." *Public Administration Review* 47:160–70.

Leeds, Anthony, ed. 1967. *Social structure, stratification and mobility.* Washington, D.C.: Pan American Union.

Leeuw, F., R. Rist, and R. Sonnichsen, eds. 1994. *Can governments learn? Comparative perspectives on evaluation and organizational learning.* New Brunswick, NJ: Transaction Publishers.

Liner, E. B., ed. 1989. *A decade of devolution: Perspectives on state local relations.* Washington D.C.: The Urban Institute Press.

Litvack, Jenny, J. Ahmad, and R. Bird. 1998. *Rethinking decentralization in developing countries.* World Bank Sector Studies Series. Washington, DC: World Bank.

Lomnitz, Larissa. 1974. The social and economic organization of a Mexican shantytown. In Wayne Cornelius and Felicity Trueblood, *Latin American Urban Research.* Vol. 4, pp. 135–56. Beverly Hills: Sage.

López-Murphy, Ricardo. 1996. *Descentralización fiscal y política macroeconómica.* Serie Política Fiscal, no 87. CEPAL/GTZ.

Lordello de Mello, Diogo. 1984. "Modernización de los gobiernos locales en Armerica Latina." Revista de Administracão Municipal, no. 172:1–66 (June).

Malloy, James M., and Mitchell A. Seligson, eds. 1987. *Authoritarians and democrats: regime transition in Latin America.* Pittsburgh: University of Pittsburgh Press.

Marino, Juana. 1997. "Crecimiento urbano y accesso a los servicios urbanos." Presentation at the 4a Red Centroamericana por la descentralization y el fortalecimiento Municipal. 21–23 July, Antigua, Guatemala. IDB, World Bank, ICLEI, IULA-Celcadel and UNCRD.

McCarney, Patricia. 1996. *Cities and governance. New directions in Latin America, Asia and Africa.* Toronto: University of Toronto Centre for Urban and Community Studies.

Mohan, R. 1994. *Understanding the developing metropolis. Lessons from the city study of Bogota and Cali, Colombia.* Oxford University Press.

Molina, J., and J. Hernandez. 1995. "Sistemas electorales subnacionels en America Latina." Lateinamerikaforschung. Arbeitspapier Nr. 20. Heidelberg: Universitat Heidelberg, Institute fur Politische Wissenschaft.

Moreno, Alvaro y César Vargas. 1995. *Características del Mercado de Crédito Territorial y Determinantes de la Demanda: El Caso Colombiano.* Serie Política Fiscal, no. 73,

CEPAL/GTZ.

Mouritzen, Poul E., ed. 1992. *Managing cities in austerity. Urban fiscal stress in ten western countries.* London: Sage Publications.

Müller, Regina 1995. *Descentralización político-financiera en Francia.* Serie Política Fiscal, no 74. CEPAL/GTZ.

Neffa, Juan Alberto. 1996. *Descentalización fiscal: El caso Paraguayo."* Serie Política Fiscal, no. 91. CEPAL/GTZ.

Nickson, Andrew. 1995. *Local government in Latin America.* Boulder: Lynne Rienner Publishers.

North, Douglass. 1991. *Institutions, institutional change, and economic performance.* New York: Cambridge University Press.

Ocampo, José Antonio, y Guillermo Perry Rubio. 1996. *Seminario internacional sobre descentralización fiscal en América Latina: Mejores prácticas y lecciones de política.* Serie Política Fiscal, no 84. CEPAL/GTZ.

O'Donnell, Guillermo. 1993. On the state, democratization and some conceptual problems: A Latin American view with glances at some post communist countries. *World Development* 21, no. 8:1355–69.

Ostrom, Elinor, Larry Schroeder, and Susan Wynne. 1994. *Institutional incentives and sustainable development. Infrastructure policies in perspective.* Boulder: Westview Press.

Perlman, Janice. 1976. *The myth of marginality: Urban poverty and politics in Rio de Janeiro.* Berkeley: University of California Press.

Perlman, Janice. 1999. "Dynamics of poverty in Brazil." Progress report on phase I. Processed. World Bank.

Perry, Guillermo E., and Marcela Huertas. 1997. *La historia de una crisis anunciada: Regulano el endeudamiento de las municipalidades y los departementos en Colombia.* ECLAC

Peterson, G. 1997. *Learning by doing: Decentralization and policy in Latin America and the Caribbean.* LAC Discussion Series Paper sponsored by the LACTD. Washington, DC: World Bank.

Piza, J. R. 1996. *El autoavaluo, una elternativa para incrementar la base gravable del impuesto predial. La experiencea de Santafe de Bogota.* Documento presentado al III Seminario del Proyecto Regional CEPAL/GTZ de Descentraliazcion Fiscal en America Latina. Octubre.

Porto, Alberto, y Pablo Sanguinetti. 1996. *Las transferencias intergubernamentales y la equidad distributiva: El caso Argentino."* Serie Política Fiscal, no 88. CEPAL/GTZ.

Prud'homme, Remy. 1994. *On the dangers of decentralization.* Policy research working paper 1252, Transportation, Water, and Urban Development Department, World Bank.

Reilly, Charles. 1994. *Nuevas politicas urbanas. Las ONG y los gobiernos municipales en la democratización latinaoamericana.* Washington, D.C.: InterAmerican Foundation.

Remmer, Karen. 1992. The Process of Democratization in Latin America. *Studies in Comparative International Development* 27, no. 4:3–24.

Ringskog, Klas. 1995. *Meeting the infrastructure challenge in Latin America and the Caribbean.* Washington, DC: World Bank.

Rodriguez, V. E. 1993. "The politics of decentralization in Mexico: From municipio libre to solidaridad." *Bulletin of Latin American Research* 12(2): 133–45.

Rojas, Fernando. 1995. The political, economic and institutional dimensions of fiscal decentralization in Latin America. New York: United Nations Development Program. Typescript.

———. 1996a. *Estrutura, funcionamiento y politicas de los fondos de cofinanciacion en paises seleccionados: Practica y principales desafios.* Serie Politica Fiscal, no. 85. CEPAL/ GTZ.

———. 1996b. *Los ingresos no tributarios locales: Potencialidades, innovaciones y nuevos desafios en el ambito local.* Margarita: III Seminario Internacional de Descentralizacion Fiscal en America Latina: Nuevos Desafios y Agenda de Trabajo. Processed. CEPAL/ GTZ.

Rondonelli, D. 1981. Government decentralization in comparative perspective: Theory and practice in developing countries, *International Review of Administrative Science.* Vol. 2, pp. 133–45.

Selligson, Mitch. 1994. "Central Americans view their local goverments: A six-nation survey," Presented to the Regional Office of Central America and Panama, USAID and Guatemala City, October 5th, 1994

Serra, M. T. 1993. "Alternative sanitation systems in LAC: An empirical inquiry." Processed. Latin America and the Caribbean Technical Department. World Bank.

Shah, Anwar. 1998. *Balance, accountability, and responsiveness: Lessons about decentralization.* Policy Research Working Paper 2021. Washington, DC: The World Bank.

Shugart, Matthew Soberg. 1996. *Checks and Balances in Latin America in an Age of Globalization.* Working Paper Series. Washington DC: IDB.

Singer, Paul. 1998. "Desafios com que se desenfrontam as grandes cidades brasileiras." Pp. 97–141 in Jose Arlindo Soares e Silvio Caccia-Bava (orgs). *Os Desafios da testao Municipal democratico.* Sao Paulo: Editora Cortez.

Skidmore, Thomas. 1993. *Television, politics, and the transition to democracy in Latin America.* Baltimore: Johns Hopkins University Press.

Stein, Ernesto. 1996. "La experiencia de PRODEL, Nicaragua." Swedish SIDA. Processed.

Strassmann, W. P. 1986. *The transformation of urban housing. The experience of upgrading in Cartagena. The World Bank.* Baltimore: Johns Hopkins University Press.

Tanzi, Vito. 1996. "Fiscal federalism and decentralization: A review of some efficiency and macroeconomic aspects." In Bruno, M., and B. Pleskovic. *Annual World Bank conference on development economics, 1995.* Washington, DC: World Bank.

Tendler, Judith. 1997. *Good government in the tropics.* Baltimore: Johns Hopkins University Press.

Torres, Blanca. 1986. *Descentralización y democracia en México.* Mexico City: El Colegio de México.

Turner, J. F. C. 1968. "Housing priorities, settlement patterns, and urban development in modernizing countries." *Journal of the American Institute of Planners* (November): 354–63.

Turner, J. F. C., and W. Mangin. 1967. "Latin American squatter settlements: A problem and a solution." *Latin American Research Review* 2: 65–98.

UNICEF. 1993. "Focusing information to focus political responsibility—Case study of advocacy and social mobilization for children linked to decentralization and elections in Colombia." By C. Fraser and S. Resprepo-Estrada. Bogota: UNICEF. Processed.

United Nations (UN). 1997. *World urbanization prospects.* New York: Dept. of International Economic and Social Affairs.

United Nations (UN). 1991. *World urbanization prospects.* New York: Dept. of International Economic and Social Affairs.

United Nations Centre for Human Settlements (UNCHS) (Habitat). 1987. *Global report on human settlements.* London: Oxford University Press.

Valladares, L., and M. Coelho. 1996. La investigacion urbana en Latina America. *Cadernos IPPUR* 10, no. 1: Jan–July.

Veliz, Claudio. 1981. *The centralist tradition of Latin America.* Princeton: Princeton University Press.

Verba, S., and N. H. Nie. 1972. *Participation in America: Political Democracy and Social Equality.* New York: Harper and Row.

Wall Street Journal. September 1998. "Cuauhtemoc Cardenas delivers state of the city address."

Watson, Gabrielle. 1995. *Good sewers cheap.* Water and Sanitation Currents. Working Paper No. 14272. World Bank. Washington, DC.

Weisner, Eduardo. 1994. *Desentralizacion fiscal : la busqueda de equidad y eficiencia. Informo de Progreso Economico y Social en America Latina 1994.* Washington, DC: IDB

Willis, Eliza, Christopher da C. B. Garman, and Stephan Haggard. 1999. The politics of decentralization in Latin America. *Latin American Research Review 34,* 1:7–56.

Winkler, D. 1997. *"EDUCO in El Salvador."* World Bank. Mimeographed.

World Bank. 1988. *World Development Report 1988.* New York, NY: Oxford University Press.

———. 1990. *Argentina: Provincial Government Finance.* LATIE. Washington, DC.

———. 1990. *The magnitude of poverty in Latin America in the 1980s,* Vol. 1. Working paper, Human Resources Department, Latin America and the Caribbean. World Bank.

———. 1991. *Mexico: Decentralization and Urban Development.* Report No. 8924-ME. LA2IE. Washington, DC.

———. 1992. *Chile: Subnational Government Finance.* Report No. 10580-CH. LA4IE. Washington, DC.

———. 1992. "Participatory Development. Interim Report." Aubrey Williams. Bank-Wide Learning Group. Washington, DC.

———. 1993. *The East Asian miracle: Economic growth and public policy.* New York: Oxford University Press.

———. 1995. *Local government capacity in Colombia: Beyond technical assistance.* A World Bank Country Study. Washington, DC.

———. 1995. World Bank Conference on Competitiveness, Chihuahua, Mexico, 1997

———. 1996. *The World Bank participation sourcebook. Environmentally sustainable development.* Washington, DC: World Bank.

———. 1997. *OED reports on urban projects in Santa Catarina and Parana, Brazil.* World Bank.

———. 1999. *Cities in transition. A global strategy for urban development and governance.* Department of Transport, Water, and Urban Development. Washington, DC: World Bank.

———. 1999. Entering the twenty-first century. *World Development Report, 1999/2000.* Washington, D.C.

INDEX